Royal Candlelight Chris
P.O. Box 3021
Fontana, California 9233
www.royalcandlelight.com
info@royalcandlelight.com
Internet TV Website: Ustream tv.com (Royal Candlelight)

ISBN-10: 1491011173
ISBN-13: 978-1491011171

Printed in the United States of America

Doc & Stella Abersold

DEDICATION

This book is dedicated to our seven children. In order of age they are: Jeff, Pamela, David, Elaine, Debra, Phillip and Nancy. They bring joy, happiness and excitement to our lives.
Along with worry, concerns, anxiety and hope.

A WORD OF APPRECIATION

AND

SPECIAL THANKS

Through the years a number of editors have published these articles. All of them have appeared in one or more newspapers. All of the editors have my special thanks.

A special word of thanks is for my wife, Stella. She was an invaluable help in compiling these articles.

She researches information, types my scribbling, reads and critiques the articles, sends them every week by way of e-mail to hundreds of readers and I love her dearly. She is my partner in life and my partner in this literary venture. As always, she is my daily delight.

G. W. Abersold, PhD

WORDS TO THINK ABOUT

BY G.W. ABERSOLD, PhD

PREFACE

The other day I had opportunity to hear Freddie Ravel perform as a piano artist. He was accompanied by his orchestra. Technically correct, melodic, impassioned and inspiring. He played his own arrangements, and explained his own style in details. His interpretations are decidedly Latin. Ravel has flair on the keyboard. His percussions all have a strong influence. Bongo drums create a solid beat.

Born and bred in Los Angeles he has a Columbian and Eastern Europe influence. Madonna, Quincy Jones and Sergio Menendez have all worked with him.

Following his performance, Freddie gave a concise explanation of his musical philosophy. After thinking about it for several weeks, I've concluded that his description is applicable for optimal living. For a final musical composition Ravel said it needs three elements: I. *A Melody, II; A Harmony, III; A Rhythm.* Just like our lives.

The **MELODY** represents a sense of purpose. Victor Frankl, who wrote the classic book, "Man's Search for Meaning," states, "Meaning is not automatically given to us." A sense of purpose sets the direction for our lives, just as melody does for a song.

Think of the singing of Tony Bennett or Barbra

Streisand. They make any melody they sing, memorable. We can also make the melodies of our lives outstanding. For instance;, the words of James Baldwin. "The challenge of living is to be present in everything you do; from getting up to going to bed."

Elsa Maxwell was a popular comedian in the 1940's and 1950's. She made fun of herself. "I have so many chins, I can't find my necklace." But she voiced a melody that brings joy. She stated, "I wake up every morning and wonder what wonderful things I will see and hear during the day."

In the book of Psalms 118:24 are these words. "This is the day the Lord has made. Let us rejoice and be glad in it." I begin each day by reciting the words. It creates a melody in my soul.

Some sixty years ago I was taking a class in college on the poetry of Elizabeth Barrett Browning. For the first time I read a few words of hers that have stayed with me all these years. They are a melody for sure. "Earth's crammed with heaven and every common bush aflame with God. But only those who see take off their shoes. The rest sit around plucking blackberries."

The second element in Freddie Ravel's composition is *HARMONY.* There are the STRINGS: violins, violas, cellos, basses: WOODWINDS: clarinets, flutes, oboes, saxophones, French horns, bassoons; BRASS: trumpets, trombones, baritone horns, and usually a guitar and a piano. Together they provide a harmony of chords that support the melodies. The metaphor is applicable for us as we seek to live the optimal life.

Life's harmony is made up of our families and

our friends. Both provide the harmony we need for optimal living. It is true that blood is thicker than water or any other thing. Family can cause harmony or discord. It is a common saying that the family is the place that must accept its members. Prodigals, regardless of their behavior, are usually accepted by their parents back into the family. Parental love is strong.

Secondly, there is usually an element of dysfunction in every family. No family is absolutely perfect. But the benefits far outweigh any liabilities. A recent article compiled by a group of family counselors identified several benefits in a family.

Companionship and social skills are encouraged. Creativity is a survival essential in every family. Budgeting is also a part of every family. Teaching every member to be industrious and self-reliant comes naturally to every good parent. The family is a learning center; even better than a school. And, finally, there is a cohesiveness that develops that encourages a sense of being needed.

Harmony is also experienced from friends we have. Just as it takes many different kinds of instruments to create harmonious music, it also takes a variety of friends, with different personalities, to make a village or family.

Freddie Ravel's last element in beautiful music is the **RHYTHM** section. The drums set the tempo. They set the beat. I call it the "spice" that brings the melody and harmony to life. To make our lives meaningful, the rhythms of SKILLS, ACTIVITIES and HABITS we develop are what give "spice" to everyday living.

Thank you Ravel for sharing the basic elements of your music.   *Amen. Selah so be it.*

WORDS TO THINK ABOUT

Contents

ARTICLES

WORDS TO THINK ABOUT

Contents *(Continued)*

WORDS TO THINK ABOUT

Contents *(Continued)*

WORDS TO THINK ABOUT

Contents *(Continued)*

WORDS TO THINK ABOUT

Contents *(Continued)*

WORDS TO THINK ABOUT

Contents *(Continued)*

WORDS TO THINK ABOUT

Contents *(Continued)*

WORDS TO THINK ABOUT

Contents *(Continued)*

The Children of Doc & Stella Abersold

Back Cover

FOREWORD

I'm often asked a personal question about my writing style and column content. As a preacher and pastor for 46 years I seldom wrote out my sermons. However, I did have very detailed outlines and for 42 years I always preached without using the notes. The only area of my life where I seemingly have a photographic memory is in my preaching – Nowhere else.

Twenty five years ago I started writing articles for newspapers and a personal readership. Today it is about 100,000. I have written for eight newspapers, but now for only five.

After compiling three books and another in the mill, I am often astounded about the variety of subjects that I've written about. The sources vary from what I'm reading, people I talk with, talk shows (radio and TV) or just thinking. For example; while talking with a newspaper editor she mentioned that she would like articles about seniors. "Navigating through life is important to them." The word "navigating" turned my mind on. I re-read Mark Twain's, Life on the Mississippi, which was about navigating. I was off and writing.

My writing philosophy is rather mundane. My motivation is twofold: for personal therapy and to stimulate the readers to think. I want them to feel something, to do something and to think something.

Sometimes an editor will request an article on a specific

topic or person. I usually comply. Otherwise my articles are very eclectic. The themes cover six basic subjects: Inspirational, Seniors, Controversial, Travel, Humor and Religion. All of them trigger my interest. However, I do respond more quickly to articles about seniors and ones on humor. Sometimes I combine the two.

My columns about seniors seem to gravitate toward: misconceptions about seniors, foibles attributed to them, problems of role-reversal, illnesses unique to seniors (Alzheimer's), and stressors prevalent among seniors.

As a sit-down comic I want to know all I can about humor. To facilitate this desire a few years ago I made a trip around the world ostensibly to study humor in various countries. I then calculated the favorite subjects and came up with the five favorite areas. 1) SEX; 2) POLITICIANS; 3) SENIORS; 4) ETHNIC; and 5) RELIGION. I've written many articles on one or more of these areas.

Amen. Selah so be it.

WORDS TO THINK ABOUT

ARTICLES

❖

ADVERSITY

The earthquake in Haiti certainly brings the Book of Job into focus. The devastation of property and people is unimaginable. Hundreds of thousands are dead, other thousands are causalities. At least three million people are homeless.

Before the earthquake Haiti was considered the poorest of third world nations. Every estimate is that it will take many years to recover. Why? That is the question for this tragedy and the question posited by Job. Why do good people suffer? Or, basically why is there suffering in the world at all?

The acts of nature are easier to grasp: Storms, floods, tornados, cyclones, volcanic eruptions, earthquakes. Atmospheric turbulence can explain some of them. Philosophical and theological problems develop when such events affect humanity-especially the innocent.

Consider the evil brought upon people by other people: the Holocaust, slavery, wars, terrorism. All are deliberate, foisted upon the innocent. Why?

What about illnesses and malfunctions of the human body and mind. From cancer to Alzheimer: Why? Some 2500 years ago there lived a man by the name of Epicurus, an ancient Greek philosopher. He expressed these thoughts way before Job or Jesus.

Is God willing to prevent evil but not able? Then He is impotent. Not all powerful. Is He able but not willing? Then He is malevolent. Not compassionate.

The word theodicy refers to this dilemma. How God can be just when there is so much suffering in the world that He created. It was invented by Gottfried Wilhelm Leibniz in the 17th century.

The Book of Job is the traditional basis for any discussion on the subject. Very little is known about him. The 42 chapters give little information about Job, focusing attention on his problems. Verse one state he was from the land of Uz. No one knows where that was. Speculation places it east of Edom; which would make him a non-Jew. It is very unlikely that he was a historical character. The book must be considered as allegorical making the truths in it universal. There are two other Biblical references to him: Ezekiel 14:14 and verse 20; and the Book of James 5:11. James speaks of the *"patience of Job."*

The Koran of Islam venerates Job as a prophet. The Missouri Synod of the Lutheran Church honors him as a Saint on May 9. The Armenian Apostolic Church honors Job on August 30. The Druze maintains a tomb for him in Lebanon. The Turkish city of Urfa claims it to be the home area or Uz.

A few years ago (1956) Archibald MacLeish came out with his classic book "J.B." Obviously it was about Job and became a Broadway hit.

The New Testament gives three good examples of suffering: First is John 9:3. Jesus confronts a blind man-from birth-and his disciples ask who sinned, him or his parents? Second is Matthew 27:46 when Jesus is on the cross. He says, *"My God, why have you forsaken me?"* Third is Paul in II Corinthians 12:7. He says he had a thorn in the flesh and he asked God three times to heal him.

In speaking of the Book of Job, Victor Hugo said, "It's perhaps the greatest masterpiece of the human mind."

Amen. Selah so be it.

AFRICA

Diversity: That is the word that best describes our world. It is best understood by viewing the great Serengeti desert in East Africa.

It is hard to imagine the strangeness of the animals. Most common in their diversity is their appearance. Consider the hyenas, vultures, elephants, giraffes, cheetahs, crocodile, hippos, wildebeests, zebras, monkeys, gorillas and of course, birds. They all vary in appearance.

The only animal that doesn't have an enemy is the elephant. Their size is the determining factor. The rhinoceros is a close second. The natural protection for the hippopotamus and crocodile is their habitat of water. In it they reign supreme.

In particular the countries of Tanzania and Kenya are the territories of most of these animals; except for the gorillas. They are mostly in the Congo.

Survival is the essence of the Dark Continent, especially in the Serengeti. For example it is estimated that 250,000 wildebeest die each year. However, 500,000 are born each year. There are millions of them.

Most of the animals spend their days grazing, sleeping or looking for their next victims. It is truly a survival of the fittest. The elements of nature are probably their greatest threats. Months without rain causes unbelievable drought and destroys food supply.

It dries up the water holes. Hippos and crocodiles

really suffer. The land becomes barren. The wind creates a blinding swirl that hinders movement for both man and beast...Then, suddenly the weather changes. Clouds form, lightning strikes and fires sweep across the plains. What foliage was left by the drought and wind is gone. Suddenly without warning, the skies become dark and rain shatters the tranquility. It is a mixed blessing. The fires are put out, the wind stops and the drought ends. But, and it's a huge but; the gullies are overflowing, the rivers are wild and the plains are flooded. Most of the African animals are again in great danger.

A few years ago I spent several days in Kenya, Tanzania and in particular the Serengeti. I saw all of the animals mentioned, plus others. Serengeti is considered by most anthropologists to be the area where mankind started. The museum there is memorable.

The Masai people go back to the 14th century. Today, they are the most distinct tribe of people in east Africa. The Masai language is called Maa. They are nomadic and have not adopted any of the cultures of the surrounding people.

They are considered warriors and live in huts called "kraal." There are 8-20 huts per village. Cattle are very important to the Masai: The source of wealth, food and power. Every part of the cow is used. Cattle are also used to pay debts.

Masai women do all the domestic work; the men protect the village and cattle from their mortal enemies-the lions. Both men and women are circumcised at age fifteen. Both sexes are tall in stature and red is the color of choice. They're known for the making of jewelry and masks for tourists.

The importance of a male Masai is based on the number of cattle he has and the number of his wives. The Serengeti was the highlight of my visit to Africa.

Amen. Selah. So be it.

AGING

Satchel Paige, the great black baseball pitcher, used to say, "How old would you be if you didn't know how old you were?" He meant that actual age was an illusion.

As an 82 year old octogenarian I feel qualified to make a few observations about seniors. History has recorded an interesting fact of seniors who made outstanding contributions to society.

Notably, there was Moses. At the age of eighty he led the Jews out of Egypt; led them for forty years in the desert; and received the Ten Commandments from God.

Aging is not the sole criterion for a meaningful life. What one does with the years and the activities engaged in is also significant. Jack LaLanne is 96 and still exercising. George H. W. Bush is still jumping and helping people throughout the world. Jimmy Carter has done more with Habitat for Humanity than as President. He's 86. Warren Buffett is still making money at age 80.

Bless Willie Nelson at age 77. He's still singing and inspiring millions. Do you like the poetry of Maya Angelou? She's still writing at 82. I have the names of scores of people over 70 that are still active and contributing to society.

Let me bring this issue closer. Men and women I know over 70 that are active and living meaningful lives.

John (82) a skier, PhD, church leader, married to Beth (81); Marilyn (78), century club-visited over 100 countries, ESL teacher, church leader, novelist and best seller; Dave (79) and

Joyce (74), mountaineers, retired school teachers, church members. Lowell (72) pastor for 34 years, Ph.D, preaches two sermons each Sunday. Pearl (89) PhD and Ralph (91) churchmen and lead discussion group at Senior Center every week. Becky (85) attends classes and excellent painter. Nora (102) active socially, exercises on stepper 20 minutes a day. Frank (80) and Betty (78) active in church, magician, drive to Apple Valley to babysit grandchildren. Bob (83) author, scientist, singer, dramatist and teacher at Senior Center.

Charles (77) editor and columnist, wanna-be comedian. Floyd (75) is an avid poker player, magician, and social activist. Wayne (78) retired military, retired city employee, lawyer and judge. George (80) and Mary (77) have been married for 60 years. They love Bunco and traveling on cruises.

Helga (80) is a remarkable woman. She swims six miles every week; walks everyday; does yoga and belongs to a book discussion group: Martha (85) active at Bally's, traveler, church-goer.

What's so unusual about seniors today?

1. Most are avid readers. They buy or borrow books constantly.
2. Seniors keep our economy going. They shop, travel on cruises and go on trips; attend movies; and keep restaurants and fast food chains in business.
3. Almost all of those I know attend church on a regular basis: Catholics, Protestants, Liberals, and Conservatives.
4. All are feisty. They are opinionated. They speak their minds. Don't ask them a question if you don't want an answer.

5. They have an active curiosity. Why, what, where, when are basic to their curiosity.

6. Seniors are notoriously thrifty. They are not spendthrifts. Maybe because they remember the Great Depression. They are always looking for bargains.

7. They have a large range of emotional responses. Some are grumpy, others are happy. Whatever their mood, they love humor. They will smile or laugh uproariously at a good joke.

8. Most seniors (70 plus) have aches and pains. They process remedies galore. They have wheelchairs, walkers and canes. None of the above inhibits their activities.

9. The 3 B's are big for seniors: BUNCO, BRIDGE, and BINGO. All kinds of games of chance are part of their activities. Laughlin always looks like an AARP convention.

10. Stella (72) and Doc (82). They have 7 children, 28 grandchildren and 10 great grandchildren. They are voracious readers, travelers and social. He writes constantly and does magic. They attend church regularly.

11. Seniors are notorious for always being-not on time-but early at any event. Check it out. For appointments, dinner, family gatherings and even church.

Amen. Selah. So be it.

ALLEGORIES

The more I read the Bible, in particular the Old Testament, the more startled I am. First I am aghast at some of the outrageous recordings. Fortunately for devoted readers, from the earliest days of New Testament history, leaders like Origen and Iranaeus believed the stories in the Old Testament should be interpreted as *ALLEGORIES*.

One of the most bizarre accounts is about Jephthah as recorded in the Book of Judges, chapter eleven. His mother was a prostitute and the people of Israel rejected him, until the Ammonites made war on Israel; then came to Jephthah to lead their forces.

Then comes the kicker: He makes a vow to God that if He (God) would give Israel the victory; he would offer as a sacrifice whatever came out of his house; first. After the victory the first-whatever- was his only child, his daughter? The vow was subsequently carried out. Call many Biblical stories beastly, this is one of the worst. Any justification for such a story is lost on me. Maybe he thought a sheep or goat would come out of the house. Whatever, the story is a poor revelation of God's love.

My second insight is about various Biblical stories. Many meaningful truths are like hidden and revealed valuable gems. For example, in II Samuel 24:24 there is an interesting story about David and God. God tells David to take a census-count the number of Israelites.

David has it done and then feels guilty over what he

had done. God tells Gad the prophet to tell David he has a choice of punishments. David chooses three days of pestilence. The sequence of events is hard to believe. God then has Gad the prophet to have David prepare a sacrifice-his penance. He is to build an altar on the threshing floor of Araunah the Jebusite. David wants to buy but Araunah wants to give it to him. Now here comes the interesting insight. David says. "No, I will not have it as a gift. I will buy it, because I will not offer to God a burnt offering that has cost me nothing."

If I understand this scenario correctly, David is saying, *"To please God I must pay a price."* To posterity he is saying, *"Any achievement demands your best efforts."* Or, in the common vernacular; it takes our best efforts to achieve success in any endeavor. We must be engaged to make things happen.

Jesus gave a similar analysis when He said, "Narrow is the gate that leads to life." The inference is obvious. Real living necessitates a narrow focus; whether it is in sports, business, the arts, marriage or parenthood.

Back to David: First of all he is reminding that there is a cost to serving God. It includes acknowledgment of faux paux. He made a serious mistake. He had to eat humble pie. The more elite of the media would call it mea culpa.

In recent months we have seen a plethora of miscues and moral violations. From Congressmen patronizing prostitutes and taking bribes to AIG executives slithering away with excessive bonuses; all of them professing innocence.

A common axiom in such public license is very simple. The American people are very forgiving. Confession of guilt is more often than not forgiven. To deny guilt is unforgivable. David's behavior is one of taking the high road. He paid the price.

This incident in David's life brings to the forefront other events in his life that were far from circumspect. Two examples will suffice. Bible students will remember his poor relationship with his son Absalom. It reached such a low that his son tried to unseat his father as king. The worst example was his relationship with Uriah the Hittite and his wife Bathsheba. David seduces her and sends him to the front to be killed.

While most people are not that gross, the story reminds us of human frailties. The Apostle Paul says, "All have sinned and come short of the glory of God." The answer is always God's unmerited favor and unconditional love and forgiveness.

Amen. Selah. So be it.

AMBASSADORS

The Gospels: Matthew, Mark, Luke and John-are distinctly different from the Epistles of Paul. The words and actions of Jesus are recorded in the Gospels. Paul, the founder of Christianity, wrote letters to churches regarding problems and explaining his theology about Jesus.

Jesus and Paul were very different. Jesus was raised in a small town (Nazareth) that was rural. Paul was raised in a large city (Tarsus) and was very urban. Jesus was home-schooled and Paul probably attended the University of Tarsus and "sat at the feet of Gamaliel" (the leading scholar of his day.)

Their differences are also reflected in the kind of language and word pictures they used. Jesus talked about fishing, weddings, dinners, sowing seeds, weeds, sheep and pigs.

Paul used big city language. He used athletic metaphors (running a race, keeping on the course, achieving the prize); the language of the military (swords, helmets and body armor.)

He was fond of using the political word, "ambassador." (II Corinthians 5:20) "We are ambassadors for Christ." We are to be representatives for Jesus. To expand the idea, we are to influence our environment.

Jesus gives a similar challenge, but with different words. "You are the light of the world." "You are the salt of the earth."

In the parlance of our modern world, we are called to be SALESMEN for our faith. Herb Cohen uses another word for salesmanship. He calls it "negotiation." If you haven't heard of him, in 1980 he wrote a classic book on selling or negotiating, "You Can Negotiate Anything." He states, "One of the greatest negotiators in history lived approximately two thousand years ago . . . I am referring to Jesus Christ."

Our world has witnessed a plethora of men and women who have influenced and persuaded hearers to their way of thinking. While there are scores, I list the following as skilled negotiators/salesman: Abraham Lincoln, F. D. Roosevelt, Bill Clinton, Sister Teresa, Billy Graham, Martin Luther King, Jr., Adolph Hitler, Fidel Castro; and of course, President Barack Obama. I believe these people possessed or possess the skills that we ordinary mortals can emulate; except of course, HITLER and CASTRO.

Herb Cohen, the aforementioned author, suggested several criteria for effective ambassadors, representatives, negotiators and salesmen.

Following the example of Jesus, we begin with a sense of PERSONAL KNOWLEDGE. Jesus knew who He was. He inferred it when He said, "I must be about my Father's business." Power to be effective comes with personal awareness. No handicap or liability is insurmountable.

The second criterion is PEOPLE KNOWLEDGE. Jesus knew those whom He persuaded; their strengths and weaknesses. The disciples, Nicodemus, the Rich Young Ruler, the woman at the well, are good examples.

To be effective ambassadors we too must understand those to be persuaded; their needs, their desires, their hopes and even their failures. Information is a great tool in our calling.

A further element is PRODUCT KNOWLEDGE. Jesus was not reticent or ignorant of His message through parables and actions: Forgiveness, eternal life, unmerited favor, a rebel spirit, to name a few. Whether it is in the field of religion, politics, business etc., a major element for success is having a message with passion.

As ambassadors for Christ our message is more than bland platitudes. The Gospel song, *"God Hath Not Promised"* graphically expresses our message.

God hath not promised skies always blue
Flower strewn pathways, all our lives through;
God hath not promised sun without rain,
Joy without sorrow, peace without pain.

Chorus
But God hath promised strength for the day,
Rest for the labour, light for the way,
Grace for the trials, help from above,
Unfailing kindness, undying love.

Amen. Selah so be it.

ANIMALS

It was either Abraham Lincoln or Mark Twain that said something to the effect that God had to have a sense of humor because he made so many funny looking people.

Someone has also said that one out of every three people is as ugly as all-get-out. Stella and I always look at the next person who comes into our home and laugh.

A change of direction: Let's look at other animals. What a funny creature is the giraffe. It's been said the camel was put together by a committee. The hippos and rhinos are something else. They are ugly. The ostrich, the lobster, the kangaroo, the baboon, the alligator, the walrus and the elephant-among others-are all "as ugly as sin;" in my opinion.

But the object of this article is to acquaint you with four animals that are unique and have something to say to us humans.

The first is the ARCTIC TERN. I first heard about the birds while watching a TV program. It was challenging the watcher to name the most durable, strongest and amazing animal on earth.

I picked the elephant. Others chose the whale, the lion, the condor and the rhino, among others.

In their opinion, the arctic tern won hands down. They are small birds, ranging in weight from 1.5 oz. to 1.4 lbs.

The tern makes the longest migration of any bird; making an annual trip of 21,000 miles from Arctic Alaska to Antarctica. They are all white with a black skull cap, red legs and a red beak. They have long tails and long narrow wings. They are often mistaken for the common puffin, but watching them skim the water and plunge quickly for their prey, they capture the mind of every watcher. They are predators. Having been known to attack eagles and moose, they are pesky critters, driving their adversaries crazy; Even humans. Terns are generally long-lived birds; Often living in excess of 25-30 years...Amazing.

Snakes do not exist in cold climates like Alaska and Canada. Frogs neither; except for the WOOD FROG. It ranges in size from 1.5 to 3.0 inches in length. They eat spiders, beetles, slugs and snails. These amphibian creatures go back 65 million years and probably hopped across the Bering land bridge from Asia. Their freeze tolerance is the most amazing thing about them. As winter approaches it burrows underneath decaying leaves and all physical attributes shut down. They stop breathing; eat nothing, circulation stops and their eyelids freeze. Blood flow and heart beats cease. They are dead. When spring approaches, they start thawing out and are resurrected. They hop around like before they froze...Amazing.

The Blue Whale is the largest mammal that has ever lived. Up to 125 feet in length, it weighs between 175 and 200 tons. It is equal to 40 elephants or 5 Greyhound buses. Its call is louder than a jet engine and can be heard for 100 miles. A newborn weighs about 200 pounds and drinks 50 gallons of milk per day. The consistency is like that of cottage cheese. The BLUE WHALE has a brain the size of a V-W. Its tongue weighs around 3 tons and its mouth can hold up to 90 tons of food and water. It is not a fish, having skin and not scales. It has fingers (in its flippers), an anus, a four chamber heart and lungs. They live about 80 years; amazing.

BONOBOS, pronounced "bo'noubou," are related to the common chimpanzee but very different. They are bi-pedil, which is uncommon in primates. Their diet is mainly fruit and high protein. They are non-aggressive and extremely sexual. The females are the dominant sex. There are very few in captivity, but around 10,000 in the country of Congo.

The female breast is larger than the common chimps. Their hands are very human-like. An example of their dexterity and intelligence: they will use a hollow bamboo as a straw and suck up termites and ants. One amazing facet is that when a new born human and a newborn bonobos are watched together, the bonobos will OUT-LEARN the human baby for the first year. Then the human will continue to learn much faster.

Of great importance is that 98 percent of the DNA of Chimps and Bonobos is the same as the DNA of us humans. What a difference that 2 percent makes….Amazing!

Amen. Selah. So be it.

ARGENTINA

I have a great antipathy to blandness. It turns my stomach. This applies to food of all kinds and also to politics and politicians. Consider Sarah Palin. I disagree with her on most things. But, I admire her intensity. Her enthusiasm is most admirable. I can say the same thing about John McCain.

On the other hand, Boehner and Reid are nauseating. They have a blandness that is suffocating.

I like public speakers, ministers in particular, that speak with passion and a sense of urgency. A standard definition of preaching is, "truth through personality." If that preacher's personality is bland, so will the truth be dull.

Amazingly, the Bible is very specific about blandness, only it's called "lukewarm." In fact, God is depicted as wanting to "spew them out of His mouth."

Perhaps the pinnacle of my enthusiasm for vibrancy is directed to the states and countries I've visited, the peoples I've met and the places I've seen. Alaska fits the bill for states. It is vibrant in all ways. It is beautiful, the people rugged, the animals are plentiful and the things to see are numerous. I place Turkey, Israel, New Zealand and Switzerland at the top of my list of vibrant countries. BUT, the most exciting country that I've visited, outside the USA, is Argentina.

The best way to learn about the people of Argentina is to watch Manu Ginobili play NBA basketball with the San Antonio Spurs. A veteran of 11 seasons, he has been instrumental in their winning several titles. He is known for his relentless scoring ability, his clutch performance, his intensity in diving for loose balls and his general playing without regard to his body. That is a picture of Argentina.

It also depicts the gauchos; the wild horsemen. They are a mixture of Wild West cowboys and racetrack jockeys. It is a thrill to watch them ride without regard to their welfare. It is important to remember that the gauchos are an inseparable part of the Argentinean culture. They are romanticized in art and literature. They represent the free spirit of the country.

The TANGO dance is the national dance. I attended a theatrical show of the dance. It was marvelous. It is both sexual and spiritual. It is dramatic and intense. It seems that everyone dances the tang.

The present Pope Francis was a world class tango dancer in his youth. He is remembered for his concern for the poor, his frugality and his skill as a dancer. I imagine that even today, when he is alone, he does a step or two.

There are several things I remember about Buenos Aires. The La Plata River that is so wide the other side can barely be seen. The natural foods are yerba mate and steaks. Argentineans are a beef eating society. And, believe it or not, every other building seems to house an Italian restaurant. I tried most of them.

This is easy to understand when considering that Italians and Spaniards are the most common ethnic groups. Of the 40,091,000 people living in Argentina, 25 million are Italian and 2 million of Buenos Aires 3,050,725 is Italians and Spaniar.

Maria Eva Duarte de Peron was born on May 7, 1919

and died on July 26, 1952. She died of cervical cancer. At the time of her death, she was probably the most powerful woman in the world. The poor idolized Evita, as she was called and her life inspired a musical and a movie. I visited her huge mausoleum in Buenos Aires, along with hundreds of other tourists.

I have two regrets concerning Argentina. I wish I could have gone to the Southern tip of the country and visited Tierra del Fuego (the land of fire) and Antarctica is not too far away. I have a great interest in both places. The former has a long history, going back 10,000 years. The native Yaghan people were first visited by Ferdinand Magellan-world explorer in 1520. The Indians lit fires to ward off the low temperatures. Later the fires warned sailing ships of the dangerous waters and rocks in the Magellan Straits.

Of the many impressive things to see and witness in Argentina, the most exciting and interesting is the Iguazu (Iguassu) Falls. It is the largest in the world. The Angel Falls are higher, but not as big. It makes the Niagara Falls look like a pond on the backside of a small farm.

It is located between Brazil and Argentina. I first became interested in the Falls when I saw the movie "The Mission" with Jeremy Irons and Robert DeNiro. The Falls are pivotal and the Guaram Indians.

Irons, as Father Gabriel climbs the Falls. I've seen them. They can be heard from 20 miles away and the mist they cause can be felt for miles. The largest of the 275 independent falls is La Boca de Diablo (the mouth of the devil.)

I rode a motor boat to its very edge and looked down. It was terrifying. A cement bridge had been built, but part had broken away. While in the boat I kept thinking about what would happen if the motor stopped. It would be good-bye, Doc.

About ten miles from the Falls the government has constructed a huge electrical power plant, using the power generated by the Falls. It provides electricity for Argentina, Paraguay and a large part of Brazil.

Amen. Selah. So be it.

BANG

Between 14 and 15 billion years ago the universe began with the Big Bang. This is the considered opinion of the vast number of scientists. No one knows what existed before that tremendous explosion. I believe God was there.

Robert Jastrow in "God and the Astronomer," wrote as an astrophysicist, "At this moment it seems as though science will never be able to raise the curtain on the mystery of creation. For the scientist the story ends like a bad dream. He has scaled the mountains of ignorance; he is about to conquer the highest peak; as he pulls himself over the final rock, he is greeted by a band of theologians who have been sitting there for centuries."

The Big Bang demands a divine explanation. So says Dr. Francis S. Collins.

The age of the universe was calculated by the data provided by Edwin Hubble. Using the Doppler effect- the same principle that enables police to determine the speed of a car-scientist's figured back to the Big Bang for the age. It wasn't until 4-5 billion years ago that our galaxy came into existence: The sun, the planets and of course our earth. Believe it or not, the Bible is accurate. It was without form and void.

Gravity was and is essential. It keeps everything in place, rotating around the sun. Then, amazingly, elements like hydrogen and helium came together and nuclear fusion began.

After billions of years, oxygen-which at first was deadly-was changed so that all living creatures could exist. Carbon was added to the mix and with addition of nitrogen and hydrogen, life was started. I believe all of this was a product of "Theistic Evolution."

By the way, the projected age of our earth has also been calculated by geologists. They have tested rocks on Greenland and found them to be 3.85 billion years old.

Another interesting factor concerns dinosaurs. About 230 million years ago they dominated the earth. A large asteroid fell on what is now the Yucatan peninsula and wiped them out. The climate and atmospheric changes led to their demise between 65 and 70 million years ago.

Life on earth began with the appearance of a single cell about 4 billion years ago; the first cells. They were the only evidence of life for over 3 billion years. Eventually they bonded together and multi cellular life appeared-500 million years ago.

In a previous article I discussed the Second Law of Thermodynamics or ENTROPY. This projects a downward spiral-a disintegration of all of life. The First Law pertains to the indestructibility of matter and energy. The combined volume in the universe is never less nor more. Things may change in form but never in essence. With this depressing state, it is also important to recognize the opposite of entropy. It is called ECTROPY. Dr. Richard G. Colling puts it this way: "Mechanisms capable of producing ORDER from DISORDER must be functioning here, or life could not exist." But this is only temporary. Then, entropy takes over.

The word is synthesis or, photosynthesis. It is through

this process that glucose, "without it, most, if not all life on our planet would likely come to an abrupt end." So says Colling. The sun is the primary contributor. This starts the process of entropy. This proves that reactions are not always destructive. "Bacteria, insects, plants, animals and humans are all examples." They are complex forms that have evolved from less organized molecules and cells."

In Genesis, chapter one, there is given a day by day account of creation: First day, establishment of night and day. Second day:, the dividing of the waters and the firmament. Day three was the creating of trees, herbs, fruit and seeds. Fourth day: the creating of the sun, moon and stars. Day five saw the creation of fish, whales and fowls of the air. The sixth day, the earth brought forth living creatures, creeping things and beasts.

Scientists give a chronology that is somewhat the same and yet drastically different; the earliest FISH fossils around 500 million years old. The earliest PLANT life fossils go back to about 440 million years. Then come the fossils of AMPHIBIANS-frogs and toads...And other animals that had reptilian appearance. About 370 million years ago.

REPTILES, the bane of most of us, appeared about 300 million years ago. The first dinosaurs go back to about 245 million years ago. The first MAMMAL fossils that appear in rocks go back to 210 million years. These are whales, possums and kangaroos. The first brains are also present. The sperm whale has a brain the size of a V-W car.

Then the PRIMATES showed up. Around 60 million years ago. While all humans are primates, not all primates are human. Monkeys are in this group. Humans came into existence between 100,000 to 200,000 years ago. Then around 45,000 years ago a group of higher developed HUMANS began to populate our earth.

Now we come to the most significant account in Genesis. Man was created in God's image. That is what makes us truly human. Scientists and believers agree that we have the capability of SELF-AWARENESS. "We can think about what we are thinking about."

Good and evil, right and wrong, compassion and meanness, pain and pleasure. We have the capability of choice: who we love and what we do. We possess moral values and the comprehension of spiritual revelations.

In the image of God we also have the potential of creativity. We can make our reactions and our environment including friends. The words "Let us make man in our image" is the use of the editorial we, us and our-nosism. (NOS-ez-em) The image thing means we are created for the eternal. God made us to live forever. This is the soul or spirit of man, given by the Divine. It transcends the physical evolution. This is the miracle of creation.

To fully understand the essence of the creation account, two significant incidents should be connected. The entire narration is allegorical. The connection between "in our image" and "breathed on the figure" is important. "Breath" in the Hebrew means "wind," "breath," "spirit," or "soul." The ultimate creation act by God was to create humans to be like the Divine by becoming eternal or immortal.

Perhaps the words of St. Augustine bring the whole creation account into perspective. "Oh God, You have made us for Yourself and we can find no rest until we find our rest in You."

Amen. Selah so be it.

BELLS

I've always been fascinated with bells; All kinds of them. The Liberty Bell; bells on cows; Silver bells at Christmas; bells in church steeples; bells at boxing fights to signal rounds. You name them and you've got my interest. They've been made out of all kinds of materials, even wood. But mostly from copper, steel, iron, gold, silver and alloys.

From all apparent historical data, bells originated in the same place we've gotten silk and spaghetti---China. The date is approximately 3-4000 BCE, or 6000 years ago.

There are two distinct references in the Bible: In Exodus, chapter 39 it speaks of bells of pure gold. They were worn as a part of clothing. In the book of Zechariah a reference is made of gold bells being placed on horses. This was a distinctive part of the harness on horses. Seemingly it was merely decorative. Bells have been placed on cows that have a tendency to wander away. Cowbells are used to locate these wanderers.

As mentioned the Chinese were the first master founders. Bells were rather obscure until the European Renaissance when Gothic architecture flourished. Great bell towers were popular. They exist today.

It was in the 19th century that metal bells, tuned to various pitches, were perfected for use in orchestras. Many churches today have hand bell choirs that perform in worship services.

Incidentally, the process of casting bells is called bell

founding. Bronze is the typical metal with 23 % tin. Very large bells add brass and iron to the alloy. Steel does not provide the resonance necessary.

Bells have had significant historical usages. At Christmas time: Jingle Bells and Silver Bells are examples. They also announce important events: war's end, weddings, funerals; arrival of ships and, of course, a call to worship.

The use of bells in a literary context is highlighted in Hemingway's classic novel, For Whom the Bell Tolls. His inspiration comes from John Donne's poem which goes, "No man is an island entire of itself. Everyman's death diminishes me, because I am involved in mankind . . . for whom the bell tolls, it tolls for thee." This poem was written by Donne in 1624.

Whenever we think of the "Liberty Bell" it seems to ring in our ears. Its history is inspiring. Its first ringing changed the world on July 4, 1776 after the first reading of the Declaration of Independence.

It arrived in Philadelphia on September 17, 1752 with the inscription on it from the Book of Leviticus 25:10, "Proclaim liberty through all the land."

There is disagreement as to the cause and time of the crack in the bell. It currently resides in the Liberty Bell Pavilion (since 1976) and is symbolically tapped each July 4th. This icon weighs 2,055 lbs, is 12 feet around the bottom and is 7 feet 6 inches from top to bottom. Long may it be tapped!

The Highland Congregational Church has one of the few (if not the only one) bells in the area. The church was established in 1884 and in 1905 the members purchased the bell from the Redlands Episcopal Church. It was also used for years by the Highland Fire Department.

It was moved in 1964 when the congregation sold the building to the Nazarenes and built the current facilities. Since steeples were originally built to house "bells," the high steeple was built for their bell. A giant crane was used to put the bell in place. The bell was rung to celebrate the end of World War I and World War II. For many years it was rung each year on November 11, at 11 A.M. in honor of Veterans Day. On July 4, 1976 (200 year anniversary of our nation) it was rung 200 times.

Today it is rung to announce every wedding in the church and every Sunday to announce the worship hour (9:15 A.M.) Its resonance is strong and loud. May it continue to ring!

Amen. Selah. So be it.

BIOS

Life is a strange phenomenon. At what point does a fetus become human? Or, at what point does life infiltrate into a glob of flesh? Biologists are prone to say that up to a point in gestation, all embryos look alike: chickens, rabbits, whales or humans. Then something happens and the human fetus appears.

As with so many concepts, we are indebted to the Greeks for bringing clarification to human thought. Example: Democracy. It is a Greek word.

They have three words for love. Eros is normally translated as sexual love. From it come the words: erotic and eroticism. Then, there is the word phileo. It usually has the meaning of brotherly or familial love or caring. The third word for love is agape. This is love at the highest level. It has a spiritual quality. It is love of man and woman and the love between God and humans.

When it comes to describing <u>life</u>, the Greeks outdid themselves. THE BIG THREE are: Bios, Psyche and Zoe: ALL MEANING LIFE.

Anthropologists tells us that we humans (Homo sapiens) began our trek through history about 200,000 years ago. We spawned from the desert area of Serengeti in Kenya. So say the Leakeys.

Of course we were preceded by the Cro-Magnins and Neanderthals. That is when BIOS began the process of biology; the study of life.

As a Christian and a believer in Biblical truth, I believe that God is behind all of life. I also affirm a belief in Theistic Evolution.

Behind the beginning of human life, 4-5 billion years ago (bya), there was the Creator God. The evolutionary process began very small with a single cell. That's what the Bible says. "In the beginning God created."

Every parent can explain the birth process that culminates in life. But human life is significantly different from animal or mammal life.

Dr. R. Colling, a micro-biologist, states that we humans are different in many ways, but most importantly we have self-awareness. We can think and process our thoughts. That's BIOS.

The second Greek word for life is PSYCHE. Basically it means, "Breath of life." This word is important because of its connection with Western medicine.

Rene Descartes (1596-1650) espoused the view that the psyche (mind) and soma (body) were totally separate. No connection.

Hans Selye MD changed medical thinking by showing the connection between worry and ulcers. Today, medicine has changed drastically, BY ACCEPTING THE FACT THAT THE MIND INFLUENCES THE BODY.

Men like Norman Cousins, Herbert Benson and Bernie Siegel became the fathers of Behavioral Medicine. Life without mental health is tragic. Recently Dr. Deepak Chopra spoke of optimal life for us humans. It included exercise, diet (the food we eat) and especially dealing with STRESS. This is what Selye called the "fight or flight" responses, bringing stress into our lives. In managing our stress we possess optimal life.

The third word for life is the Greek word ZOE. It is commonly associated with Zoology-the study of animals-or, zoo-where animals are kept. However, it has a deeper and more spiritual meaning. In the Greek New Testament, ZOE has a special meaning. It is often modified by the adjective aionios or eon. This means eternal or everlasting. It comes out as "everlasting life." Zoe can also have a temporal meaning-this life. A good example is John 10:10. One translation of this verse says, "I am come that you might have life and that you might have it more abundantly-RIGHT NOW."

This grammar lesson has a meaningful theological identification. In Matthew 22:37 and Luke 10:27, Jesus said we should love God with all we have: bios, psyche and Zoë...Body, mind and soul. That is LIFE at its best.

Amen. Selah. So be it.

BUCKETS

The 2007 hit movie The Bucket List is humorous, poignant and provocative. Starring Jack Nicholson and Morgan Freeman; Jack is white and a billionaire. Morgan is black and owns a mechanic shop. Jack has been married four times and cynical. Morgan has a large family and a loving wife and is a man of faith. They both are terminally ill and end up in the same hospital room. Jack owns the hospital. After recovering from surgery they develop an unlikely friendship.

Morgan is a master at trivia and with a stale marriage he has made a list of things he would do if he could. Jack finds the list and challenges Morgan to do them. He's got the money and owns a jet plane. Together they go skydiving, car racing, go to Africa and Paris and China. In the end Morgan's marriage is revived and Jack unites with his one daughter and grandchild. Jack speaks at Morgan's funeral and his cancer goes into remission. He lives to be 81. The cremated remains of both were buried on top of Mt. Everest where the voice of God could be heard; so said Morgan.

In one of their discussions Morgan tells Jack of two questions asked of every person to gain entrance into the Egyptian heaven: "Have you had joy in your life?" and "Did you bring joy to other people?" Obviously the title of the movie is a play on words of dying-kicking the bucket.

Former President Bill Clinton is a fan of the movie. He has made a list of things to do before he "kicks the bucket."

He wants to climb Kilimanjaro, run a marathon and live to see his grandchildren.

I also have a Bucket List. I'd like to visit Galapagos, Churchill, Manitoba where polar bears roam the town, the Congo to see the silver back gorillas, my brothers and uncle back east and New Zealand again. But I probably won't make any of them. However I am a senior, 82 years old, and I have a Bucket List for happy, meaningful living. My mantra is, "Life is worth living." U.S. News recently published several criteria for a happy retirement.

GOOD HEALTH: Someone has said, "Getting older is not for sissies." Why? ...Because our health is always in jeopardy. Doctors are our bed partners. Pharmacies are our senior centers.

Feeling well is essential for happiness. In addition to genetics; exercise, sleep, good eating and medication will contribute to good health.

A SIGNIFICANT OTHER: Every study indicates that married or co-habiting seniors are happier than singles. And they live longer.

A SOCIAL NETWORK: Friends are more important than having kids. Studies say that a strong social network brings 30 percent more contentment.

Grandkids had no impact on a retiree's level of contentment.

THEY ARE NOT ADDICTED TO TELEVISION: Couch potatoes are not happier. Unhappy people watch more TV than happy seniors.

The implication is clear: The busier the senior, the happier the senior.

<u>INTELLECTUAL CURIOSITY</u>: Libraries and book stores love seniors. Seniors engaging in brain stimulating activities are two and a half times less likely to suffer the effects of Alzheimer's.

<u>A RELIGIOUS FAITH:</u> All studies I've read about senior happiness include the element of spiritual faith. It develops contentment now and hope for the future. The Bible says, "They that wait upon the Lord shall renew their strength."

<u>A SENSE OF HUMOR:</u> In the above mentioned movie Jack and Morgan share a great laughing moment. Jack has a favorite, expensive coffee ($100.00 a pound) and Morgan tells him how it is made.

The civet animal is native to Indonesia. It eats a coffee berry and defecates it whole. When dried the defecation is washed off and the coffee bean is ground. They laugh uproariously.

Laughter always brings happiness. Laugh a little and live a lot.

Amen. Selah. So be it.

BUDDHISM

There are about 390 million Buddhists in the world. The vast majority are in Southeast Asia; Indonesia, Thailand, Vietnam, Cambodia, etc. While it began in India, there are only about 7 million there today. There are a few similarities between Buddhism and Hinduism. For instance: a belief in reincarnation and karma. Karma is a principle based on cause and effect. The experiences that one has today are based on the actions of one's past life. Reincarnation is transmigration from one life to another. At death the soul is reincarnated from this life into another life.

Both Hinduism and Buddhism also have a unique way of greeting one another. In facing each other they clasp their hands together as if praying and bow. The significance of this gesture is that they are saying, "I salute (honor or respect) the god in you."

Buddha means "a fully enlightened being." It was the title given to Siddhartha Gautama the founder of Buddhism. He is also referred to as the Bhagavat. (Lord) Scholars set the beginning of Buddhism in the 6th century (BCE), before the Christian era.

Gautama was born in the lap of luxury. He was a prince in a ruling family in Nepal. At the age of twenty-nine he left the luxuries of home, a wife and his son, to become a wandering ascetic. He followed this life for six years. It was as dissatisfactory as his previous life. He came to the belief that a middle path would be best. That would bring him enlightenment. One evening while meditating under a banyan tree, he has "a spiritual awakening." Disciples start following him and he becomes the Buddha.

In his first sermon he proposed the basic path to enlightenment: 1) pain is inextricably part of mankind's everyday life; 2) that our cravings of all kinds are the cause of this pain; 3) that the way off this treadmill is to free oneself from these cravings; and 4) this can be achieved by following the Eightfold Path.

This Path includes:
1) Right understanding;
2) Right purpose;
3) Right speech;
4) Right conduct;
5) Right livelihood;
6) Right effort;
7) Right alertness;
8) Right concentration.

The word "true" is used as a substitute for "right." The eighth step "goes to the heart of the Buddhist ideal." Right concentration induces a special state through deep meditation. "In this way the Buddhist hopes to achieve complete purity of thought, leading ideally to NIRVANA." Nirvana is the final state of liberation from the cycle of birth and death; compared favorably to heaven; even though Buddha avoided such metaphysical designations.

Zen is often associated with Buddhism. It is a part of it, formally called Chan. Budhidharma was the founder of Zen.

By the way, Phil Jackson of the Lakers is an advocate of Zen, as well as Tiger Woods.

The Buddha taught that our physical form, sensations, perceptions are an illusion. Nothing exists independently or eternally. To Buddha, even a blade of grass is transitory. Nothing is permanent. Don't take anything too seriously. Holding on to what does not actually exist will only lead to suffering. Buddha taught that we should not seek divine intervention in this life. The behavior of Buddhists is worthy of note. They are "not to kill," "not to steal," "not to speak falsely," "not to take intoxicants."

Spiritual leaders (monks) vow: "not to eat times not appointed," "not to view entertainment deemed as secular," "not to wear perfumes or bodily ornaments," "not to sleep in beds that are too high or too wide," and not to accept money."

Buddhism sees all things as subject to decay and division that liberation comes only by overcoming selfish desire and craving.

Amen. Selah. So be it.

CHANGELESS

MIT is well known throughout the world as a great scientific institution. Some years ago a professor was called before the governing body of trustees. Reportedly he gave the same final exam each year to his students and then collected the test. Somehow the exam had been stolen and he was called to account. His humor is classic. "I give the same test every year for sure," he said. "However, in science the answers change every year."

When I was in my high school science class we were told the atom was the smallest unit of matter. TV was unheard of. I learned to drive in a Model-T. Ever hear of out houses? We had them.

No NBA, NFL, NHL, PGA or pro-tennis. Jackie Robinson was years ahead. Talking movies and I were born the same year, 1927. We never heard of Vietnam or Pakistan. Pot belly stoves and iceboxes were the norm. I wore knickers to school. Flying to the moon was just a song. Landing on it was thought impossible.

Transplants and cloning...No way! No McDonalds, Burger King, Jack In the Box, frozen foods, motels, cruise ships, Delta, Southwest, Alaska, etc., antibiotics; I could go on and on.

Air-conditioning...We sweltered in the heat and froze in the winter. The proliferation of book stores, freeways, fine restaurants, schools, ear phones and movies still amaze me.

As a retired minister, I've witnessed tremendous

changes in the religious field. Catholics and Protestants now are compatible. Catholics have mass in English and eat meat on Fridays. Protestants have mega-churches and seldom mention hell or sin.

The Dead Sea scrolls and the Nag Hammadi scrolls plus archeological discoveries have brought new understanding of the Bible. New Translations have also brought new insights. For example take the virgin birth of Jesus. It was a common belief in other religions including Roman Emperors. The word "virgin" in Isaiah 7:14 is a mistranslation. The word almah does not mean virgin, but young woman. In Hebrew the word for virgin is bethulah and it was not used.

With all of the changes in our society and belief systems, is there anything that has stayed the same and outlasted the test of time? Yes, absolutely. JESUS.

In the Book of Hebrews (in the Bible) chapter 13 verse 8, it states, "Jesus Christ the same yesterday, and today, and forever." The authorship of the book is unknown, but the verse is vital to Christianity. In the light of the thousands of denominations and branches of Christianity, (Catholic, Protestant, Eastern/Oriental Orthodox) and all claiming to be the "true believers" and all having distinctly different beliefs; how can the verse be believed?

The tragedy of Christianity is that the followers of Jesus obscured, changed, diluted and perverted the message of the Jesus of history to the Christ of faith. The Apostle Paul, Martin Luther, John Calvin, John Wesley and all other founders of denominations imposed their priorities on what the Gospels said about Jesus. In the process they obscured, changed, diluted and perverted the message.

The basic question is still about the unchanging message of Jesus. In my opinion it is: loving God completely, compassion for others. God's universal love for mankind: the kingdom within us, His eternal presence, and the Golden Rule.

Hazel Hurst is considered the founder of the "seeing eye dog" movement. She was asked what the most difficult thing was in training such a dog. To everyone's surprise her reply was, "to teach a dog to raise the horizon of its vision; to see life from the level of a six foot man."

It seems to me the task of Christians is to raise our vision to see life as Jesus saw it.

Amen. Selah. So be it.

CHRISTIAN

E. Stanley Jones was a great Methodist missionary to India. In one of his books he says, "Jesus was the greatest photograph God ever had taken." The implication is clear. If you want to know what God looks like, look at Jesus. Likewise, if you are curious about God's view points, examine the words of Jesus.

In John 10:30 it says, *"I and my Father are one."* John 1:1 is very specific, "In the beginning was the Logos (Word) and the Word (Jesus) was with God and the Word was God."

The Gospel writers are clear in their portrayal of Jesus as a reflection of God. The Apostle Paul picks up on the same theme. *"At the name of Jesus every knee shall bow."* Then, "Every tongue shall confess that Jesus Christ is Lord." However, for the purpose of this article I will limit my conclusions to the four Gospels. My method is called "profiling." It is more commonly used by the FBI in identifying criminals; in particular serial killers.

The method is also used by other disciplines in their search for clarity of personality types. Since history does not give a picture of the historical Jesus. I will use the aforementioned method.

Since Jesus was a Semitic Jew of the first century, He was short of stature (about 5'4"), dark complexion, with a hooked nose, dark hair and eyes. He was muscular with a wiry physique, since He was a carpenter and builder. Jesus was also a farmer. He knew about crops and weeds. He was acquainted with animals: camels, cows, donkeys and pigs. His family was into the fishing business and it is safe to say He was also.

A weakling could NOT have walked around as Jesus did. I've been to Israel. It is hilly and rocky. I've walked where He walked. It was rough going; even more so in that day.

Jesus' emotional reactions also define His profile. His emotional reactions are chronicled several times. When Lazarus died and the news was received by Jesus, the word is that "Jesus wept."

The conflict between Jesus and the Pharisees is well known. In His frustration with them Jesus reportedly called them "whited sepulchers." Perhaps the most visible emotional expression is when Jesus cast out the money changers from the Temple. He used a whip to do it. He was angry.

Another insight into the personality of Jesus is to remember His interaction with people: women, children and the physically ill.

He always treated women as special. Whether Mary Magdalene, the woman taken in adultery, Mary and Martha or His mother. Jewish men of that day thanked God every day that they were not a woman. Jesus respected them. Many scholars believe Mary Magdalene was the key leader in the early church. Even on the cross, Jesus told Apostle John to care for His mother.

Think of those who were healed: the lame, the blind, and the lepers. Jesus' compassion is indicated again and again.

Then there is His intelligence. At the age of twelve He confounded the elders with it. His wisdom was exceptional. It was revealed in His confrontation with the Scribes and

Pharisees. He can be described as sharp as a tack, politically astute and a scholar.

But one attribute stands out above all else. He was focused. He was passionate about life and what He wanted to do. He was willing to die for what He believed. And He did.

No one has ever lived as He did; impacted the world as He has; and challenged millions of people to follow in His footsteps through the centuries as He does.

Amen. Selah. So be it.

CHRISTMAS

Christmas or the Mass of Christ, as it was originally called. Jesus' disciples knew nothing about it. Neither did the Patristic Fathers.

The birth of Jesus was not celebrated by Christians until hundreds of years after His birth. Pope Julian was the first to use the word in 345 A.D. At that time there were two competing religions: Christianity and Mithraism. Because of Emperor Constantine, Christianity won out. They immediately engaged in syncretism. This was the process of incorporating other beliefs and practices into Christianity.

So it was with December 25th. It was the birth date of Mithra, the god of Mithraism. It became the birth date of Jesus.

Helena, the mother of Constantine, arbitrarily established the location of Christian sites in the Holy Land; for example, the location in Bethlehem of the birthplace of Jesus. I've been there. The Cathedral is entered through a small door. At the back of the Chancel is a stairway descending about 20 feet. At the bottom is an ornate altar and a copper star with a one foot hole in the middle. Looking into the hole there is a light about twelve feet below. That is the place where Jesus was born. So it is believed.

Did you know that the Wise men never came to the manger? The Gospel of Matthew states they came "to a house." Tradition says there were three magi. Only because three gifts are mentioned: gold, frankincense and myrrh.

Again, tradition says they were named: Balthazar (the oldest), Melchior (middle-age), and Caspar (a young man).

Consider the time of the year-December. I've been to Jerusalem and Bethlehem in December. It was rainy, snowing and cold. It is comparable to the mountains in December; hardly the time of year for sheep on a hillside. There are huge limestone caves in the area that shelter the animals. The time of the manger story is most likely to have occurred in the spring of the year.

A few years ago the Art Department of Cal State at Long Beach had a Christmas display on campus. Several sidewalks were lined with giant Christmas cards-designed by students in the Department. The winning exhibit was a card with Santa Claus hanging on a cross. It symbolized the commercialism of Christmas. Where does God fit into this crass secularism?

It's time to wake up to the realities of Christmas. Guizot was a great French painter. One of his remarkable paintings depicts the shepherd scene. The lower left shows several shepherds gazing up into the sky. Dimly portrayed-in the upper right-is several angels, singing. It is so real one can almost hear them; "Glory to God and Peace on Earth." BUT, surrounding the shepherds, fast asleep, are several sheep dogs. They don't see or hear the angels. The depiction should be obvious. I'm afraid too many professing Christians are like them-missing the real message of Christmas.

Dan Brown, in his recent best seller, "The Lost Symbol," speaks of the "potentiality of God within each of us." In the Bible we find that man was NOT created inferior to God. In Luke 17:20 we are told, "The Kingdom of God is within you." Genesis says we are created in the image of God. Emmanuel is the real message, "God with (in) us.

Forty years ago I was Protestant Chaplain on the Ship Hope in Tunis, Tunisia. Upon arriving there I was asked to preach each week at the Anglican Church-the only Christian Church in Tunisia. Their priest had become ill and went back to England.

On Christmas Eve I participated in three services: at the church, on the ship and with the Catholic priest at the Midnight Mass. I ended my sermon at the Anglican Church by telling the story of Handel's great oratorio, The Messiah. Written in 21 days, it was sung for the first time in 1741. The British king was present at the presentation. I reminded them that at the singing of the Hallelujah Chorus, the king stood and the entire audience did the same. This practice continues to this day. As I began reciting the words, "He shall reign forever and forever, hallelujah" to my amazement, the audience stood; A tribute to the King of kings.

Years ago Admiral Richard Byrd was on a discovery expedition in the Antarctic. He decided to spend six months several hundred miles, alone, away from the base camp. A half submerged cabin in the snow was built and he was left alone to study the bleak environment. After several weeks of isolation he became stir-crazy and ventured outside.

A sudden snow storm wiped out the whereabouts of his cabin. He knew that if he didn't get back soon he would die. It he went the wrong way he would be lost and death would be his. He placed his eight foot staff in the snow and began circling it, ever increasing the radius. Eventually he found his way back to safety, by keeping his eyes on the pole and looking for the cabin.

To me, this is a parable of the human condition. Our ultimate hope is the center of our focus-the Christ of Christmas.

Stella and I wish you and yours
a very Merry Christmas.

Amen. Selah so be it.

CLAY FEET

Many people, including myself, have used the phrase, "feet of clay," at one time or another. It is used to describe an "unexpected flaw or vulnerable point in the character of a hero or any admired person." An example: "Yes, he is admirable, but you should know that he has feet of clay."

For your literary curiosity, the phrase originates in the Bible. In the Old Testament, the Book of Daniel chapter 2, verses 31, 32 is the reference to feet of clay. Daniel interprets a dream for Nebuchadnezzar, founder of the great Babylonian Empire. The dream is about him. There is a great idol with a golden head, silver arms and chest, brass thighs and body, and iron legs. However, his feet are made of iron and clay. Daniel tells the King that his feet of clay make him vulnerable. The prophecy was about the breaking apart of the Empire.

Numerical categories are often used in religious descriptions. Everyone knows of the Ten Commandments. Most everyone knows of the two greatest commandments given by Jesus.

The Seven Deadly Sins as emphasized by Catholicism are: <u>Pride</u>, <u>Avarice</u> <u>Envy</u>, <u>Wrath</u>, <u>Lust</u>, <u>Gluttony</u>, and <u>Sloth</u>. It is interesting to bounce opposing virtues against them: Humility, Generosity, Love, Kindness, Self Control, Temperance, and Zeal.

What are some of the major evidences of clay feet among men and women today? In many ways their lives are credible and everything about them seems above board. But the subtlety of clay feet is insidious into all of their lives. The first <u>one</u> I call FLIP-FLOP. When a person is reluctant to stand for tried and true values, the way out is to waffle, to change one's mind or to flip-flop: Feet of clay.

While we commoners are prone to waffling, political leaders are notorious: McCain, on immigration, the first President Bush on "no more taxes," Lieberman on everything and Specter of the Republicans. Just to name a few.

My second evidence of feet of clay is old fashioned GREED. It is another subtle attitude that weakens character. It involves more than money, even though it includes the striving for monetary wealth. It is the incessant drive to accumulate more and more at the expense of others; regardless who they are. Two good examples are Halliburton and BP-British Petroleum. Their consuming passion is greed at the expense of "little people." Former Vice President Cheney is their poster man.

Before running for V-P he was the CEO of Halliburton and when he left them, he received a 34 million dollar bonus. He also met with them-in private- several times while being V-P. Greed is evidence of feet of clay.

Someone has said, "Every sinner has a future and every saint has a past." The past of saints is often their feet of clay. Their past is expressed with arrogance; especially relative to their expression of spirituality. They think God has resigned and put them in charge.

The "feet of clay" syndrome can be evident in a myriad of ways. For Abraham Lincoln it was a wife with mental problems. With others it can be overeating, or smoking (Obama,) or alcoholism (George W. Bush,) or drugs (Willie

Nelson.)

A similar adage comes from Greek mythology; the legend of Achilles. His mother (Thetis) dipped him in a magical river when he was a baby to make him invincible. BUT, she held him by his heel and that was his weakness. He was killed by a poisoned arrow in his heel. The use of "Achilles heel or tendon" refers to an area of weakness. Very much like "feet of clay."

Amen. Selah so be it.

COFFEE BEAN

Derek Angelo shared with me a most insightful story. It's about a carrot, an egg, and a cup of coffee.

"A young woman went to her mother and told her about her life. She did not know how she was going to make it and wanted to give up; she was tired of fighting and struggling. Her problems were severe. Her mother took her to the kitchen. She filled three pots with water and placed each on a high fire. Soon the pots came to boil. In the first she placed carrots, in the second she placed eggs, and in the last she placed ground coffee beans. She let them sit and boil without saying a word.

In about twenty minutes she turned off the burners. She fished the carrots out and placed them in a bowl. She pulled the eggs out and placed them in a bowl. Then she ladled the coffee out and placed it in a bowl. Turning to her daughter, she asked, 'Tell me what you see.' 'Carrots, eggs, and coffee,' she replied. Her mother explained that each of these objects had faced the same adversity: boiling water. Each reacted differently. The carrot went in strong, hard and unrelenting. However, after being subjected to the boiling water, it softened and became weak. The egg had been fragile. Its thin outer shell had protected its liquid interior, but after sitting through the boiling water, its inside became hardened. The ground coffee beans were unique, however. After they were in the boiling water, they had changed the water. . . 'Which are you?' she asked her daughter. 'When adversity knocks on your door, how do you respond? Are you a carrot, an egg or a coffee bean?

Am I the egg that starts with a malleable heart, but changes with the heat? Did I have a fluid spirit, but after a death, a breakup, a financial hardship or some other trial, have I become hardened and stiff? Does my shell look the same, but on the inside am I bitter and tough with a stiff spirit and hardened heart?

Am I like the coffee bean? The bean actually changes the hot water, the very circumstance that brings the pain. If you are like the bean, when things are at their worst, you get better and change the situation around you. The choice is yours;" And mine; and you; every one of us.

In Scott Peck's book, The Road Less Traveled," the first paragraph has only three words. Life is difficult. No one can deny it.

There can be monumental invasions into our tranquility like illness, death of loved ones, economic and family problems; or, the accumulation of the many irritations of everyday living. How do we respond to them? Like the CARROT?

Karl Barth, one of the great thinkers of the past century reminds us, that, "there is a saving element in every situation." Accepting defeat should never be an option. There is an old adage that reminds us that whenever a door is closed to us, another one opens up: A saving element.

Recently, Larry Stamper, retired Methodist minister and former Mayor of Burbank, sent me an e-mail that gives pause for we seniors. He said, "I see many seniors becoming more conservative in their thinking, more set in their ways and inflexible." This indictment is reminiscent of the EGG affect.

They are suspicious of life, calloused and merely waiting for the end of life. Years ago I read a statement by Johann Wolfgang von Goethe, German playwright (Faust), poet, novelist and dramatist. "WE MUST ALWAYS CHANGE, RENEW, REGUVENATE OURSELVES; OTHERWISE WE HARDEN."

The challenge of the fore mentioned mother is relevant. Become a COFFEE BEAN.

Amen. Selah. So be it.

COLONIES

My considered opinion is that Will Durant was the greatest American historian, ever. His opus is the "History of Civilization." The eight volume work combines an amazing array of facts with thoughtful and meaningful insights. He once observed that most of history is a record of what's happening in the middle of rivers, without what is happening on the shore. Will Durant avoid his own indictment? For example, he records the existence of Roman colonies. To advance Roman culture and dominance over newly conquered territories, the Roman Senate established the colonies.

These garrisons were settled by representative citizens from Rome. In addition to soldiers for protection, there were farmers who sent much of their produce back to Rome. Additional citizenry was composed of artists, engineers, teachers, architects, slaves for scut work, government officials, religious leaders, etc; Everything to make up a normal community. A basic consideration was complete families; parents and children. The most important purpose of the colonies was to influence the so-called ignorant pagans of the ways of cultured Romans. This concept could work today. Incidentally, in the Bible's Book of Acts, Chapter 16, the author calls the city of Philippi, a "colony." It was the Apostle Paul's first missionary venture into Europe.

Later on Paul uses the analogy of a colony to Christians who were a "colony of heaven;" Also changing the word to "ambassadors." The purpose was similar to the Roman colonies; to influence the "heathen" to become followers of Christ.

I heard a beautiful illustration of a subtle influence the other day. Dr. Lowell Linden told the story of Alfaro Valences. As a young man, his parents sent him from the Philippines to the United States to study law. The first day on campus a fellow student asked Alfaro if he could be of help. Being a Catholic, he asked directions to the nearest church. He was given directions.

On Sunday it was pouring rain and he decided to stay home. However, the other student showed up with two umbrellas and offered to walk with him to the church. Alfaro asked the fellow student where he attended and the student said it was close by. He then asked if he could go with him. It was a Methodist Church. He liked it, began to attend regularly and became a member.

Shortly thereafter he decided to be a minister and attended seminary. He returned to the Philippians. When the Bishop announced the appointments, Alfaro misunderstood where he was to go and so he went a thousand miles away to a primitive area.

Arriving there, no church existed. Not knowing differently, he went to work: preaching and visiting people. For several years the Conference forgot about him. Several years late, Alfaro notified them that he was a pastor of a church with thousands of members. Sometime later he became Bishop Alfaro Valences.

Dr. Linden concluded this account with the words: "The hero of the story is not the Bishop, but the unknown college student who had two umbrellas, who influenced him.

My dad died at the young age of sixty from silicosis (black lung.) He had worked in a coal mine and foundry. It was the Great Depression. Work was scarce and we were poor. Dad never owned a car. We walked everywhere, including five miles to and from church. Dad was quiet and unassuming; only a six grade education. However, every week we would stop at various homes and walk a friend of his to church.

In the course of my growing up, I knew of four families who started going to church; five men and women became leaders in the church; two others became ministers.

The power of a subtle influence is evidenced in all three stories: Roman colonies, Bishop Alfaro Valences and my Father. There is hope for all of us.

Amen. Selah. So be it.

COMFORT

The other day I attended a funeral service for someone I'd known for many years. The service brought to my mind the need for comfort for those who are sorrowing.

There are three basic spiritual needs that we have. The first is the need for forgiveness. We don't live very long until this need surfaces in our minds. It's not accidental that Jesus spoke often about forgiveness. Even in the Lord's Prayer. The cross has long stood as a reminder of God's love and gift of salvation (forgiveness).

The second need is for a comforting presence. Jesus said, "Yea, I am with you always, even to the end." Again, the Bible says, "Underneath us are the everlasting arms (of God.)

And, third of course, is the need to be comforted in times of grief. In Isaiah we find the words, "I am He (God) who comforteth you." The ultimate source of comfort for those who sorrow is our God. In times of our grief there are three other sources of comfort; for example, the universality of our condition. Everyone, at some time or another has experienced the loss of a love one. This binds us together. Be a life long or short, there comes an end. The Bible describes it as "the span of a man's hand." Or like "a flower in the field." Here today and gone tomorrow. Or like "a vapor that disappears in the sky."

The commonality of our plight is a source of comfort. Family and friends offer prayers, light candles and think thoughts for mourners. The sadness caused by loss becomes an opportunity for family togetherness. Disagreements are forgotten in the presence of loss and all who have loved the deceased share the commonality of grief.

A further source of comfort is our memories. While time well diminishes them; there will always be a residue of memory. Words of advice, experiences and activities that come to mind; such memories of things enjoyed will never be erased.

Angelo Patri had a beautiful insight. "In one sense there is no death. The life of a soul on earth lasts beyond its departure. You will always feel that life touching yours, that voice speaking to you, that spirit looking out of other eyes. They live on in your life and in the lives of all others who knew them."

Another source of comfort is our faith. Those things we believe. Jesus said, "I am the resurrection and the life. Those who believe in me shall never die." The Apostle Paul said, "To be absent from the body is to be present with Christ.

The Psalmist said, "Though I walk through the valley of the shadow of death, I will fear no evil, for Thou art with me." Albert Einstein proved that matter is ultimately indestructible. We affirm that the spirit of our loss is also likewise indestructibility.

Teilhard Chardin, the great Catholic theologian said, "It is utterly absurd to believe that the human spirit is so poorly devised that it would contradict its highest aspirations."

There were some things we wished to share with the deceased. We believe that we shall meet again and can share with them.

As mentioned before our God is the ultimate source of

our comfort. *"My God, even my God, is He who comforts you."* We do believe in God. He hears our prayers and sees our tears. We believe our loved one is with Him. We pray that He will share with them our love and appreciation. They made the world a better place and enhanced our lives.

The song writer has lifted the spirit of many with these words: "God hath not promised skies always blue, Flowers strewn pathways all our lives thro'; God hath not promised sun without rain, Joy without sorrow, peace without pain. But God hath promised strength for the day, Rest for the labor, light for the way, Grace for the trials, help from above, Unfailing sympathy, undying love."

Amen. Selah. So be it.

COPTICS

The Coptic Orthodox Church is one of the least known and most important segments of Christianity. The word "Coptic" originated in the age of the Pharaohs of Egypt. In fact, Coptic and Egyptian are synonymous. They are considered descendants of the Egyptians.

As a church they believe it was started by John Mark, the supposed writer of the second Gospel. Theoretically it is older than the Catholic Church since the Holy Family fled to Egypt to escape the massacre of the infants by King Herod. (Matthew 2:15)

No one knows how long they stayed in Egypt but wherever they stopped, a sanctuary was erected. I personally have visited several.

Today there are several thousand Coptic Orthodox Churches in Egypt with approximately 9 million members. They make up about 15% of the Egyptian population. In addition to another 1.2 million Copts who practice their faith in other countries. They have also achieved academic and professional status in the world. Dr. Boutros Ghali was the 6th United Nations Secretary-General. Dr. Magdy Yacoub, M.D. is one of the world's foremost heart surgeons.

Dr. M. Gayid, M.D. is my personal internist doctor and Dr. Marian Beshara, M.D. is Stella's physician.

Back to ancient history. Saint Mark preached in Alexandria, Egypt in 48 A.D. and was martyred in 68 A.D. The next great ecclesiastical leader was Saint Athanasius, the Pope of Alexandria for 46 years. Patristic Fathers Origen and Clement were both Coptic.

Athanasius is remembered for three main reasons. He formulated the Nicean Creed in 325 A.D., which is repeated in most Christian churches today. Second, and very important, he was the first person in antiquity to formulate the 27 books known today as the New Testament. Several others followed in his wake. Third, was his refutation of the heresy of Arius; he denied the divinity of Jesus. Arius did this by saying, "There was once when he (Jesus) was not. He did not exist before he was born. Therefore Jesus did not have the same nature as the Father and consequently was not divine."

Athanasius was adamant in quoting John 1:1, *"In the beginning was the Word (Jesus) and the Word (Jesus) was with God and the Word (Jesus) was God."*

Believe it or not, most churches that quote a creed are Arians. Their creeds affirm Jesus as the "Son" of God. This means there was a time when He (Jesus) did not exist. He is also famous for saying, *"God became man that we might become God."*

In the early years of Christendom there were five major centers: Jerusalem, Antioch, Constantinople, Rome and Alexandria. All had pretentions for greatness. The unique claim is Alexandria was its great library, established by Alexander the Great. It is reported that Anthony gave over 200,000 scrolls to it. It was considered the largest library in ancient history with close to a million volumes. Unfortunately it was burned to the ground; which, incidentally ushered in the Dark Ages.

NO ONE KNOWS WHO DID IT. But many scholars

believe it was set ablaze by the foes of the Coptic prominence. What a tragedy.

Orthodoxy is basic to the Coptic beliefs. They contend that the Catholic and Protestant Churches have moved away from it; particularly through the acceptance of the views of Augustine.

However, one position where they agree with Catholicism is concerning the Sacraments. They endorse Baptism, Confirmation, Penance and Confession, Communion, Unction of the sick, Matrimony and the Priesthood.

Other pertinent facts: The Coptic's were the first ones to use the title "Pope." In 1971, His Holiness Pope Shenouda III became the 117th Pope and Patriarch of Alexandria.

The Coptics were the majority of the Egyptian population until the thirteenth century. Egypt is the only country outside of Israel that Jesus visited.

History records the Emperor Diocletian killed more Christians than any other Emperor, including Nero. Between 500,000 and a million Coptic's were martyred.

Amen. Selah. So be it.

CRUISES

Cruising is a major part of tourism today. Bigger ships are being built. They are also plushier. They plow the seas to every port on the globe. In many respects, all cruise ships are the same: NCL, Princess, Carnival, Holland American, Celebrity, Royal Caribbean, etc.

The main emphasis on all of them is food. It's offered 24 hours a day. The only difference is seating arrangements. Some are casual, others more formal. Excursions are offered at every port docking. The prices are going higher every year. The kind is dependent on the location. For example Alaska offers helicopter rides to glaciers. Mexico has jungle trips.

All sea days provide activities from morning to late at night. Bingo, parlor games, water sports, etc. Of course every ship has a casino-open only when ships are at sea. Shopping, shopping, and shopping; on shore or on the ship. Specialty cruises are also popular: for singles, for religious groups and for homosexuals are examples.

Recently Stella and I went on a Mexican Riviera cruise aboard the Princess Sapphire. They offered all the usual amenities plus an unusual one. Every Princess we've ever been on had religious services. This trip was no exception. There was a Friday evening (Sabbath) service for Jewish cruisers; plus a Sunday morning Interdenominational worship service. In addition, during the days at sea an informal Bible study was held in the Chapel, which we attended.

The Sunday worship was lead by Paul Chalmers,

Assistant Cruise Director. There were about 100 people present and Paul led us in singing. How Great Thou Art, and Amazing Grace. A volunteer crew member played the piano. Paul is a native of Corby, England and single. Prior to working for Princess he studied at the University and majored in musical theater. He is a member of the Anglican Church. His sermon is too long to print, so I'll only provide excerpts from it. Paul begins with a provocative question. Could we be really happy if we lived in a paradise like the Garden of Eden? Probably not! Why? ...Because in spite of an idyllic environment each of us has a proclivity to worry. We will not allow ourselves to enjoy what we have.

Paul talks of a girl who had everything hut had developed the habit of worry-no matter how wonderful things were. The Gospel message is for us to enjoy life-to live fully.

In addition to worry, life becomes more futile if we engage in judging. Jesus said, *"Judge not that you be not judged."* Judging involves more than evaluating the character of other people. It includes life's experiences. What happens to us. Is it good or is it bad? Do we possess the capacity to make a truthful judgment call?

Consider the tale of the wise old farmer whose one prized horse ran away. His neighbor lamented this horrible loss. The farmer responded with, good or bad, how do I know? The next day his horse returned with 50 other horses. His neighbor was thrilled, but his response was, good or bad, how do I know. The next day his son broke both of his legs trying to ride a horse. Again, the neighbor lamented. The farmer again said, good or bad, who knows? The next day his country went to war and every young man was conscripted.

The son couldn't go to war where all were killed. Good or bad, who knows?

Jesus said don't judge what happens. The two essentials for happiness are compassion and forgiveness. These are two of Jesus' favorite topics. They lead to a meaningful life. Thanks, Paul

Amen, Selah, So be it.

CRUISING

"Viajar es vivir" is a Hispanic dicho or proverb. It means "to travel is to live." I can't think of any philosophy of life more appropriate for seniors.

Stella and I recently made a fourteen day cruise to Hawaii with 2598 other passengers. At least 90 percent of them could be called seniors. There were about fifteen teenagers; very few kids that I could tell; and the rest were young adults or middle aged.

Discounting the food, which the seniors gobbled down with an amazing alacrity, they participated in a myriad of activities. They certainly utilized the exercise facilities. The several dance floors were filled with them. They even took dance lessons from ballroom to line dancing. Since we were going to Hawaii, the hula was a favorite for lessons.

Ukulele lessons…You bet-cha! They even put on a recital composed of hula dancers, singers and ukulele players. Another group of volunteer singers put on a concert in the piazza. One thing, above all other activities that seniors participated in was reading. Every senior seemed to have a book in hand. All cruise ships have extensive libraries. Why else but for seniors? From serious books to romance and mystery, they (we) are always reading.

They dress up, attend all shows, get their pictures taken, and watch movies and football games. The Golden Princess has a huge outdoor screen, so there was a constant screening of movies and sporting events. They make leis, learn how to fold napkins, play bingo, gamble at the casino, go to the art auction, shop 'till they drop-on land and on the ship-attend AA, service clubs, Bible studies, single groups, keep the bars busy and sing at karaoke. The biggest attractions for everyone are the Las Vegas type shows, lectures and performances by entertainers.

Of the fourteen days at sea, rough weather characterized ten of them. The storms were so bad that we could not dock at Kawai: 40-45 mile an hour winds and 15-20 feet high waves. We also could not dock at Maui. The floods were so bad all streets were covered with mud and no electricity on the island. Weather is unpredictable everywhere.

There were several highlights for me. First, we had a handicapped room twice the size of a regular room; a large balcony, a king sized bed, doors big enough for a walker or wheelchair or scooter; and best of all, a bath room and shower four times the size of the usual ones. Wow!

Second, the lectures by Dr. Sharron Faff were outstanding. She lives on the Big Island and is a Naturalist and Geologist. She really knows the islands. They are three to four million years old: their historical development since the Polynesian invasion; their take-over by Christian missionaries and descendants and the natural disasters. She covered all of them.

Joshua Seth is a lecturer on hypnotism and mentalism. He's also an outstanding entertainer. Every performance was greeted by a packed out house. He thrilled the audience with his knowledge.

Third, and most impressive for me, a retired minister, were the worship services (2) conducted by the cruise director,

David Bradshaw. A former actor and Anglican Churchwarden, he has been with Princess for many years. He even provided copies of the services for the worshipers.

Perhaps the best thing about a cruise is the many new friends you meet. Too many to mention, but you know who you are. I cannot think of a better way to have a vacation than by taking a cruise-anywhere.

Amen. Selah. So be it.

CUBA

Curiosity motivated me to visit Cuba the latter part of July. My previous visit had been before Castro took over and made it into a communist country. Back then the key words were Batista, torture, crime, mafia, ignorance, gambling and Hemingway.

This time found that in the words of a young man I met named Jose, "We have education, medical care, no crime, drugs or bombs and no freedom." Or as Gregorio told me, "In the United States you can fulfill your fantasies and dreams, while we cannot."

The most harrying experience I had was when I was interrogated by the police and accused of making statements to the detriment of Castro and the Cuban government. I had read an article just the week before where several journalists were sent to prison for the very same accusation. After an hour of questioning I was ordered to cease and desist from such activities.

There were three experiences that elevated my spirit and gave me insight into the Cuban psyche. First, I visited Cojimar, the fishing village where Hemingway caroused and wrote his classic book, The Old Man and the Sea. Since he is still revered as a saint and is admired by everyone, including Castro, I wanted to visit La Terraga-the name of the restaurant he frequented. Memorabilia was everywhere and fortunately I met Gregorio Fuentes, the fishing buddy and supposedly the man who inspired Hemingway's book. He is now 97 years of age, dapper, articulate and belligerently defensive of Hemingway. Last year he broke the nose of an Argentinean journalist who spoke despairingly of Hemingway. I culminated my visit with Fuentes by buying him a drink.

The second insight came from visiting a hospital outside of Havana that was built for the children victims of Chernoble. Over 15,000 have been treated there for cancer, tumors, burns and other problems caused by the radiation fall out.

The Cubans have developed a treatment from the placentas that aids in their healing. The combination of environment, sea water, and the sun along with the traditional use of surgery, radiation and chemotherapy has enabled them to help all but the eleven who died. Diet is also a significant aid in the rehabilitation of the children.

Perhaps the most significant event that I experienced was in meeting Rosita. She is a dentist and is also a participant in the underground economy. CNN did a special on this practice a few weeks ago and I saw it working.

As a dentist Rosita is typical of all the people who are paid by the government from 200 – 300 peso a month or about $10.00 American. In addition they receive housing, food stamps, and medical care. Because of the U.S. embargo, the economy is poor and Castro has suggested a free enterprise economy that is illegal but also legal – in other words, it is winked at. As an expression of this practice, Rosita and her husband run a bed and breakfast facility in their home.

Since she can only practice dentistry two days a week because of the paucity of dental materials, she runs the bed and breakfast on the side. But it was not this practice that impressed me most. She is a Presbyterian and treasurer of her church. In June, 1995 the congregation entered their new Sanctuary for the first time. It is absolutely beautiful. The vibrancy of her faith and the energy is her life and the hope she projects was inspiring.

Her minister's wife Mrs. Dora Arce wrote a booklet entitled, <u>A Christian Woman in the Revolution.</u> In reading it, one can well understand Rosita and her family, for Christianity is alive and well in Cuba.

Cuba is a beautiful mostly green island with sandy beaches. It has the softest sands imaginable. The people are smart and aggressive in business and sports. They are survivors. They are attractive people. Many express their private opinions that Castro is an old man and past his prime. By and large they resent those who have fled to the U.S.

Their infrastructure is old and worn. As one man said, "For change to come there must be three things, 1) a bad economy, 2) persecution and 3) someone to step up to lead. We have the first two but no one on the horizon to replace Castro." When change comes, look for a bonanza for American business.

Amen. Selah so be it.

DAD

It has been 65 plus years since I was under the direct discipline of my father. And yet, I remember very vividly his counsel by way of actions. With a limited education – only six grades – he lived his years honestly and with integrity.

I learned from him. Give an honest day's work for an honest day's pay. Be thrifty; as much as possible, stay out of debt. Help others in need. Don't be ashamed to wave our flag. Be patriotic. Attend church. Let your actions speak louder than your words. Not bad for an uneducated man, born in 1903. I've tried to emulate him.

I read somewhere that one goal in life is to learn. We do that by looking around us at all times and listening to others. In that way we receive knowledge and understanding. In some ways our lives are shaped by heredity. Many reputable psychologists also add our environment; nature and nurture.

There's an old saying that says, "A knife is sharpened on stone. Steel is sharpened by fire. But people are sharpened (learn) by other people."

An impediment that we often face is human discouragement. It is easy to get down on life. A phrase in a novel I recently read said, "No man is lost while yet he lives."

I like what Jon Stewart said the other day. "These are tough times but they are not the end times." No discouragement there.

Dr. Lowell Linden used a figure of speech in his pastoral prayer when he prayed for the Divine to help us when we are caught in LIFE'S FISHNET...Caught without hope of getting out. God answers that prayer.

It seems to me as I observe the human situation-including myself-we can do just about anything we put our minds to. It has been said, "Only the weak blame parents, their race, their times, lack of good fortune, or the queries of fate." But, as I recall, the author also reminded the readers that we each have the power within to make today different from yesterday.

There is an old Chinese proverb that reminds us that a journey of a thousand miles begins with the first step. Actions must follow ideas and thoughts. A good synonym for actions is DEEDS.

With due respect for my Democrat affiliation, I was most impressed with the words of newly elected Republican Senators Rubio of Florida and Paul of Kentucky who both spoke of the great heritage of America. Our freedom must be respected and worked for. It is not automatic. I liked what they said. Actions do speak louder than words.

Louis L'Amour was a marvelous novelist. He was also a distinctive and persuasive philosopher. For example, he has one of his characters say, "The goods of this world are soon lost. Fire, storm, thieves, and war are always with us, but what is stored in the mind is ours forever." This statement is very reminiscent of Jesus' words about hoarding (lying up) treasures where bugs and rust destroy or thieves steal them. Rather, we should preserve eternal values in heaven. Where is it located? Jesus said the Kingdom of God (heaven) was within us. What better place than "the mind." As L'Amour said, "it is forever." *Amen. Selah. So be it.*

DASH

Without a doubt the most provocative question ever asked is, "What is life?"…The "how" to deal with it has been discussed and cussed from time immemorial.

Even Hugh Hefner has an opinion. "The challenge of life is to live it to the hilt;" Whatever that means. I like what James Baldwin has to say, "The challenge of life is to be present in everything we do; from getting up in the morning to going to bed at night."

Jesus even spoke about life. "I am come that you might have life, and have it more abundantly." Obviously He was talking about more than our sum total of breathes and heart beats. Some theorists describe life as Birth, Living and Death. No meaning, no purpose. The Bible sometimes falls into that "slough of despond." Methuselah is said to have lived 969 years. That's all he is noted for. The Book of Numbers reiterates a similar mundane record; so and so begets so and so.

Does the name Linda Ellis sound familiar? Her poem, THE DASH, is enjoyed by millions. It is responsible for changed attitudes, a shifting of directions and motivations. The dash refers to the line between the dates of a person's birth and death. It usually appears on obituaries and on tombstones. As one writer puts it, "the poem will get you thinking differently about life and what's truly important."

Three verses of the poem are:

For it matters not how much you own,

The cars, the house, the cash.
What matters is how we live and love
And how we spend our dash.

So think about this long and hard
Are there things you'll like to change?
For you never know how much time is left
That can still be rearranged.

So, when your eulogy is being read
With your life's actions to rehash
Would you be proud of the things they say
About how you spent your dash?

Harry Ward Beecher is reported as saying, "God asks no one if they will accept life. The only choice they have is what they will do with it."

Jesus lived only 33 years and the same for Alexander the Great. Think for a moment what they both accomplished. Both, in their own ways, changed the world.

Moses began his life's work at the age of 80. I personally know several men and women in their 90 are who are continually enriching our world with their thoughts and actions.

I owe a big "thanks" to Dave Bradshawe, Anglican churchman and Cruise Director for the following story. It is about a woman named Rose whose "dash" was amazing.

"The first day of school our professor introduced himself and challenged us to get to know someone we didn't already know. I stood up to look around when a gentle hand touched my shoulder. I turned around to find a wrinkled, little old lady beaming up at me with a smile that lit up her entire being. She said, 'Hi, handsome. My name is Rose. I'm eighty-seven yours old. Can I give you a hug?' I laughed and enthusiastically responded; 'Of course you may!' and she gave me a giant squeeze.

'Why are you in college at such a young, innocent age?' I asked. She jokingly replied, 'I'm here to meet a rich husband, get married, have a couple of children, and then retire and travel.' 'No seriously,' I asked. I was curious what may have motivated her to be taking on this challenge at her age. 'I always dreamed of having a college education and now I'm getting one!' she told me. After class we walked to the student union building and shared a chocolate milkshake. We became instant friends and every day for the next three months we would leave class together and talk nonstop. I was always mesmerized listening to this 'time machine' as she shared her wisdom and experience with me.

Over the course of the year, Rose became a campus icon and she easily made friends where she went. She loved to dress up and she reveled in the attention bestowed upon her from the other students. She was living it up. At the end of the semester we invited Rose to speak at our football banquet. I'll never forget what she taught us. She was introduced and stepped up to the podium. As she began to deliver her prepared speech, she dropped her three by five cards on the floor.

Frustrated and a little embarrassed she leaned into the microphone and simply said 'I'm sorry I'm so jittery. I'll never get my speech back in order so let me just tell you what I know.' As we laughed she cleared her throat and began: 'We do not stop playing because we are old; we grow old because we stop playing. There are four secrets to staying young, being happy, and achieving success.

-You have to laugh and find humor every day.
-You've got to have a dream. When you lose your dreams, you die.

We have so many people walking around who are dead and don't know it! There is a huge difference between growing older and growing up. If you are nineteen years old and lie in bed for one full year and don't do one productive thing, you will turn twenty years old. If I am eighty-seven years old and stay in bed for a year and never do anything I will turn eighty-eight. Anybody can grow older. That doesn't take any talent or ability. The idea is to grow up by always finding the opportunity to change. Have no regrets. The elderly usually don't have regrets for what we did, but rather for things we did not do.'

She concluded her speech by courageously singing 'The Rose.' She challenged each of us to study the lyrics and live them out in our daily lives. At the year's end Rose finished the college degree she had begun all those years ago. One week after graduation Rose died peacefully in her sleep.

Over two thousand college students attended her funeral in tribute to the wonderful woman who taught by example that it's never too late to be all you can possibly be."

Amen. Selah. So be it.

DEFENSE

Of all the things that have been said and will be said to describe Jesus, none is more accurate and beneficial than: "He was the most effective and helpful therapist who ever lived." Even by current psychological standards for human behavior, His views are valid.

The emotional needs of people today are basically the same as they were 2,000 years ago. Guilt, fear, depression, worry and bitterness are still plaguing the vast majority of people. Guilt is either self-imposed or outer imposed; the latter by parents, significant others, organizations like the church or a perceived Deity (God.)

Forgiveness is the ultimate therapy and it involves extending it and accepting it. Self-forgiveness is in many ways the most difficult. But Divine forgiveness, as extended by Jesus, is completely healing.

Fear is devastating. It is immobilizing. It is akin to paranoia. Fear of failure is a persistent emotional disease. It often leads to aberrant behavior like what the Apostle Peter experienced in the Garden of Gethsemane. It affected him so drastically he even lied. Jesus offered him understanding and that revolutionized Peter's life. The expectations of others can trigger a persistent fear; Again, failure. Jesus' influence was powerful in its calming effect. This was paramount in every one of His encounters.

Anxiety and worry stimulate all kinds of physical traumas from high blood pressure to psychosomatic illnesses.

Jesus brought those suffering into resolution by reminding them of God's care: the hairs on their heads were numbered by Him, even the lilies were His.

Bitterness is an insidious and malignant disease of the emotions. It distorts any inclination to forgive. It can be caused by a small slight or a subtle resentment. Jesus was extremely astute in offering the therapy of "Judge not that you be not judged."

It seems to me this issue is simply one of SURVIVAL. Survival of the fittest, if you please. It means dealing with those issues that weaken our psyche. Sigmund Freud was right when he developed "Defense Mechanisms." One therapist has said, "When you get right down to it, survival is a matter of emotional defenses." Consider a few of Freud's pearls of wisdom. His answer for loneliness, rejection, disappointment, fear, failure, anxiety, grief, anger, tears.

1. <u>SUBLIMATION or COMPENSATION</u>. It allows us to act out unacceptable impulses by engaging in behavior that is more acceptable. For example: Instead of expressing anger toward a loved one, engage in competitive sports, play an instrument or any stress relieving activity.

Often because of a sense of inferiority, guilt or anger, an individual will compensate by going into a helping profession like teaching, the ministry, or law enforcement.

2. <u>RATIONALIZATION or JUSTIFICATION</u>. This defense mechanism is often the favorite of the more intellectual. "The devil made me do it." It prevents anxiety and also protects self-esteem. "People tend to attribute achievement to their own qualities and skills while failures are blamed on other people or outside forces."

3. <u>PROJECTION.</u> This is a great escape/defense mechanism. It involves ascribing to other people our own unacceptable behaviors. It is blaming others for our failures, thus easing our own anxiety.

4. <u>DISPLACEMENT</u>. Oh my. This is a beauty. Have you ever had a bad day at work, then gone home and taken out your frustration on family and friends? Or kicked the dog? It's called "displaced aggression."

5. <u>ACTING OUT.</u> The individual deals with stress by engaging in "maladaptive behavior;" Such as drinking alcohol, using drugs, eating excessively, becoming sexually promiscuous. The end result is often: becoming an alcoholic, drug addict, overweight or sex addiction.

"Freud believed that defense mechanisms helped shield the ego from the conflicts created by the ID, SUPEREGO and REALITY."

Amen. Selah so be it.

DESIGN

Genesis Chapter one verse one has long been the source of great controversy between science and religion. "In the beginning God created the heavens and the earth." The following verses describe the process of creation by number of days. However, the key word in the aforementioned verse is "beginning." Theologians and scientists alike have disagreed on the time-frame.

Archbishop James Ussher set the time of creation at 4004 B.C.E. For centuries scientists left the time open by affirming that the universe always was and will always be. Then along came the Big Bang theory in the mid-twentieth century. Most scientists accepted the view of Judaism, Christianity and Islam that the universe had a definite beginning. The difference between them is substantial. Religion asserts God as the source of the Big Bang. Science declares the Big Bang came into existence out of nothing.

So, the conflict continues. The only difference is that religionists have changed the word "creation" to the term, Intelligent Design; or as many religious scientists call it, "theistic evolution."

I am a definite believer in the Intelligent Design theory, in that I affirm the creation of the universe 13-14 billion years ago, the creation of our earth, 3-5 billion years ago and of mankind 100,000-200,000 years ago.

What began with the Big Bang caused an evolution of the above and is continuing today. This causes disagreement with fundamentalist Christians and with many scientists. Many of them have one thing in common. They both believe they are right and those who disagree with them are wrong.

Scientists by and large accept only facts that can be replicated. In 2000 there were 11 million employed college educated scientists in the U.S. Over 6000 scientific articles are written every day. Hypotheses, theories and supposed facts are constantly changing. Einstein said, "No amount of experimentation can ever prove me right; a single experiment can prove me wrong."

Scientific infallibility is a myth. I'd rather endorse Intelligent Design than rely on the speculation of science. It is unreliable. Many scientists also denounce ID by questioning the many natural disasters, poverty in our world, drought areas and global weather changes. The question? Why would a benevolent God (ID) permit such a world?

My answer is simple. The universe and earth are not complete in the creative process. Earthquakes, volcanic eruptions, hurricanes, etc. are part of the process. Even diseases and Katrina tragedies are the result of human failures and decisions to live in potentially dangerous places. Some cancers are caused by smoking and industrial mistakes. It's us not God.

In the creative process, initiated by ID, man has the power of choice for good or ill. Societal dilemmas are the result of human exploration and exploitation.

William Paley, back in the early 1800's, presented the now famous example of the watch and its maker. The analogy is often ridiculed by scientists. But I believe it is relevant to my argument. Complexity demands intelligence. An example of this complexity is the fact that in the human brain there are 100 billion neurons, each linked with 10,000 other neurons. It is foolish to think that a watch, so intricately made, could assemble accidentally. A maker, designer or intelligent being must have made it. So it is with the universe, our earth and mankind.

My favorite scientific story involves a professor at MIT. He was questioned because his final exams were stolen and passed around to the students. The exams were the same every year. He laughed at the questioner's concerns and said, "Yes, the exams are the same, BUT THE ANSWERS CHANGE EVERY YEAR. Science is unreliable.

When I was in high school, the science teacher taught that the atom was the smallest unit of matter. That theory has certainly changed.

I believe that LIFE and MATTER began with INTELLIGENT DESIGN; and I call the Designer-GOD.

Amen. Selah so be it.

DREAMS

ONEIROLOGY is the scientific study of dreams. Throughout the course of recorded history, they have been a topic of speculation. The contents and biological purposes are not fully understood. In spite of large businesses that purport to explain them.

Day dreaming has been defined as "a visionary fantasy experienced while awake, especially one of happy, pleasant thoughts, hopes or ambitions." People in creative or artistic careers seem to be more prone to daydreaming. Engaging in it stimulates their minds with new ideas. Closely related to these subconscious experiences are visions. A vision is critical for human success in every endeavor.

In the Bible, the book of Proverbs, chapter twenty-nine, verse eighteen, are very insightful words, "Where there is not VISION, the people perish." There is no equivocation in this statement. While negative in essence, it also contains an element of positiveness. A vision can motivate success, change hope and optimism. Of all mammals, only we humans possess the capability of being visionary. In many ways our basic understanding of dreams and visions has a common pedigree.

Dreams are unconscious during sleep and visions are the product of calculated decisions. However, there is an element when they are synonymous. Martin Luther King, Jr. could just as well have said, "I have a VISION," as "I have a DREAM."

Visions are essential for wholesome, meaningful living. Without them our nation, our families and you and I will die mentally and probably physically-eventually. Bobby Kennedy was a true visionary. It was said of him, "He saw life not just as it was, but also AS IT COULD BE."

Another asset that we humans possess is the power of CHOICE. Mammals from the smallest monkey to the largest whale have many things in common. Even whales have in their flippers the vestiges of appenditures. The DNA of chimpanzees and humans is ninety-eight percent the same. The great separation factor among all mammals is the human capacity to make CHOICES.

The difference is between instinct and choice. We can choose what to eat, where to live, when to work or where to go. We can choose to get in out of the rain or snow. The difference is obvious. One of the best illustrations of this concept is found in the Book of Joshua, chapter twenty-four and verse fifteen. Joshua is giving the Israelites his farewell address. He says, *"CHOOSE you this day whom you will serve."*

President Barack Obama recently challenged his listeners with the words, "Hard times are great opportunities." The potential of choice is ours. The origin of the following statement is unknown, but the idea is relevant. "When the going gets tough, the tough get going." How? ...By choosing.

Another asset that humans possess is the capacity to BELIEVE. Vision and choice undergird this asset. And likewise, belief makes vision and choice possible. In the Gospel of Mark 9:23 Jesus says, "If you can believe, all things are possible." Going back to Herb Cohen, he says that Jesus exercised the power of belief like no one else.

Barbara Parker is a creative novelist. In one of her novels she has a recovered wayward declare, "God does not turn His back. He never abandons His children. You can have a great sin, but God gives you something good with it, too. It's always there if you look." So it is…Vision, choice and belief.

Amen. Selah so be it.

DRUMS

Louis L'Amour, Max Brand and Zane Grey are considered the best of the Western novelists. In my opinion, if you read one Grey or one Brand novel, you've read all of them. The only differences are names and places. Not so with Louis L'Amour. He adds a distinct feature. He parallels James Michener in his research.

The flavor of food is enhanced with the addition of salt and pepper, spices, etc. L'Amour adds interest and intrigue to a bland novel with the addition of items of historical interest; or the other way around. He enhances dull history with colorful episodes of imagination.

A native North Dakotan, he early on traversed many paths, experienced many things and worked at many jobs. All of these, in one way or another, found their way into his novels. He lived with bandits in Tibet. He was a cowboy, a miner, longshoreman, lumberjack, drifter, and elephant care taker, a boxer, a movie script writer and among many other things a World War II hero as a tank officer. He wrote well over 100 novels and the copies of his works number in the millions. He wrote the Sackett series and four books about Hopalong Cassidy. My favorites are Hondo, The Walking Drum, The Haunted Mesa and The Last of the Breed.

L'Amour was also a devoted family man. On February 19, 1956 he and Katherine Elizabeth Adams were married and they had two children; Beau Dearborn and Angelque Gabrielle. Louis died on June 10, 1988. To read his books one receives lessons in history, geography, poetry and philosophy.

For example, The Walking Drum. Kerbovchard is the hero. He is a soldier of fortune in the Middle Ages. His exploits are full of adventure as he seeks to set his father free from slavery. The book is chuck full of accurate history; much of it about Muslims and their culture.

While Europe was wallowing in the Dark Ages, the Moors were at the height of their Renaissance. The cities of Cordoba, Constantinople and Baghdad were unbelievable- which L'Amour depicts. The concept of a "walking drum" is intriguing. It refers to a cadence. Its beat determines the pace of the marchers. L'Amour enlightens us with a phrase in his book.

"I wonder what it is that starts the drum of a man's life to beating...FOR EACH OF US WALKS TO THE BEAT OF OUR OWN DRUM; AN UNHEARD RHYTHM TO ALL OUR MOVEMENTS AND THOUGHT."

Whether we like it or not we each have motivations, impulses that drive us. For some it is powerful and altruistic; for others it is equally powerful, but destructive.

I share with you four prime examples of the former: Patrick Henry, Henry Thoreau, Jimmy Carter and Nelson Mandela. They march and do march to their own drum beat.

Henry is known for his Revolutionary statement, "Give me liberty or give me death." His drum beat is obvious. Thoreau's is also apparent. "I went to the woods that I might live deliberately, and not come to the end of life and find I had not lived at all."

In my opinion, Jimmy Carter has been ill-abused. In spite of the fact he achieved more in 4 years than Reagan,

Clinton or Bush did in 8 years. His highlight is the peace accord between Begin and Sadat. It stands today.

Nelson Mandela spent most of his years in prison. Yet, he became President of South Africa and was mainly responsible for the destruction of apartheid.

All four have something in common. They are dreamers. They do not accept life as it is, but rather what it may become. They are not literalists. They do not accept the status quo. They dream the impossible dream. Above all, they march or marched to their own drumbeat. Just like Louis L'Amour.

Amen. Selah. So be it.

EASTER

Twelve years ago I went around the world. A major part of the trip was to discover the country of Turkey: A historical and biblically important country. There are more references to Turkey in the Bible than any other country; of course with the exception of Palestine. One of its more famous cities is Nicea; located about 100 miles from Istanbul. In the time of Constantine it was the place for the first Church Council. The Council of Nicea in 325 A.D was held almost 300 years after the death/resurrection of Jesus. Among many decisions made was the time and date of the celebration of Easter. It applies to today. Easter is always celebrated the first Sunday following the first full moon following the vernal equinox-the first day of spring. Thus, April 9th, 2009. Without a doubt, Easter is the most important day in the Christian calendar; a much more important day than Christmas.

The day before Easter, Stella and I stopped at the Jack-in-the-Box on Hospitality Lane. A homeless man was there and we began talking. After wishing him a "Happy Easter," he politely informed me that the correct designation was "Happy Resurrection Sunday." I had forgotten. He was correct. Incidentally I gave him $5.00 for his reminder.

The story in Luke Chapter 24 is an excellent insight into the significance of that resurrection. First of all, the RESURRECTION makes sense out of our FAITH. In the account, the risen Lord confronts Cleopas and Jacob on the road to Emmaus, about 7 miles from Jerusalem.

He doesn't discuss the Virgin Birth, as so many do today in making it the litmus test for being a Christian. Every Roman Emperor professed to be born of a virgin. Neither do they discuss the matter of Biblical inerrancy or the rapture or the trinity. None of those words are even mentioned in the Bible.

What did they discuss...The resurrection of Jesus. The Apostle Paul put it succinctly; "If Christ be not risen, then is our faith in vain." This affirmation turned a group of wimps into witnesses. The Book of Acts described them as "turning the world upside down."

John Masefield penned the classic narrative poem, "The Trial of Jesus." In it he gives Pilate's wife the name of Procula. The centurion is named Longiness. Pilate's wife had encouraged him to set Jesus free. He just passed the buck and washed his hands. On hearing that Jesus is alive, Procula sends Longiness to find out the truth. When he returns, her question is, "Do you believe it?" His answer is provocative. "I believe He has been set free, where neither Roman nor Jew can confine His truth;" Which is our faith.

Second, the RESURRECTION makes sense out of Death. I don't want to be morbid, but death is not the end of our existence. One writer has described death as the "vestibule to eternity." Palm Springs is often described as the "waiting room for heaven." Neither description is as appropriate as what the Apostle Paul said. "O death where is your sting. O grave where is your victory?" The Psalmist gave a previous insight into death when he said, "Yea, though I walk through the valley of the shadow of death, I will fear no evil, for, God is with me."

Eugene O'Neal wrote a religious play, called "Lazarus Laughed." The setting is in Athens where Caligula wanna-be Emperor and later was-is riding through the streets. Everyone is bowing except Lazarus (brother of Mary and Martha and who was raised by Jesus.) Caligula threatens him with death. Lazarus laughs and says, "Caligula, don't you know that Death Is Dead?" So it is…Now and forever.

Third, the RESURRECTION also makes sense out of LIFE. Cleopas and Jacob had their hearts warmed. Their lives were changed completely. Jesus said two things about life that I like. "I have come that you might have life and that you might have it more abundantly;" And this about the resurrection. "I am the resurrection and the life. He (she) who believes in me, though he (she) die, yet shall he (she) live; and whosever lives and believes in me shall never die."

I am a fan of Michael J. Fox. In his recent book, "Always Looking Up," he wrote, "Life is a gift." This is from a man who has Parkinson's disease. He lives life victoriously. He is not a victim. What a contrast to the philosophy of the Romans. On their catacombs (burial places) were found the letters NFSNNC. Interpreted it meant, I was not, I was, I am not, I DO NOT CARE. A completely pessimistic view of life.

I'm supposed to be an authority on the Early Church and Stella and I have done considerable research on their celebration of the resurrection. Did you know that for 300 years no church displayed a cross; it was 400 years before a crucifix was displayed. The Early Church had a liturgical process that was unique. They began each Sunday with an emphasis on the resurrection. They prayed the Lord's Prayer, observed the Sacrament of Holy Communion, and sang

Psalms.   This was always followed with a communal dinner on the grounds. The afternoon was spent dancing and telling jokes; especially making fun of Satan. I kid you not. Life was celebrated as an expression of joy and fun. May this spirit be revived!

Amen. Selah. So be it.

ECCLESIA

The Rev. Dr. Joshua Beckley is a modern Renaissance Man. He's a scholar, minister, musician, preacher, husband, father, grandfather, business man, politically savvy and administrator. He is also a significant religious leader in the Inland Empire. He is the Senior Pastor of the Ecclesia Church at 1314 Date Street in San Bernardino. Mrs. Lynda Beckley serves the church by being CFO, Chief Financial Officer.

The Church was started on May 16, 1991 with 15 members and today there are well over 3000 members. It won't be long until it will be the largest church- black or white- in the Inland Empire. While its membership is primarily black, all nationalities are made welcome.

Dr. Beckley was born in 1955; he's 58 years old - in Hattiesburg, Mississippi. In 1956 the family moved to Joliet, Illinois. Two major events occurred in Joshua's early years. He learned to play the clarinet- and later the saxophone-and be became a Christian. After high school he went to Vandercook College of Music and received the B.A. degree. His focus was on woodwinds: clarinet, saxophone and flute.

Joshua had accepted Christ at age 16 and felt called to preach and was licensed at age 19 by the 2nd Baptist Church of Joliet. At age 22 he left Joliet for Los Angeles with no idea what he would be doing.

Providentially he met Dr. E. V. Hill and served his church from '77-'79 when he began a long ministry with Rev. Chuck Singleton of Loveland Church in Ontario. Singleton guided Beckley into his present style of preaching called Expository. It consists of Scripture centered with Biblical explanations; in contrast with Topical preaching.

He is an avowed Fundamentalist in his understanding of Scripture. Even though he is able to read Hebrew and Greek, he accepts the Bible literally; meaning that every word is inspired by God.

His energy is boundless. He moves around like Rev. T.D. Jakes and quotes the Bible like Billy Graham. He uses "power point" to a minimum. A major difference between him and the above men is his use of humor. It not only keeps the audience alert, it is used to clarify his ideas.

Dr. Beckley received his earned doctorate in 2010 from Redlands University. He previously had received his M.A. degree from the International School of Theology that was operated by the Campus Crusade for Christ. He is also a graduate of Golden Gate Theological Seminary.

Normally his musical abilities are evident as he plays during the hymns and praise songs. He is the church's answer to Kenny G.

The service is usually divided into three parts. First is the music involving the congregation with a choir of about 40 singers leading praise songs; or a band leading Gospel songs like Amazing Grace. The second part is Dr. Beckley's sermon. The third part is the closing invitation to come forward for a commitment. This lasts about 20 minutes.

Beckley is a devoted husband and father. He and Lynda have three children: Anton, Aliea and Anell. They have six grandchildren: Cameron, Christian, David, Dominic, Jayden and Lailani.

Dr. Beckley's profile is easy to read. He's expressive, verbal with strong views on most subjects. His sermons are punctuated with vivid word pictures accompanied with passionate gestures. He loves what he does and the people he serves. Laughingly he says, "I'll preach 'till I die."

He's equally involved in serving the community. He is co-founder of the Inland Empire Concerned African American Churches; sits on the Board of Trustees for the Christian Community College of Redlands; a member of the Alliance for Education; a member of Priscilla's Helping Hands; a board member of Affordable Housing Solutions of San Bernardino; a board member of New Creations Church in Beaumont; a board member of Ecclesia's Economic and Community Development; and a member of the Century Club of San Bernardino City Schools.

In addition, Pastor Beckley has a way of manipulating the resources of the city for the benefit of his church. The property now owned by Ecclesia Church was owned previously by the Emmanuel Baptist Church of East Highland. They left because of the blight of poverty in the area. Dr. Beckley and his church bought it (for 1 million 300 hundred thousand) for the same reason Emmanuel left. He saw the needs of the area and wanted to do something about the problems.

And they have and are. For example Dr. Beckley and his church have been able to finance the purchase of several homes near the church. In them they have established buildings for: education and help students get their GED; another building to distribute clothing; another to help with finding jobs; another to supply food; another to establish a

Daycare. These programs are constantly expanding to meet the needs of the community.

Amen. Selah. So be it.

ENTITLEMENTS

As a musician I am aware of a phenomenon known as "perfect pitch." Certain musicians have the ability to detect the pitch of a note in any song in any key. I've known several of them, and their skill is amazing. A by-product of their talent is not so good. If any singer or instrumentalist is slightly off pitch, it rubs them like scrapping a piece of chalk on a blackboard. They lack appreciation for so much pretty good music; Irritating at best.

Jesus illustrated this in the Gospel of Luke chapter 18:10-14. Obviously He wasn't happy with the Pharisee. Why? Because the presumption of the Pharisee of his spiritual perfection. His arrogance is typical of many with exceptional talent.

The contemporary analysis of those in that category is called "entitlement." Tiger Woods confessed that his success as a golfer and subsequent economic success contributed to his belief that he deserved whatever he wanted. Mel Gibson has the same attitude. So does Laurence Taylor. Reverend Jimmy Swaggert is part of that group. I could go on and on. It seems that anyone who achieves a level of success in any endeavor is vulnerable to the insidious feeling of entitlement. Society is prone to; think that those who are obsessed with entitlements are the poor. Not so. No group is more entitlement prone than members of Congress. That's why they are against term limits. They assume they, are entitled to life terms.

Other examples that might clarify this condition from the positive side are: John Elway, Peyton Manning, Tom Brady, Tim Duncan, Steve Nash, Jack Nicklaus, Phil Mickelson and Derek Fisher. They do not reflect a craving for special treatment. They are all sport figures.

Other professions that seem to encourage such entitlement attitudes are: education, political, and TV personalities. People like John Edwards and Larry King. They have what I call an EX CATHEDRA mentality. When the Pope speaks; ex cathedra he is considered infallible – immunity from error.

Confidence should not be equated with arrogance. Humility is never a part of arrogance, but humility and confidence are great partners.

I've spent considerable time thinking of people that possess those two traits without a spark of entitlement. They have impacted our world for good. I've decided on seven. Two are women, three are black, two are Jewish and one is a billionaire. Three are avowed Christians. One was a comedian. Only three are alive today.

Mother Teresa was a Catholic nun. Her life's work was helping the poverty people in Calcutta, India. Hers was selfless giving without expectation of reward.

Albert Einstein is considered one of the most brilliant persons who ever lived. His thoughts gave the basis for the nuclear bomb and space travel. I particularly appreciate his discovery of the indestructibility of matter.

Michelle Obama is an inspiration; as a mother and a role model for all women. She seems to be smarter than her husband.

Martin Luther King changed the face of civil rights. His role in changing the image of all blacks cannot be minimized. Nelson Mandela is a living martyr. Apartheid was destroyed in South Africa because of him. His international influence is monumental.

Warren Buffett is one of the richest men in the world. He still lives in his first home and drives an old car. His homespun philosophy is contagious. I wish I knew him.

A story about Jack Benny speaks volumes about him. He belonged to the legendary Friars Club in Hollywood. They had heard he had just signed a multimillion dollar contract. They agreed to ignore complimenting him when he arrived at their meeting. He came in bubbling and surprisingly said, "I've just had the most delicious glass of ice water I've ever had." He has an amazing humility.

From all the information we have, none of the seven were afflicted with a sense of entitlement. P.S. A note from the son of Warren Buffett. "Entitlements are the worst thing ever and I see entitlement coming in many guises. Anybody who acts like they deserve something 'just because, is a disaster.' . . . Peter Buffett, "Life Is What You Make It."

Amen. Selah so be it.

EUGENICS

Eugenics is a very strange word. It came into prominence several years ago and then faded away. However, it has achieved recent prominence because of a paper written by a Harvard University scholar. His basic theory is that blacks, Hispanics and other minorities are mentally inferior to Caucasians-whites.

Martin Kramer is a Senior Fellow at the Shalem Center in Jerusalem and a faculty member at Harvard University. His basic proposal was to limit the births of "superfluous young men" among Palestinians in Gaza. Palestinians called his proposal "an incitement for genocide." Students at Harvard have argued that "such racist ideas had no place at their University." U.S. national television had a field day with Kramer's' viewpoints for several weeks.

The subject of eugenics is a popular source of discussion in Israel. In general it relates to Arabs and Palestinians in particular.

Hitler was blamed for establishing human breeding farms for "Aryans." "In the 1930's and 1940's, the Nazis developed large scale sterilization and euthanasia programs for the mentally and physically disabled."

Death camps for races they believed were "genetically inferior" were sent to the death camps. Over nine million Jews, Gypsies, Masonic Lodge members, were among those killed.

It was in the 1920's that America experimented with

genetics as a "tool" for social change. The United States became the world center of eugenic study and social policy. Amazingly, "from 1907-1960 more than 100,000 innocent Americans were sterilized in more than 30 states."

After World War II, the eugenic movement fell into disfavor. However, a few splinter groups like neo-Nazis, KKK and a few religious radicals continued spreading the eugenic philosophy.

A key spokesman was Stanford University physicist William Shockley. He suggested offering cash incentives to people with low IQ scores who would agree to sterilization. Professor Shockley was a Noble Laureate and an acknowledged racist. In spite of this he was responsible for the resurrection of the new eugenics movement.

On September 21, 1975 the New York Times Magazine reported an amazing account. They reported that doctors in major cities "were routinely performing hysterectomies" on mostly black welfare recipients as a form of sterilization." These operations were referred to as "Mississippi Appendectomies." There is another word that is close to eugenics — genocide.

When Hitler and his Nazis committed genocide, Stalin was a close second. He slaughtered millions of Jews, Germans, Polish and dissident Russians.

Historical anthropologists say that in the early 1500's there were 22 million Indians in Mexico. By 1600 there were only 2 million. Some were victims of venereal disease spread by Cortez and his men. Others were slaughtered by his soldiers; Eugenics under the guise of religion.

Recently a Bible scholar calculated the number of

people killed by the Jews after their slavery in Egypt. His number was 10 million; all supposedly under the command of Jehovah.

One of the worst eugenic/genocidal atrocities was Armenian victims by the Turks from 1915-1923. One and a half million Armenians were killed in concentration camps out of a total of two and a half million Armenians in the Ottoman Empire.

THESE FEW EXAMPLES ARE ONLY A DROP IN THE BUCKET. THERE ARE HUNDREDS THAT HAVE OCCURRED IN THE LAST TWO CENTURIES.

Martin Kramer is blight on the ethical values of our nation. But he is not alone. A few years ago there was a talk-show host on KFI in LA who advocated that whenever any man or woman reached the age of 65, they should be euthanized.

Well-bodied as well as the sick, disabled, blind, deaf and crippled. Eugenics and genocide are both evils that need to be expunged from all societies.

Amen. Selah. So be it.

EVOLUTION

The Bible is not a scientific book. It is very vague about the whys and wherefores of creation. Genesis 1:1 merely states that creation occurred "in the beginning."

Today's science is able to clarify the beginning with the Big Bang theory. This happened between 14 and 15 billion years ago. Our earth came into existence between 3 and 5 billion years ago.

Human evolution is a burgeoning field of study. The Leakey family was pioneers in the origin of mankind in Africa. The generally accepted date of 100,000years is accepted by most anthropologists.

The migration throughout the globe goes from 60,000 years ago. The migration across Siberia, through Alaska and down through North and South America goes back to about 40,000 years ago.

The Bible gives interesting data from the earliest days of human development. Mankind is given the task of ruling and developing our planet. We are in charge.

I endorse Theistic Evolution or the Intelligent Design theory of creation. That means that God created the process. In so doing, mankind (you and me) were endowed with a unique intelligence and the power of choice; Far and away more extensive than any other resident animals on our planet.

Joe Mays-a good friend of mine-recently gave me a most interesting concept. He suggested that in creation, while man has intelligence, many of the other mammals have distinctly different abilities. For instant the bird: from eagles, condors and hawks to pigeons and sparrows. They can fly and soar, which we can't. But with our intelligence we build airplanes, helicopters and gliders. With rockets we can climb higher than any of the birds; God given intelligence.

What about fish: sharks, catfish, salmon, etc. We can't breathe under water. But we build submarines and some of us can even snorkel. What about the cheetahs? They are considered the fastest animals on earth; Running at speeds of up to 80 miles an hour. That is nothing compared to our race cars.

Camels are called the ships of the desert. Mankind, with air-conditioners can live for years in the desert. Polar bears inhabit the coldest of temperatures. But we build heated homes and even heated cars. Get the point? Mankind supplements the absence of certain traits by using his/her God given intelligence.

From what we know, animals do not think, rationalize or choose. They live by instinct. Aside from our intelligence, the next trait we possess, that separates us from other species of creation, is our spiritual potential. We have a soul that contains our values and spiritual essence.

Back in the early part of the last century, Hazel Hurst developed the Seeing Eye dog program. When asked about the most difficult problem in training a dog to assist the blind, she surprised everyone. It was teaching dogs to raise their vision from looking at the ground to looking from the view of a six foot man.

We, who are unique, created in the image of God, have a higher vision. Jesus challenged His followers to "love our neighbors." So we build and develop hospitals for the sick, retirement centers for the elderly, rehab centers for the invalid, food banks for the hungry, civil rights for everyone, medications for illness, and churches to assist our worship of God. He has certainly placed eternity in our hearts. (Ecclesiastes 3:11)

Amen. Selah. So be it.

EXCUSES

I was watching Joel Osteen on TV the other day. He told of an 86 year old woman who showed him a diploma she had received a few days earlier. It was from an accredited university. Joel asked why she had waited so long. Her answer was simple. "I always had an excuse, even though my mother was always urging me to get a degree. She was just married; several children; no money; sickness; husband's death; too old, etc. However, four years ago I relented and at my Mother's intense urging, I went to college." Osteen said, "Your mother's looking down from heaven and I'm sure she's proud of you." The 86 year old responded, "Heaven, my foot. She's sitting right over there and she's 106 years old;" Excuses, excuses...Perseverance, Perseverance.

These words are often followed by: success; success, success. History is filled with examples of those who have followed this formula. Think of Moses. God calls him to do a job. But he's Mr. Excuse. Too old (80), can't speak and he's wanted for murder. Convinced, he perseveres and becomes the greatest figure in Jewish history.

Those who have physical handicaps or mental disorders most often use excuses for failures or not doing something. Those who don't, often use their problems as motivators for success. There are always those who refuse to alibi.

What about Socrates (480-389 B.C.) and Aristotle (384-322 B.C.)? Both of these Greek philosophers suffered from epilepsy. Alexander the Great also was epileptic. Just think what these great men accomplished. It is believed by most Bible scholars that Apostle Paul also had epilepsy. Enough said about him.

Ludwig Beethoven was deaf when he composed his 9th symphony. Stephen Hawking, probably the world's greatest scientist, has had Lou Gehrig's disease most of his life.

Stevie Wonder was blinded as a child, but today he is a world famous pianist and singer. Both John F. Kennedy and Robert Kennedy had learning disabilities.

Marilyn Monroe was speech impaired. Nelson Rockefeller was dyslexic. George Washington could barely write his name and had very poor grammar. Abraham Lincoln suffered from deep depression.

Franklin Delano Roosevelt, at age 39, his legs was paralyzed by polio. He was also elected president four times.

I have a list of over 100 individuals who were physically or mentally disabled and became famous in spite of their difficulties. But Helen Keller (1880-1968) stands head and shoulders above them all. From birth she was visually and hearing and speech impaired. In spite of these setbacks she became an author, activist, lecturer, humanitarian who lived an active physical life. She wrote 14 books and traveled the world. She also obtained graduate degrees and lectured constantly to bring a message of hope to millions of disabled people.

What do all these people have in common; from Ludwig Beethoven to Helen Keller plus countless others? One very important item the vast majority of the people listed had in common; they were or are concerned about other people.

They lived to serve. Helping others was there modus operandi. Religiously they were diverse. None of them were so-called evangelicals. Most were Catholics, Methodists, Deists or Presbyterians; strongly humanistic and caretakers of the disenfranchised.

In the 1980's Montana was one of the five Northwest States designated as "white homeland" by the Aryan Nation, made up of white supremacists. They targeted Jews, non-whites and gays. Harassed and even murdered them.

In Billings, Montana, with a population of around 100,000 experienced a number of hate crimes. On December 2, 1993 a brick was thrown through the window of 5-year-old Isaac Schnitzer's bedroom. The reason: A menorah had been stenciled on the window. The police advised his mother to remove the menorah. The few Jewish families in the city were appalled.

A <u>handicapped</u> Christian mother went to the minister of the First congregational United Church of Christ. They wondered what would happen if a Christmas tree in their window wasn't safe.

The clergyman called other ministers and after one week, there were more than six thousand Billings homes decorated with menorahs.

Known Christians and businesses were vandalized; even churches. Wherever there was a menorah, the words, "Jew lover" was painted. By the following Easter the handicapped woman's message of peace and tolerance had prevailed. Intolerance was mostly eliminated.

I personally think that it finally dawned on the hate-mongers that JESUS WAS A JEW. *Amen. Selah. So be it.*

EXPECTATIONS

As a senior male, in relatively good health, married, age 83, I feel qualified to speak for other seniors. From about age 65 (normal retirement age) there is an increasing gnawing on the mind of most seniors. There is a yearning for genuine happiness. The demands of a job cease to plague the retiree; the family is on their own; relaxation that includes travel is a distinct possibility and the vision of happiness is real. What it will comprise is very ethereal. No more pressures; no more expectations from others...Dreamers, all. None-the-less happiness is something hoped for.

From the same age 65 most seniors think seriously of their mortality. They want longevity to live many more years. An accident or serious illness is not considered.

The Psalm 90: verse 10 states that mankind's allotted years are three score and ten (70). Insurance companies' project that both men and women will live close to 80 years; Hopefully fifteen more years beyond 65. But in Genesis 6:3, it states that humans can expect to live 120 years. That's fifty-five more years. That's real good longevity. (37 years for me)

Let's limit this article to the first desire and goal-HAPPINESS. Right off the bat, we can say that it is subjective. In general, what is happiness for me may not be happiness for you. It is based on individual interpretation. One thing we know for sure about happiness. It is a by-product. It is not to be sought in itself. It is experienced because of something else.

Sadness and happiness are similar in this respect.

Sadness is a by-product. It is experienced because of illness, the loss of a loved one, the economy, world events, etc.

There is a singular difference. Sadness is precipitated by events affecting us. Happiness most often is the result of something we do: An achievement, a relationship, a new baby, satisfying a hunger (meal), listening to music, watching a sunset or sunrise, doing something for others, etc. It comes because of our actions.

Lowering our expectations is a good way to increase times of happiness. Years ago, Jack Benny, the legendary comic, visited regularly with his cronies (like George Burns) in their favorite restaurant in Beverly Hills, Calif. One day he was late and the group knew he had received a multi-million dollar increase in salary. They decided to ignore it, no mention of it; let him stew. He rushed in, obviously excited and happy. With somber faces they watched and finally he said, "Gentleman, I've just had the greatest experience." Now get this. "I've just had THE BEST GLASS OF WATER IN MY LIKE." They all were overwhelmed; a good example for us. What does it take to make you or me happy?

Stella (my wife) has a low threshold for happiness. If she buys an item, priced high, that's on sale for a minimal amount, she is radiantly happy for days. She's also excited for weeks in the anticipation of going to Laughlin and playing the PENNY slots.

Believing what I've just written, I plan my own happiness by: finishing this article, reading a good book, watching a funny movie, having lunch with a good friend, watching people, practicing my magic, planning future activities, etc; of course, not all at once.

Cultivate laughter. IT STIMULATES HAPPINESS. Norman Cousins, years ago proved that laughter triggers the secretion of endorphins from the brain. It in turn eases body aches and pains.

When I give lectures on cruise ships I always begin with a joke. Then I urge the audience to share it with their table companions. It's amazing how the joke gets around the ship. Laugh a little and live a lot happier.

Someone has said that happiness is the spice of life. Tasteless food is horrible. Spices add to its taste and our enjoyment. (From salt, pepper to basil and garlic) Happiness is truly the spice that enhances living.

Amen. Selah. So be it.

FAITH

Faith is an essential ingredient in every religion; but especially in Christianity. In the Old Testament Book of Habakkuk 2:4 the prophet declares, "The just shall live by faith. In Romans 1:17 Paul copied the prophet and declared the same admonition.

When Martin Luther started the Protestant Reformation, "the just shall live by faith," became his battle cry. Luther objected to the Book of James because that author said, "Faith without works is dead."

Aside from the religious dependence on "faith," it is also vital for living and life itself. Faith is essential when driving a car. Driving on the right side is expected in most countries. It is expected that drivers driving the other direction will stay on the opposite side. That's where faith comes in. You drive on your side and have faith that on-coming drivers will stay on their side.

Have you ever written a check? You do so with the expectation (faith) that you have money in the bank to cover the check.

Many scientists mock the unseen spiritual aspect of religion. However, faith is vital for all scientific endeavors. Consider the law of gravity. There is no way men could have gone to the moon without their belief (faith) in the law of gravity. Its force took them there and brought them back.

Or, the belief (faith) that two parts of Hydrogen plus one part of Oxygen (H_2O) will make water. It is faith that is basic to assume these conditions will always work.

One of the most famous and best loved chapters in the Bible is Hebrews chapter eleven. It's right up there with the 23rd Psalm and I Corinthians chapter thirteen. The Hebrews chapter is called the "faith chapter." It contains a roll call of the great spiritual leaders in the Old Testament. It begins with Abel, the son of Adam and Eve; and closes ambiguously with "the prophets."

It begins with a definition of faith, that I have trouble understanding. "Now faith is the substance of things hoped for, evidence of things not seen." (King James Version)

THE WAY translation says, "What is faith? It is the confident assurance that something we want is going to happen. It is the certainty that what we hope for is waiting for us, even though we cannot see it up ahead."

J. B. PHILLIPS translation says, "We have full confidence in the things we hope for. It means being certain of things we cannot see."

THE MESSAGE translation says, "Faith is the firm foundation under everything that makes life worth living."

Thirteen men and two women (Sara and Rahab) plus the prophets are listed as persons of faith. Some are prominent like Abraham and David, and others are little known like Abel and Barak.

An analysis of these people is provocative. Abraham and Isaac lied about their marriage. Noah was a drunk. Jacob was a deceiver. Moses was a murderer. Rahab was a prostitute. Japheth had his daughter sacrificed. Samson was involved with Delilah and David was a womanizer.

All of them had periods of doubt about God. They were

skeptical about His will. WHAT A PORTRAYAL OF HUMAN FRAILTIES AND DIVINE TOLERANCE.

The Book of Hebrews concludes with what I think the greatest affirmation in the Bible is. In Chapter thirteen verse eight, the writer states categorically, "JESUS NEVER CHANGES. HE IS THE SAME YESTERDAY, TODAY AND FOREVER."

Amen. Selah. So be it.

FIGHT/FLIGHT

In November 1981 I received a PhD degree with dual majors, Behavioral Medicine and Humanistic Psychology. The focus of the first major was psychosomatic illness with an emphasis on stress and its affect on the human body.

My interest was stimulated by listening to and reading a book by Norman Sheely, M.D. from Madison Wisconsin. His premise was that we can add thirty years to our lives by learning to manage stress. I also became very familiar with the work of Hans Selye, M.D. (1907-1982) from Canada. He was the first one to connect the stress of worry to the endocrine system and ulcers. He formulated the classic phrase, "the flight or fight" syndrome. It means "confrontation or escape." His metaphor was an example of our pre-historic ancestors, confronting a saber toothed tiger. Immediately his eyes would dilate, his heart would beat rapidly, adrenaline would flow to his limbs, hunger would vanish, the sex drive would disappear and he would collapse in his cave.

After a rest, his heart would slow down, his breathing became normal, and he became ravenously hungry and very sexual...The flight syndrome.

There aren't any saber toothed tigers around today. But there are many different stressors today. Dr. Selye differentiated them between <u>dis</u>-stress and <u>eu</u>-stress. The first is bad or negative kind of stressors: death of a spouse, divorce, a care taker, loss of a pet, and accident, etc. A eu-stress is a good or nice stress: getting up in the morning, a promotion, your birthday, a vacation, getting married, etc. Both kinds of experiences are stressful.

Dr. M. Lazarus, Ph.D. of Stanford University added a different dimension to the list of stressors. He called them "hassles"; loss of car keys, getting stuck in traffic, late for an appointment, burning the roast, spilling a paint can, the IRS etc, all stressors.

In the process of my study, I studied with Norman Cousins, Ph.D., Carl Simonton, M.D., Bernie Segal, M.D., Irving Katz, Ph.D., Victor Frankl M. D. and Ph.D. (1905-1997) Plus many others.

I came to certain conclusions about stress. First, everyone is affected by it, but no two people respond the same way. What is stressful to me may not be stressful to you. The degree of intensity may also vary.

Second, at times eu-stress can be as deadly as dis-stress. During the Vietnam War I pastored a large Methodist church in Orange County. One of the church families had a son in Vietnam. They received word he had been killed. They were obviously grief stricken. Two weeks later they again received word from the U.S. Army that a mistake had been made and he was on his way home. The mother had a heart attack and almost died. The good news almost killed her. It was stressful.

Third, both kinds of stress are cumulative. For example, the affects of the loss of a spouse or a divorce can last for several years. Taking responsibility for the care of a loved one or friend is extremely stressful, plus hassles, plus housework, or maintenance, all add up to a lot of stress.

Fourth, stress causes or aggravates the major causes for

death and other sickness. Major killers are: heart attacks, cancer, strokes and accidents. I'll bet you a nickel that the last time you had the flu, headache, or sore throat, a few days before you had a stressful experience.

Fifth, and closely related to number four, is the fact that stress lowers the immune system. Our immune system is weak at three distinct times: when we are babies; when we are elderly; and when we are under stress.

The stress ridden person has a tendency to engage in what I call "maladaptive behaviors" or negative compulsive actions. They begin drinking too much (booze and a myriad kinds of alcoholic beverages); they beginning eating too much or too little (becoming anorexic or bulimic); they engage in sexual promiscuity; they have sleeping problems (too much or too little); they engage in drugs and become addicted and they often become very abusive-especially to members of their family.

Studies have shown that 60% of our stress is job related; which includes limited income, pressure to perform and domestic responsibilities. Forty per cent of our stress is family related. The imposition of a spouse, parents, siblings, relatives and others can be unbelievably stressful. The sequence often begins with expectation, subtle pressures that erode one's tranquility. The shoulder and neck muscles tighten; a nervous stomach and periodic headaches are evidence of stress. The mind becomes clouded with depression. The psyche (mind) affects the soma (body) in many ways.

My next article on stress will deal with ways to manage it.

Amen. Selah. So be it.

FOOLISHNESS

Any casual Bible reader should be grateful for the plethora of translations that are available. They bring clarity to obtuse, obscure versions in the King James Version. (KJV) Most Bible scholars readily admit that the KJV is one of the worst translations ever written. Besides its use of "old English," the original sources were extremely faulty.

There are thousands of good examples, but for the purpose of this article I'll use only one. Proverbs 19:3. "The foolishness of man perverteth his way; and his heart fretteth against the Lord." It's hard to understand its meaning? You bet. Now here is a translation from THE WAY. "A man may ruin his chances by his own foolishness; and then blame it on the Lord." WOW. If you don't know the meaning of the word "fretteth" you're not alone. I'm with you. How much more meaningful is the verse with a modern translation. Again, this is but one example of such incomprehensible verses in the KJV.

What does Proverbs 19:3 really mean? "A person can ruin his future by his own foolishness and then turn around and blame God for the mess he's in." A parallel thought is when people make a mess of their lives and blame their parents, their friends or their teachers, their family, their church or even their country. It's called misdirection; anyone but themselves.

The word "foolishness" intrigues me. Synonyms can enlighten: crazy behavior, thoughtlessness, silly, senseless, unwise, absurd, ridiculous, ludicrous and devoid of wisdom, to name a few. An example of a foolish act is when we ignore the future. The belief of "we only go around once" encourages living in the now. Forget the road ahead.

No one can afford such absurdity. Saving for the future; getting a good education when you are young; taking care of your health. George Burns said, "If I knew I was going to live this long, I would have taken better care of myself."

The future may be long or the time could be short. Indifference to it is pure foolishness. Then blaming bad luck or God or His will seems so counterproductive. Consider life as we know it. Birds are born to fly. Cut their wings or incarcerate them and their aliveness is diminished.

Dogs are descended from wolves that primarily live in packs. They are social creatures. Domesticated dogs are animals that covet affection. You know this if you've ever had a dog for a pet. Deprive them of it and you are the loser. Flying and affection are basic to their nature.

Back to blaming God...The propensity for it is indigenous to our nature. We often refuse to accept responsibility for the outcome of our choices. As did Adam and Eve in the Garden of Eden; Eve blamed the snake and Adam blamed Eve. It's part of our nature. However, the most audacious effect in the Blame Game is to blame God for every mishap or tragedy. Many of these are the result of our own lack of common sense; Foolish behavior.

Amen. Selah so be it.

FORGIVENESS

There are two basic beliefs in Christian theology that are easy to grasp and clearly presented in the Bible. The love of God and His redeeming love through Christ. Both can never be diminished. They are extended to all humanity.

Merit is never demanded nor is it expected. The only condition is recognition of its availability. God's love and salvation are gifts.

Brit Hume, Fox network news reporter, has committed a grievous error by denouncing Tiger Woods' religious tie with Buddhism. He categorically states that only in Christianity can he (Tiger) find forgiveness for his unfaithfulness to his wife. Therefore he should denounce Buddhism and become a Christian.

Hume's ignorance is only exceeded by his arrogance. All religions, including Buddhism, affirm the love of God and divine forgiveness for transgressing. This is true whether God is called God, Jehovah, Elohim, Allah, Supreme Creator, Intelligent Designer or the Ground of Our Being.

Clarification of truth comes from many sources. For me, truth often invades my mind by way of novels. Many of the better novelists include moral values along with their stories. Among them I include Dean Koontz. He is a master of the thriller with a different twist. His plots are such that the outcomes are unexpected.

An example is "Your Heart Belongs to Me." At age thirty-four Ryan Perry seems to have the world in his pocket;

along with his billionaire status. His story resembles the story of Job in the Bible. He begins to lose everything that means anything to him: Samantha his lover; his friends; and above all, his health. He is diagnosed with incurable cardiomyopathy. His only hope is for a heart transplant. Without it he is given six months to live. Sounds like Job, doesn't it?

In the process he is given a new heart and after a year everything is great. Then, strange things begin to happen. An unexpected box of chocolates, a pendant and a note saying, "Your heart belongs to me."

Ryan is distraught and afraid. He is also being stalked, by the twin sister whose heart spared his life. It is revealed to him that his doctor had taken him to China where the government is harvesting body organs and selling them to wealthy people throughout the world.

It dawns on him that it was his greed-for life-that had corrupted him. Through a series of events he changes his life. He begins to work cleaning up stables of excrement for a monastery, after giving away all his money. He finds redemption and happiness. For him, serving and helping others is the only way. His life became meaningful. Such is the story and moral truth emphasized by Dean Koontz.

Another example of Koontz' writing is his book, "One Door Away from Heaven." It radiates an indomitable spirit and inspiration. Hope is a constant message. A crippled girl, a confused young woman, a burned out PI and a boy and his dog are vehicles of suspense, humor and wonder. Even the evil Preston Maddoc cannot conquer their indomitable spirit. Both are good reads. *Amen. Selah so be it.*

FREEDOM

The other day I read a most provocative statement about life. "Old age is like a Bank Account. You withdraw from it what you've put in." With this in mind we should make deposits of a lot of happiness in the Bank Account of memories.

Since my memory isn't always what I hope it to be, I help it along. I have pictures of where I've been and who I know. I place them in small albums of 30 or 40 pictures each. In looking through them periodically, I find great joy and happiness. In this way I am drawing from my Bank Account.

Happiness is so elusive. It's here today and gone tomorrow. The perception of happiness is always subjective. It varies with the individual. It seems to me there should be a few guidelines for joy and happiness. Recently a friend gave me the following suggestions.

I. FREE YOUR HEART FROM HATRED and BIGOTRY. Both of these attitudes are corrosive to our spirits. They destroy tranquility. In my years as a minister and therapist, I've never known anyone who harbored hatred and bigotry that was not unhappy and bitter.

Some years ago Norman Cousins wrote an article for the New England Journal of Medicine. In it he described the physical and emotional affects of such negative attitudes. They are always accompanied by anger, depression and vitriolic outbursts. Physical ailments are also present: ulcers, cancer and heart attacks, among others. Hatred and bigotry do not foster happiness.

II. FREE YOUR MIND FROM WORRIES and FEARS. These two attitudes can destroy any semblance of happiness. They must be gotten rid of. But it's easier said than done. Hans Selye M. D. developed the concept of the relation between the mind and body. The mind that worries and fears will soon impact the body, causing unhappiness. Worry and fears are really mind-blowers. Not in the sense of extravagant benefits but mental and emotional traumas. Grant me the serenity to accept the things I cannot change. Probably sleepless nights are the greatest of these traumas.

III. LIVE SIMPLY. Our world is becoming more complex every day; which makes the simple life more difficult to actualize.

There aren't too many places where we can go to escape heavy traffic and a burgeoning population. We are constantly pressured to "keep up with the Jones" with "things" that clutter our existence. They make the "simple life" very difficult.

Henry Thoreau solved this problem by moving to Walden's Pond. He said, "I went to the woods that I might live deliberately and not come to the end of life and find I had not lived at all."

A common problem in life today is BURN-OUT, which contributes to unhappiness. It is often caused by busyness. A sure cure is to consciously start eliminating our unnecessary activities said Dr. Norman Cousins.

IV. GIVE MORE/EXPECT LESS. To give with the expectation of receiving commensurate benefit is "fools gold." I'm always appalled at ministers who encourage giving with the expectation of receiving a return of "ten-fold."

Even given monetarily for the benefit of a tax break seems a selfish action. Compassion is the ultimate motivation. Reward is the last thing in the mind of a "Good Samaritan." It is the essential ingredient for happiness.

Amen. Selah so be it.

FRIENDS

There are four factors in my life that bring meaning to it: Family, Friends, Flag (country) and Faith. They have two or three things in common. All four are in a constant state of change. They expand and contract in a state of flux. Each is also made up of values that enhance my life.

The four also differ in significance. For example Faith may be more important than one or more of the other three. Age or physical mobility may limit one's Friendships.

When it comes to Family, Stella and I are very fortunate. Together we have seven children, twenty-eight grandchildren and ten great grandchildren. The latter group seems to be increasing annually. Our family is ethnically diverse; Anglo, Hispanic, Black, and Greek. I'm the oldest of the clan (82), but I have a couple of aunts back east older than me. We are also religiously diverse: Catholic, Protestant, Muslim, Mormon, Jehovah Witness, and Agnostic and indifferent. Sports are a favorite topic of conversation and somewhat, politics.

We all keep in touch. Three of four times a year 20-35 gets together for food and fellowship. Several are always in school; 4 or 5 out of work; and a couple is sick. All are hard workers and fiercely defend each other.

Friends are important to me. Most of what I've said about FAMILY can apply to FRIENDS. However, there are a few differences. Many of my friends are older than I am. Most of them have an ailment of one kind or another; arthritis, glaucoma, cancer, bad backs, hard of hearing, poor eye sight.

My friends travel, shop, eat out, and have strong opinions. Whether it's politics or religion, they have strong views. They love jokes and tell them. They are voracious readers and always have a book they are reading. Many are ultra conservative and some are racists and bigoted. Above all, differences of opinion do not sever our friendships.

My third "F" is FLAG or country. Patriotism is important to me. I'm well aware of the flaws in our country; too much government, two unwanted wars, excessive taxation, illegal immigration, deregulation, crooked politicians, etc. But the USA is still the greatest nation in the world. I've been a Democrat since the days of Harry Truman. I support President Obama, but dislike Pelosi and Reid.

I respect every ex-military and current serviceman. I am an avowed patriot. Thank God for America, flaws and all.

My FAITH is important to me. For over sixty years I've been a professing Christian. Serving in it has been my vocation and avocation. I am aware that most of the Bible was plagiarized from Egyptian religions. Also, that the Apostle Paul plagiarized over 200 verses from Greek philosophers and poets.

The Bible does not give a satisfactory answer to the problem of suffering. Rabbi Abraham Hershel and Rabbi Harold Kushner both affirm the prevalence of allegory in the Old Testament. There are over a dozen major differences in the resurrection account in the four Gospels. In chapter fifteen of I Corinthians, Paul says repeatedly, "according to the scriptures." This is incredible since no scripture existed. Paul's writing preceded all of the Gospels. Someone obviously inserted these words years after Paul's death.

I do not believe in the inerrancy of the Bible. However, I do believe it contains the truths about God and Jesus. The discrepancies in the resurrection do not bother me. The central truth is the resurrection of Jesus, which I believe. Whatever discrepancies are evident in the Gospels do not violate the reality of the resurrection of Jesus. The old adage is applicable, "Don't throw the baby out with the bath water."

The love of God, the mercy of God, the redemption we have through Christ, and the hope of eternal life are all fundamental to my FAITH. These are but a few elements in my statement of faith.

Amen. Selah. So be it.

GELATOLOGY

The word "Gelatology" is not well known in academic or medical circles. Words such as Oncology, Cardiology, Hematology; the "ology" means "the study of"' cancer, the heart, blood and laughter. Gelos means laughter in Greek. Several medical schools have departments that are focusing attention on the healing benefits of humor and laughter. Such is the case at Loma Linda. Dr. Lee Berk is one professor involved in the study. A few years ago I interviewed Dr. Berk on the subject of his research. He confirmed his early dependence on the work of Norman Cousins Ph.D.

I was in the class when Dr. Cousins related an outstanding experience. He began by establishing a baseline blood sample. He then went into a self-imposed hypnotic state and then let his mind concentrate on negative things (war, fatalities, anger, jealousy etc.) At his signal another sample of blood was taken. The result between the two samples was startling. The white blood count (immune system) had DROPPED significantly. He then began the same process of hypnosis but reversed the suggestions (peace, joy, happiness, etc.) An amazing result transpired. The white blood count had increased 95%. In other words, his immune system had doubled.

Dr. Beck copied the same process with different results. He had several young people have blood tests. In the first one, the white blood count went way down. In the second test the white blood count increased 125 percent. Amazing evidence of how the mind affects the body.

All of this information should be viewed in the light of Norman Cousins' previous experience with terminal illness. His collagen illness was diagnosed as terminal. But through laughter and mega-vitamin C, he became well.

Psalm 126:2 states, "Then was my mouth filled with laughter and my tongue with singing." Obviously laughter is not an aberration but indigenous to being alive. It is undoubtedly important.

A study published in Psychology Today said that every day we need at least four hugs and twenty laughs. A baby laughs at least twenty times an hour. The benefits of laughter are magnanimous. It is a trigger; a stimulus in four distinct ways.

FIRST, it triggers the secretion of ENDORPHINS from the brain. They have the same molecular formula as morphine. Both are painkillers.

SECOND, it stimulates white blood cells (as per Cousins and Berk) that increase the potential of the immune system. White blood cells act as Special Forces that attack and destroy the enemies of infection that invade the body, causing sickness. Negative thoughts and emotions weaken the immune system.

THIRD, it stimulates and nourishes the brain's thinking process. Before one laughs, there must be a comprehension of the "punch line." For example, a couple was about to have breakfast, when the wife remembered she needed milk. "Honey, would you go to the store and get us a carton of milk?" She continued, "And if they have eggs, get us six." He returned with six (6) cartons of milk. The amazed wife retorted, "Why six cartons of milk? The husband said, "Because they had eggs." Think about it.

The FOURTH benefit of laughter is that it minimizes stress and alleviates tension in the body. Laughter has been described as giving the organs of the body a massage.

A few years ago I traveled around the world, making a study of humor. Several observations were obvious. Every nationality made fun of another one. I also learned that the Chinese seldom tell a joke, but they love cartoons. In every country I visited I would ask, "What is your favorite joke?" In Paris, a French gal said, "What's the difference between men and mosquitoes?" I didn't know, and she said, "Mosquitoes only bother me in the Summer time." At each country I tabulated the favorite kinds of humor/jokes. The most favorite was SEXUAL jokes. In Turkey they loved to tell homosexual stories. The double entendre and insinuations were prominent.

The second favorite was jokes about POLITICIANS. Their ignorance and infidelities were favorites. Germany and England in particular told political stories.

The third favorite, believe it or not, was jokes about SENIORS. In Spain, particularly Madrid, there were benches every few feet filled with seniors swapping jokes about themselves. The fourth favorite was ETHNIC humor. I include blonde jokes in this group. There's no dearth of material for either ethnic or blonde jokes.

The fifth favorite was RELIGION. Ministers, nuns, the Catholic Church, celibacy, pedophiles; nothing seemed sacred. I never told them I was a retired minister.

I'm often asked how I remember jokes and where do I

get them. The answers are simple; from friends, TV, reading, other comics. When traveling Stella and I often play a game: "Tell me a joke about . . . ." I also clip jokes or write them and scotch tape them in my date book. I'm always on the look-out for a good joke.

Amen. Selah. So be it.

GENESIS

Alan Dershowitz is a legal mind par excellent. A Law professor at Harvard, he has handled scores of cases-and won most of them. In his book, The Genesis of Justice, he gives a startling observation. He believes that many cultural and religious mores in our modern world originated in the stories found in the Book of Genesis. Most Jewish and Christian scholars believe that the stories in Genesis should be viewed allegorical and not historical accounts.

Rabbi Abraham Heschel and Rabbi Harold Kushner are typical of contemporary scholars. The Apostle Paul in the Book of Galatians, chapter four, affirms the allegorical view.

Way back when, during the time of the early church Patristic Fathers, most of them believed the Torah was NOT historical but mythological or allegorical. Consider a few of the cultural and religious influences.

I. THE POWER AND PRIORITY OF PERSONAL CHOICE. From Adam and Eve to Joseph, this principle is emphasized again and again. Monarchies, dictatorships, tribal rulers, religious dynasties, etc., have all ruled by fiat; Acquiescence to pre-determined decisions, without an opportunity to choose.

II. Another influential event in the creation involves God's punishment of Eve. Because of her disobedience, she and her descendants were forever to be subservient to Adam and males. That dominant attitude has prevailed throughout the world for thousands of years. Religion, particularly

Christianity and Muslim have perpetuated this view.

It wasn't until 1920 that women were granted the right to vote in the United States. The Southern Baptist Church, the largest Protestant denomination, believed until 1998, that a woman should "submit herself graciously" unto her husband. A casual reading of the Pauline Epistles will reveal who pushed that view-the Apostle Paul.

III. Our culture and religious beliefs have also been influenced by the story of Cain and Abel. Remember how and why Cain killed his brother? It was Fratricide. God set Cain up by disapproving of his sacrificial offering, preferring Abel's animal sacrifice. That made Cain jealous and angry, so he killed Abel. From that event came thousands of years of wars, conflicts, feuds and family estrangements.

The issue was simple. How do we worship God? Just think of it. Christianity separated from Judaism over circumcision. The Eastern Orthodox churches broke off from the Roman Catholic Church over priests marrying. Protestants (Martin Luther) were started because of indulgences. Arminanism (Methodists) and Calvinists (Baptists) disagreed over baptism.

With the Church of Christ it was Holy Communion. The Pentecostals: speaking in tongues. Seventh Day Adventists, worshiping on the Sabbath (Saturday.) The worship of God by Cain and Abel started the entire mess of splintered religions and denominations.

IV. One further thought, on the positive side. The standout men and women of the Old Testament have two things in common. Whether it be Adam and Eve, Cain, Noah, Abraham, Jacob, Joseph, Samson, Esther, Ruth, David and any other, all faced disastrous experiences. Cause enough to give up. But, and it's a big "but," each one went on and created a successful, meaningful and productive life. What more can any of us ask for? All of us have fallen short, failed or didn't measure up at one time or another.

Victor Frankl, the father of Humanistic Psychology and Holocaust survivor, described this potential as "THE INDOMITABLE POWER OF THE HUMAN SPIRIT."

The above examples should encourage us all. If they can, we can also.

Amen. Selah. So be it.

GRIPES

I have a major gripe. A beef, if you will. It is directed at our government and the Church. Both are floundering. Both have lost their way. Both are a long way from their original purpose. Bluntly and concisely they both were: OF THE PEOPLE, BY THE PEOPLE and FOR THE PEOPLE. Both institutions have forgotten this description of what that should be.

Consider the plight of both. Government is plagued with unbelievable debt, a high rate of joblessness, fighting two wars and festering unrest. The churches of all denominations are losing members, declining attendance and have financial woes. Both our government and churches are more concerned about perpetuating the organization than considering the needs of us, the people.

We are fighting unwanted wars, paying unreasonable taxes and dealing with growing joblessness; and dissension in the Congress. Members of Congress and Ministers are more concerned about their positions than meeting the needs of we; the people.

Listen to the messages of both. Both preach FEAR of terrorism and hell. We must consider that mistreatment always leads to retaliation. This is true historically whether it be with Arabs, Blacks, Native Americans or the poor. Remember. Poverty always is followed by an increase in crime. The members of churches retaliate by staying away from church.

What should both do? WHY CAN'T OUR GOVERNMENT BE AS CONCERNED ABOUT THE POVERTY, JOBLESSNESS, THE ECONOMY AND HEALTH OF WE, THE PEOPLE AS THEY ARE BOUT HAITI, IRAQ AND AFGHANISTAN? No wonder confusion is rampant among Republicans and Democrats alike.

The church advocates boring services, and bland music. They specialize in secular programs, suppers and rummage sales. No wonder attendance is declining. History reveals a sad commentary. Whenever an institution forgets its constituency, they DECAY and DECLINE.

Now for a change of pace; here are three basic messages that should be a part of every church's emphasis. The first one is in Chapter 15 of the Gospel of Luke. Some years ago I was on a bus tour in Europe. A British passenger had a book entitled, "The World's Best Short Stories." The first one was what is called, The Prodigal Son. It is a parable told by Jesus. In reality it should be called "The Parable of the Loving Father." Most Bible scholars believe the father is Jesus' understanding of God.

In verse twenty there is a memorable picture of God. The Father RUNS to meet the wayward son. The parable is universal in the application of the message. God is anxious to greet us and accept us without reservation.

The second message is in the Gospel of John, chapter three, and verse sixteen. "For God so loved the world He gave His only begotten Son, that whosoever believes in Him shall not perish." The verse is considered by many to be the most beloved verse in the Bible. Whatever, the truth of it opens up the concept of "inclusion" for all mankind into the Kingdom of God.

Belief in God is the key to salvation. The word "Him" has the antecedent of "for GOD" so loved the world. Whatever word that is used to refer to God is acceptable: Allah, Jehovah, Elohim, Intelligent Design or the Ground of our Being.

This smacks of "universalism," rightly so. How can millions and billions of people that have populated and will populate this earth be excluded from divine favor. "God so loved the world." The author of this Gospel was truly inspired in his inclusionary emphasis.

The third emphasis is also in John's Gospel; chapter 21:7. It describes a very provocative incident. When the disciples arrived at the empty tomb, Jesus was gone and the linens were lying in a heap. Except the napkin, that had covered His face was folded "in a place by itself."

Why this extra attention? In the culture of that day, if the Master was finished eating and stepped away from the table, he would wad up the napkin and toss it onto the table. Meaning, "I'm done." But if he folded the napkin, it meant, "I'm coming back." The significance should be obvious.

Amen. Selah so be it.

HAPPINESS

The year was 1937. Our nation was in the throes of the Great Depression. President Roosevelt was in his heyday. The Japanese began their invasion of China. Hitler began his domination of Germany. Russia was on the march. There was seven million unemployed in the USA. And, Stella was born.

Also, a little known program was started at Harvard University in 1937. Two hundred and sixty eight (268) sophomores were recruited in a study measuring, "a formula for a good life." It was to evaluate some mix of love, work and adaptation for as long as they lived. "This study continues to be diligently maintained to this day.

A current report states, "Never before has science been able to report such fascinating and thoroughly time-tested results of HAPPINESS." The status of the study was reported in the June 2009 issue in the Atlantic Magazine. The happiest people in the study had a HEALTHY OUTLET. Consider that the participants were probably born in 1917 (?), they are in their late eighties or early nineties today.

In the beginning, all was fine: In their prime years they made lots of money and had great careers. They had beautiful families and large homes. Unfortunately, in later life many of them ended up with mental and/or physical problems. The happiest both mentally and physically had/have major outlets: sports, charitable activities or the ability to laugh; a sense of humor. One assessment says, "A person without a sense of humor is like a car without springs, jolted by every pebble in the road."

The second powerful lesson the study found was: DON'T TAKE YOURSELF TOO SERIOUSLY. Obviously it was strict rules that contributed to the participant's unhappiness. There seemed to be a basic humility and an acceptance of life's pains and problems for the happy ones.

Scott Peck, M.D. states categorically, "Life is difficult." Or as the Book of Job says, "Man is born to trouble as sure as the sparks fly upward." Don't take life too seriously. Life is short at best and should be enjoyed every moment.

Have you heard of Chris McCandless? He graduated from college in the early 1990's; left his home and went to the wilds of Alaska. He was fed up with society's rat race. In the bleak Alaskan wilderness he eventually succumbed and died of starvation. He seemed to regret his isolation and wrote these last words in his journal, "Happiness is only real when shared."

According to the Harvard study, McCandless was right on. The unhappiest were those who spent too much time by themselves. "The happiest subjects in the study were those who sustained meaningful, healthy relationships with friends and family." HAPPINESS MUST BE SHARED.

We just can't give too many hugs or send enough "I miss you." Henry Ward Beecher said, "God asks no one if they will accept life. Our only choice is what we do with the time we have."

Albert Schweitzer concluded his opus, "The Quest for the Historical Jesus" with these meaningful words: "He comes to us as One unknown, without a name, as of old, by the lakeside, He came to those men who knew Him not. He speaks to us the same word: "Follow thou me!" and set us to the tasks which He has to fulfill for our time. He commands. And to those who obey Him, whether they be wise or simple, He will reveal Himself in the toils, the conflicts, the sufferings which they shall pass through in His fellowship, and, as an ineffable mystery, they shall learn in their own experience Who He is.

One thing I know: the only ones among you who will be really happy are those who will have sought and found how to serve."

Amen. Selah so be it.

HARVEY

Bob Harvey recently shared two delightful stories with me about kids. A little girl developed a rare blood disease and desperately needed a blood transfusion. Death was imminent if she didn't get it.

A search was made for a compatible donor. Her little brother was the only one whose blood matched hers. He was asked if he would give her blood and he readily agreed. After the transfusion the little brother turned to the doctor and said, "Now am I going to die?" He thought he was giving his sister all of his blood.

Another story: A little girl was sitting at the kitchen table drawing a picture. When questioned about what she was doing by her mother, she said, "I'm drawing a picture of God." "But, honey," her mother said, "no one knows what God looks like." "But, Mother" she said. "They will know when I get through."

Jesus would have loved these stories and may have told them. The truth in the story is that each of us has our own image of what God looks like. Recently one author was asked what he thought Jesus would do if He came back today and saw the church. The cogent answer is provocative. "He'd find the closest available place and throw up."

In my graduate days in Seminary, a professor told us, "You are either a Jesus Christian or a Paul Christian." The older I get and the more I study Christian history, the more convinced I am that he was right. Jesus was not a Christian.

The Apostle Paul started it. One writer says that Paul franchised the Christian faith. He changed the Jesus of history to the Christ of faith. His theology became normative for Christianity.

A comparison: Jesus was a rural person. He never traveled (as we know) more than 120 miles from His home. He spoke of animals like goats, dogs, swine, donkeys and sheep. Also harvesting, sowing seeds, weeds, weddings and children. Fishing was a favorite topic. He knew about trees: sycamores, fig and olive. He used home spun stories to illustrate truths. They were called parables.

Paul, on the other hand, wouldn't have known the difference between a barn and an outhouse. He was a city boy-born and bred. Paul was educated. He wrote constantly and traveled all over the eastern part of the Roman Empire. He knew Greek philosophy and the writings of Plato and Seneca. In fact, he plagiarized over 200 verses in his Epistles from Greek authors.

Paul never mentions Jesus' birth, His life, His parables, His miracles or His disciples other than Peter and James. The early followers of Jesus and Paul were in constant conflict. They even tried to kill him and he had to escape over a city wall.

The history of the Church has been filled with strife, genocide and conflicts ever since the Council of Nicea in 325 A.D. The Apostle's doctrines have been the source of most of those conflicts. Paul was volatile, argumentative, and confrontational from the get-go. Jesus was peaceful, loving and a teacher. Personally, I would like to be more a Jesus Christian. *Amen. Selah so be it.*

HERESIES

There is a major misconception about Christianity that very few believers ever think about. They assume the church appeared on the historical stage FULL BLOWN. One day Jesus was alive (resurrected) and the next day the church was in existence. Not so.

To put it mildly, chaos was in charge for several hundred years. A pivotal question is, "who was running the church when all the disciples of Jesus were dead? History records the spread of the Gospel created churches throughout the Roman Empire. Leaders, called Bishops, created their own fiefdoms.

Beliefs, later many of them called "heresies," arose. It wasn't until 325 A.D. at the Council of Nicea-called by Emperor Constantine-which the first attempt of structure was established. In their dedication to the cause they preached and wrote treatises for and against various opinions circulating among the churches. Since there wasn't a set group of books that were recognized as Scripture, there was constant turmoil.

There was even friction among the Patristic Fathers. For instance, it wasn't until 467 AD that there was a general acceptance of the 27 books in what we call The New Testament. Several of the Fathers were later condemned as heretics. The establishment of the Roman Catholic Church was completely political.

It was the beliefs and writings of Saint Augustine (354-

430AD) in the 5th century that brought a measure of solidarity to the Christian faith.

Augustine was undoubtedly the greatest influence upon the Catholic Church's views on dogma, tradition and theology. He set the norm for: original sin, celibacy for priests, predestination, authority of the Bible, confession, sacraments, purgatory, eternal punishment and the benefits of martyrdom.

For hundreds of years the subject of heresy was a dominant concern. Seemingly it started from the gitgo of the 2nd century, following the deaths of the twelve disciples. At that time Christianity was competing with Judaism, Gnosticism, Emperor Worship and Mithraism as the dominant religion in the Roman Empire.

Christianity was also fragmented by scores of writings from the many Bishops in the Empire. For example, Origen alone wrote over 2000 books and treatises.

Sermons and letters were written for and against: Gnosticism, Docetism, Arianism, Trintarianism, Marcionsm, Universalism, Unitarianism, etc.

Several of the heresies that were rejected, in a very subtle way are emerging in current religions thought. Also, most of the early heresies sprang from Gnosticism which in turn had its origin in Greek philosophy.

1. *Gnosticism* – It refers to spirit knowledge and mysticism. For them the body was evil and denied that Jesus had a natural physical body.
2. *Docetism* – It endorsed Gnosis, that matter was evil. Jesus was a phantom, and had a spiritual resurrection.

3. *Universalism* – Augustine said, "There are many who do not believe in endless torment." Among the early church Fathers were: Origen, (185-253) St. Jerome, Gregory of Nyssa and Clement of Alexandria.

4. *Marcionism* – First to formulate a New Testament with only ten books. None of the Old Testament.

5. *Arianism* – Arius was declared a heretic for declaring that Jesus was a created being. Emperor Constantine was a follower. The Apostles Creed infers that with the phrase, "we believe in Jesus, the Son of God.

6. *Trintarianism* – The word "Trinity" is not found in the N.T.; a few inferences like at the baptism of Jesus. The heresy was in declaring that instead of three distinct persons, the Trinity was three expressions of one God-example of a person who is a husband, father and a son.

7. *Pelagianism* – Pelagius was a contemporary of Augustine. He viewed humanity as good and morally unaffected by the "Fall." He believed the "Fall" affected only Adam and Eve and not the human race. He was declared a heretic in 418 A.D.

These are but a few of the many heresies dealt with prior to Augustine. Orthodoxy emerged very slowly. It came about only as the Catholic Church became firmly entrenched and assumed the power of excommunication. This ushered in the Dark Ages and eventually the Protestant Reformation.

Amen. Selah so be it.

HINDUISM

The population census of earth has been set at approximately 7 billion people. Religiously, the number of Hindus is third largest, after Christianity, Muslim and then Hindus at 900,000; the vast majority live in India. Others are in Bangladesh, Nepal, Sri Lanka, Pakistan and Indonesia. Only a few thousand reside in the USA.

Amazingly, it has no single founder. A basic facet of Hinduism is its plurality. It assimilates all other religions and rejects none. Believers affirm that Hinduism had no beginning. It always was and will always be. It has existed forever. As one writer says, "This profoundly varied religion places a heavy emphasis on attaining freedom from the perceived world and on eliminating ties to the material plane of existence."

The word Hindu means "Indian" and is derived from the Sanskrit word "Sindhu." It was further popularized by the Arabic term "al Hind"; referring to those living by the river Indus. To give some encompassing dimension to this subject, I will focus on several facets of belief.

The first is their veneration, respect and even worship of cows and other mammals, fish and birds. The cow is a utilitarian animal. It symbolizes all other creatures. It represents life and the sustenance of life. It is generous, taking nothing but water, grass and grain. It gives and gives and gives of its milk. "The cow represents Hindu values of selfless service, strength, dignity and ahim'sa, or non-violence."

Traditionally they abstain from eating beef. Most Hindus are vegetarian.

In consideration of ahim'sa it is relevant to think of Mahatma Gandhi. His protest with non-violence toppled the British colonialism of India. M.L. King emulated Gandhi.

Reincarnation is a fundamental belief of Hindus. It is virtually universal in India. Webster gives a succinct definition of it. "It is the belief that the soul upon death of the body, comes back to earth in another body or form-rebirth of the soul in a new body." To fully understand the concept of reincarnation we must see it in the context with karma. Karma is a principle of cause and effect. The actions in a past life may have an effect on one's present situation. Or, what we are enduring today may be caused by what we did in a previous life.

Hindus accept the doctrine of transmigration and rebirth. People are born over and over again. The process of spiritual growth determines one's release from the cycle of birth, death and rebirth. The life rituals in Hinduism are three in number: Birth, Marriage and Funerals; the prenatal rite. At birth the father whispers the child's name into its ear. It takes place from six to eight months after birth and is followed by prayers and a reception.

Marriage is the most important rite. Marriages are arranged by the parents: The bride's father pays a dowry to the groom. The ceremony is climaxed with prayers and a feast.

When a Hindu dies the body is usually cremated. Since they believe in reincarnation the body is not necessary. The ashes are usually scattered on a body of water. Perhaps the best known concept of Hinduism is what is referred to as the "caste system." It has been a distinctive part of Indian religious and social life for centuries. There are thousands of castes, each one different from the others.

In some ways Plato's Republic was similar to the Hindu dividing society into groups. Brahmins were the priests; Kshatriyas were the warriors; Vaishyas were the merchants; Shudras were the crafts people.

The castes divided and multiplied exponentially. For example consider the Shudras (craftspeople). There are hundreds of various crafts. Then there are the suppliers, the sellers by the hundreds. Rules and traditions would be created for each one. The tragedy of it all was that your caste was for life.

The lowest caste of all was the "untouchables." While this rendering is now illegal (1950), it is still practiced. They do the "grunt" work, the menial tasks such as street cleaning and clearing away the dead. Sister Teresa worked with this group in Calcutta.

Hinduism has four goals: righteousness, earthly prosperity and success, pleasure and spiritual liberation.

Today India has about 2500 different languages. It is a rising democracy. Its population (1,173,108,000) is second only to China (1,330,141,000.) In comparison: the USA (310,233,000); Indonesia (242,968,000); Brazil (201,104,000); and Pakistan (177,277,000). Incidentally, only Brazil and Indonesia do NOT have an atomic bomb.

Amen. Selah so be it.

.

HOMOSEXUALITY

Prejudice seems to have plagued humanity from the beginning of recorded history. Racial, religious and nationality prejudice are often the vehicles of it. Seventy years ago I became aware of all three. In the segregated town I grew up in we were ignorant about blacks, Catholics and Polish people. It was easy to be prejudiced.

The Civil Rights movement, World War II and the election of John F. Kennedy did much to erase the biases by us WASPS. However, there is a growing bigotry that W.S. Coffin has called: Homophobia, the Last Respectable Prejudice.

Webster's Dictionary defines homophobia as, "an unreasoning fear of or antipathy toward homosexuals and homosexuality." Obviously in our land of free expression both homosexuals and heterosexuals have the right to their own opinions and the expression of them.

While "gay marriage" has been the focus of much of the discussions, the deeper question is revolved around the state of homosexuality. As with the previously mentioned prejudices, fear is the basis of this phobia. Ignorance always breeds prejudice.

Unfortunately, as Dr. Coffin states, "The church has led in the oppression of homosexuals." As usual, in this article I speak only for myself. As a Christian minister who is a comfortable heterosexual, I share Bishop Desmond Tutu's conclusion: "The Lord of the Church would not be where His church is, in the matter."

It is important to observe that there are perversions in both expressions of sexuality. The extremes bring disrespect and misunderstanding on both homosexuals and heterosexuals; Bizarre behavior by the first and superiority by the second.

I hope to provide insight and clarification for this "respectable" prejudice both from the Bible and modern science.

There are thousands of verses in the King James (KJ) Bible. Yet, there are only seven (7) verses that refer to homosexuality. In the books of Leviticus, chapter twenty and Romans, Chapter one; No other of the sixty-six books mentions it at all. "Obviously homosexuality was not a big issue for biblical writers."

All discussions on the subject eventually focus on the cities of Sodom and Gomorrah. Sodom, a synonym for the sexuality is derived from that city. The story is simple. Angels are going to warn Lot, the nephew of Abraham, to flee the city. The male citizens seek the angels for the purpose of raping them; Thus the initial introduction of homosexuality.

For Bible students, this next thought is basic. In four references: Ezekiel 16:49; Isaiah 59:3; Amos 4:11 and Zephaniah 2:9. All four refer to the two cities. NOT A ONE REFERS TO SEXUAL PROCLIVITY. They are condemned for "pride, excess food and indifference to the hungry, ignoring the needy, blood on their hands, and filling their houses with violence and fraud." The Jews were compared to Sodom and Gomorrah in the above words.

Another thought. If the few verses in Leviticus are singled out to condemn homosexuality, why do fundamentalist Christians ignore: the advocacy of slavery, stoning all who commit adultery, polygamy that was regularly practiced.

Prostitution was considered natural in the Old Testament times. Walter Wink categorically states, "There is no Biblical sex ethic. The Bible only knows a love ethic."

There is a plethora of scientific information regarding the biological differences between gay men, lesbian women and straight men and women.

Consider just a couple of scientific observations. "Gay men have similar brains to straight women and gay women have similar brains to straight men." They were born that way. A recent copy of the journal "Human Genetics" reports, "The arrangement of a mother's genes affects the sexual orientation of her son." This supports the debate that there are "gay genes." Gay men and lesbian women are born that way. Their homosexuality is not a choice.

Amen. Selah so be it.

HOPE

The saga of Michael Jackson continues even after his Memorial Service. That which concerns me is the harsh judgmental statements made about him and his life.

The congressman from the state of New York is typical of the self-righteous bigots who have a holier-than-thou attitude.

I'll never forget a statement I heard years ago. The most judgmental of people are those who have: 1) Just quit smoking, 2) Have just lost weight, 3) A reformed whore, or 4) Have recently become "saved."

In evaluating the life and teachings of Jesus it is difficult to ignore the priorities that He had. Perhaps the most important was His condemnation of the self-righteous. Whether it was the person praying and thanking God he was different; or, the story of the women taken by the religious zealots and accused of adultery. The two, (Jesus and the accused) were surrounded by those who were ready to stone her.

Then the scene says that Jesus reached down and wrote something in the sand. What did He write? No one knows. But Jesus said to the judgmental, "Let those who are without sin, cast the first stone." One Biblical scholar indicates that perhaps Jesus wrote a catalog of the sins of the stone throwers. The end result was that all of them skulked away.

A moving story: It is filled with great theology and great practical advice. The first theological truth has to do with FORGIVENESS. Jesus seems to equate attitudes and actions in the same catalog of sins; Self-righteousness and adultery. The practical advice is a challenge to change one's behavior and the acceptance of divine forgiveness.

James Lehrer, noted TV commentator, wrote a book based on the life of John Quincy Watson. He was a B-29 pilot in World War II, was shot down and imprisoned in a Japanese prison camp. Tortured, he was brutally beaten and would never be able to have children. Upon his freedom, he entered the Seminary and became a Methodist minister. He was later elected a Bishop of that denomination.

Near retirement, he sees the man who tortured him and follows him to San Diego. He's then confronted by the dilemma between bitterness and forgiveness. His ultimate choice makes this real story a dramatic one. Needless to say, forgiveness is the only viable answer for a Christian. We need it from God, and we must extend it. Remember. "Forgive us our sins as we forgive those who sin against us."

The second theological truth is implied rather than spoken. It is HOPE. Without a doubt it is indigenous to all people. We can understand the importance of hope when we consider the tragedy of hopelessness. As a therapist I've often had the responsibility to counsel those who grapple with despair. The cloud of doom hovers over them.

Another image would be to describe their lives as having no light at the end of the tunnel. One of the best illustrations of hope is revealed in the movie, "The Shawshank Redemption." The two main characters are Tim Robbins and Morgan Freeman. Tim is unjustly convicted of murder and is sentenced to life imprisonment at the Shawshank prison.

Morgan had killed a man when he was young. He's now up in years.

In a moment of reflection, Tim says a very provocative thought. "It is a terrible thing to live in fear, WITHOUT HOPE." He follows this statement up with the words, "It is music to the soul and mind."

Whatever you might think about Jesus, consider the fact that in every instant He was involved, He offered HOPE to the needy. The real answer to despair or hopelessness is faith in God.

Amen. Selah. So be it.

HORSES

Midrash: parable, illustration, allegory. All four words have one thing in common. Their usage brings insight and clarification to truth. Usually it is a single truth.

Midrash has a definite tie with Judaism. Parable identified with Christianity, mainly because of Jesus' usage. The other two are part of the English vocabulary.

Dave and Joyce Freeland recently shared a beautiful story with me. It is an account of two horses in a field. There is something quite amazing. One horse is totally blind. His owner has chosen not to have him put down, but has made a good home for him. If you stand nearby and listen, you will hear the sound of a bell. Looking around for the source of the sound, you will see that it comes from the smaller horse in the field.

Attached to the horse's halter is a small bell. It lets the blind friend know where the other horse is, so he can follow. As you stand and watch these two horses, you'll see that the horse with the bell is always checking on the blind horse, and that the blind horse will listen for the bell and then slowly walk to where the other horse, trusts that he will not be led astray. When the horse with the bell returns to the shelter of the barn each evening, it stops occasionally and looks back, making sure that the blind friend isn't too far behind to hear the bell.

A few years ago a friend told me a most interesting story. Its origin has an overtone of religious compassion. It seems that the Creator of the universe had desired a provocative method of judging earth's inhabitants.

Obviously the standard for entrance into heaven/paradise/nirvana was an expression of compassion. Those who were practitioners of this virtue gained immediate entrance. Those who did not, were sentenced to a most interesting state of punishment. They were sent to a place of an eternal condition of starvation, in the presence of a huge banquet; an unbelievable buffet.

There was a major problem. Each person had unmovable slats attached to each arm, with a fork in each hand. Their arms were unbending. What a punishment. There was only one way out. Show concern for others. A solution was devised by those "seeing the light."

With unbent arms, they would fill the fork with food and FEED others. Compassion was the key...Helping the Needy.

Michael Jackson has really been in the news. We've been inundated with his exploits and personal failures. His history, to say the least, has been tragic. Fred Astaire is reported as saying that in his opinion, Michael was the greatest dancer in history.

His lyrics are poignant and inspiring. His music, and at times his dancing, has left me on the outside. I'm of a different generation. However, there is one thing that has gotten very little attention. The media has all but ignored it. Perhaps Michael Jackson did very little to advertise his actions.

According to reliable sources, he contributed between 400 and 500 million dollars of his own money to a myriad of charities; schools, hospitals, churches and various organizations in the USA and around the world; Compassion in action.

NOW BACK TO THE HORSES. Like the owners of these two horses, God does not throw us away just because we are not perfect or because we have problems or challenges.

He watches over us and even brings others into our lives to help us when we are in need. Sometimes we are the blind horse being guided by the little ringing bell of those who God places in our lives. Other times we are the guide horse, helping others to find their way....Good friends are like that...you may not always see them, but you know they are always there. Please listen for my bell and I'll listen for yours.

Amen. Selah so be it.

INERRANCY

It is common knowledge that the ultra-conservative wing of the Republican Party is made up mostly of fundamentalist Christians. The basic tenet of this group is a belief in the infallibility and inerrancy of the Bible. This means that every "a", "and," and "the" is directly inspired by God. Little attention is paid to the fact that most Bible scholars affirm the truth that the Bible-Old and New Testaments-are not historical or scientifically accurate.

The books were written by men and the originals were copied again and again. In fact, there is NOT an original copy of the Bible; Old or New Testaments. The King James Version, compiled in 1611, is based on one of the most inaccurate of translations. And yet, the litmus test for fundamentalists is a belief in the inerrancy of the Bible, the KJV.

Two basic considerations must be made. Several events in the Bible have a previous history. For example, the story of Noah and the flood. The Epic f Gilgamesh was recorded hundreds of years before Noah. It parallels the entire story.

The laws of the Israelites, especially the Ten Commandments are recorded in the Code of Hammurabi: Many of the events in Jesus' life are similar to those from Egyptian and Persian stories.

The second item has to do with authorship. Who recorded God's words, since they were often only His thoughts? For instance, He said "Let us make man in our own image." It is, therefore, reasonable to assume that many authors were recording their own views and attaching God's name to them. In describing God and recording what He wanted man to do, they were exercising editorial license.

This license is reflected in various literary styles. The major one was (is) the use of allegory. Rabbi Abraham Heschel states that all the stories in the Old Testament are allegorical. Rabbi Harold Kushner makes a very similar statement.

Saint Paul uses the word "allegory" in his Epistles when referring to the stories of Abraham. The Early Church Fathers- Irenaeus, Origen, Tertullian and others-all declared the Old Testament to be allegorical. This means there is not ONE interpretation of the ideas and incidents in the Bible; So much for inerrancy.

A casual perusal of the Bible highlights at least three obvious conditions. First, it is a book of VIOLENCE; from the killing of Abel by Cain to the crucifixion of Jesus and the Book of Revelation.

One researcher has estimated the Israelites slaughtered at least ten million Gentiles in the Old Testament; All under the supposed orders of God; or so said the writers. Add to that the millions of people killed during the Catholic Inquisition and the Protestant Inquisition. Truly, the Judea/Christian religions have been a source of violence in our world.

Psalm 137 gives a horrible example of what the Bible says about God when it says that God ordered the people to take the children by their heels and bash their heads against a wall. I don't believe in a God like that. Do you? The writers had an agenda of their own and couched it in the dictates of God.

The second idea that pops out is the rampant ETHICAL FRAILITIES of the Biblical participants. This includes sexual promiscuity, drunkenness, lying, deceitfulness, rapes, stealing, and disrespect of parents, slavery and etc; All with Divine endorsement. Many of them like Abraham are included in Chapter eleven of the Book of Hebrews, as people of great faith.

Consider Cain who murdered his brother Abel or Noah and Lot who were drunks. In his stupor, Lot impregnated his two daughters. Abraham tried to kill his two sons and lied twice about his wife, claiming she was his sister. Poor Jacob; He deceived and lied to his father and brother, with the assistance of his mother. Moses killed a man and David's conquest of Bathsheba and subsequent murder of her husband are well known. The list goes on and on. The record of the Bible with its frail heroes sounds like the Greek and Roman mythological heroes.

The third area deals with CONFLICTS. The Old Testament has many examples, but for this article, I'll stick with the New Testament. They begin with the conflict between Joseph and the community over Mary's pregnancy. He resolves it by marrying her. There is the conflict between Herod and the wise men.

Peter and the brothers James and John conflict over their respective stations in the kingdom. Peter conflicted with Jesus and later with the Apostle Paul. Paul seemed to constantly be in conflict. Originally with the followers of Jesus: Then with the disciples and the Jewish community. He and Barnabas split up with strong disagreements. He and James-the brother of Jesus conflicted on several issues; along with Peter. The Bible records his conflict with Mark and Demas. A casual reading of the Epistles reveals his arguments with the churches he established. His conflicts became so violent he was beaten, stoned, put in prison and put out of cities.

Violence, questionable behavior and conflicts have characterized the Judea/Christian religions from the beginning. With all of these facts it seems illogical to accept the inerrancy view. Yet, I affirm the Bible contains the essential truths. THE MESSAGE OF GOD'S LOVE, HIS FORGIVENESS AND SALVATION THROUGH HIS SON JESUS.

Amen. Selah. So be it.

INSIGHT

Insight and knowledge comes to each of us from many sources and directions. Self-sufficiency is a worthwhile objective. However, the Bible gives us a clear admonition, "No one lives unto themselves." Or, as the song writer and poet has said, "No man is an island."

The purpose of this article is to enlighten readers regarding at least three sources of insight: historical, artistic and religious.

Edward Gibbon (1737-1794) has often been called, "the first modern historian of Ancient Rome." Will Durant (1885-1981), in my opinion, was the greatest of all historians. In evaluating their views on the decline of the Roman Empire, a summation has several interesting insights.

First, there was an increasing realization of legions deployed to foreign lands. This depleted the number of forces available to protect Rome itself.

Second, this brought about an increase in taxation on the citizenry; a feeling of anxiety and a sense of frustration. The base for taxation was also declining. Believe it or not, too many businesses were out-sourcing to other countries.

Third, there was the increase of immigrants; many of them were slaves, whose presence drained the economy.

Fourth, and it was emphasized by both Gibbon and Durant, there was the erosion of ethical values. Gibbon blamed the Roman Catholic Church. While Durant acknowledges the spiritual malaise, he does not blame religion but the profligate lives of the Romans.

The parallel with our current situation is too similar to ignore. We either learn from the past or we will be doomed to repeat it.

Another insight has artistic overtones. It involves words, their usage and the changes in meaning. The Bible uses the word "peculiar," as in "you are a peculiar people." Today the word means "strange," "odd," or even "crazy." However, the original meaning was simply "different."

The word "sincere" basically, it means "free of deceit or hypocrisy." It is often used to end a letter. However, since the time of Michelangelo, sculptors had used the word sincere to hide the flaws in their work. The sculptors would smear hot wax into any cracks in the stone and then spread stone dust into the wax.

This was considered cheating and any work that was "pure" was called sin-cere or "without wax." The Latin was "sine cera." When the stone was a pure piece of sculpture it was called sincerely or without wax. When we use it, it means, "my words are true." Various aspects of art certainly add to our insight.

Religion certainly increases our knowledge as well as insight. For example it is impossible to eliminate the Egyptian influence on the Jewish, Christian and Muslim faiths. In the Book of Genesis 45:8, Joseph says, "He (God) has made me a father of Pharaoh" Obviously speaking of Moses. By the way, the name Moses is an Egyptian word not Hebrew.

Historians affirm with certainty that the concept of monotheism originated with the Egyptians; mainly through the belief and work of Pharaoh Akhenaten. The view of many scholars is that he and Moses were one and the same. If not, he decidedly influenced Moses; especially regarding monotheism.

To my way of thinking the most important concept in the New Testament is the INCARNATION. It is pivotal to all that Jesus said and did; God sending His Son into the world; taking on the form of man-Emmanuel; "God with (in) us."

Tom Harpur is a former Anglican priest and a professor of Greek and New Testament at the University of Toronto. He capitalizes the above idea by saying, "the central truth of all religion is indeed the incarnation of the divine in the human."

The following quote by St. Augustine should trigger your insight. "The very thing which is now called the Christian religion EXISTED AMONG THE ANCIENTS ALSO, nor was it wanting from the inception of the human race until the coming of Christ in the flesh, at which point the true religion, which was already in existence, BEGAN TO BE CALLED CHRISTIAN."

St. Augustine really blew my mind when he wrote about Socrates. He (Socrates) lived about 500 years before Christianity. "He was as grand a Christian as any churchly saint or martyr."

Amen. Selah. So be it.

JESUS

Did you know that Jesus was not a Christian? He never ever professed to be one. In the Book of Acts Chapter 11 verse 26 it states that the disciples of Jesus were first called Christians at Antioch. The best guess of Bible scholars is that it was 40-50 years after the death of Jesus.

He never even founded a church or a denomination. He left those responsibilities to the likes of the Apostle Peter, Martin Luther, John Calvin or John Wesley. Jesus never wrote a Gospel or an Epistle. He left that to others. In fact, the only reference that Jesus wrote anything is in the Gospel of John 8:6. He wrote in the dirt and then erased it. Amazingly He never engaged in discussions or debates about theological ideas. Such events then and now only create divisions among Jesus' disciples.

History records that at the Council of Nicea in 325 A.D., the delegates ended up with physical confrontations. Can you imagine the wars that have been fought in Jesus' name? There was inquisitions and holocausts galore. Jews, Arabs, Armenians, Native Americans, Mexican Indians.

The history of Christianity is a sad story. All of the above have been committed in the name of Jesus. His emphases are a long way from the messages proclaimed from the pulpits of today.

The tragedy of the New Testament involves the Apostle Paul. Very little of the life of Jesus is recorded by Him. The Apostle ignores almost all of the teachings of Jesus. He turned the Jesus of history into the Christ of faith.

With this in mind it is relevant to discuss the priorities of Jesus. There are many, but only one for this article. It is the priority of LOVE and RELATIONSHIPS. In John 15:12 Jesus said, "Love one another as I have loved you." In announcing the two great commandments, He said for His disciples to love God and their neighbors. Strange as it may seem, His disciples did not follow His advice. Divisions prevailed among the twelve. Relationships were often strained. Judas and the big three (Peter, James and Jon) bickered.

The Gospel of Thomas states that the disciples resented Mary Magdalene. "He loves her more than us." A casual reading of Acts reveals the Apostle Paul's conflicts with Peter, James (brother of Jesus) Barnabas and Mark. Factions existed in most of the early churches. The Gospel of love was simply ignored.

I've been ordained for fifty-seven years and have pastored ten churches. There were always factions in those churches. In fact, I've never known of a church that didn't have conflicts.

The Eastern Orthodox broke away from Roman Catholicism. The Protestants broke away from the Catholics. Today there are hundreds of denominations, all splintered with various causes.

Sociologists, they state that problems always develop in organizations over money, sex or power; Desire at times for all three. Bigotry, intolerance, racism, prejudice, hatred and the like are totally incompatible with the teachings of Jesus.

Many of you have read the book The Shack by Wm. Paul Young. The subject of relationships is prominent. To facilitate a good relationship, "self-limitation is essential. In choosing to limit oneself, we are honoring relationship."

One way to "avoid the will to hold power over another is to choose to limit oneself." This is done by NOT winning a competition with your kids, by always being right; by touching the infirm; by visiting the needy; by being compassionate; by not knowing all the answers, etc.

One of the most meaningful relationships I ever had was with a person who would frequently say to me, "I never knew that." Even though I knew they had. That is what limiting is all about; A wholesome relationship results.

Amen. Selah so be it.

JOSHUA

Serious musicians are very acquainted with the names of Joshua Bell and Itzhak Perlman. They are world class violinists. Bell was born in Bloomington, Indiana and began taking violin lessons at the age of four. He was shortly afterward diagnosed as a prodigy.

At age fourteen he appeared as a soloist with the Philadelphia orchestra. In his 42 years, he has received numerous awards. Currently he is a guest lecturer at the Indiana University Jacobs School of Music. Bell made his Carnegie Hall debut in 1985 at age 18. Since then he has traveled the world impressing musicians, Queens and Presidents with his abilities.

On January 12, 2007, the Washington Post columnist Gene Weingarten initiated an interesting experiment. Wearing a baseball cap; Bell played his $3.5 million Stradivarius (made in 1713), incognito for 45 minutes at the metro station in Washington, D.C. About 2000 people passed by and only one person recognized him and only seven stopped by to listen to the violinist. A total of $32.17 was collected. Two days before the experiment he had performed before thousands at a concert in Boston. Incidentally, Weingarten won the 2008 Pulitzer Prize for his article on the experiment.

In his article, he emphasized the importance of perception, taste and people's priorities. He also raised certain questions: "Do we perceive beauty? Do we stop to appreciate it? Do we recognize talent in an unexpected context?"

He further challenges his readers by challenging us about the things of beauty we miss. Fail to hear, see and appreciate. Weingarten put it this way: "If we do not have a moment to stop and listen to the musicians in the world, playing some of the finest music ever written, on one of the most beautiful instruments: WHAT OTHER THINGS ARE WE MISSING?"

God has given us senses to use to brighten and improve our lives: sight to see, ears to hear, tongues to taste, noses to smell, hands to touch, minds to think, hearts to love. If we don't utilize them, we are the losers.

THERE IS ANOTHER SIGNIFICANT AREA OF OUR LIVES THAT WE OFTEN IGNORE. We are also spiritual creatures. It is only by maximizing this awareness that we can bring meaning out of adversity.

Many tragedies in life are because of our own doing. Take Michael Vick as an example. He brought several losses on himself by what he did: loss of freedom, loss of income, loss of respect, to name a few.

People who smoke all of their lives or overeat bring early death upon themselves.

But what about those in the helicopter the other day that were killed when hit by a plane over the Hudson River? Several were Italian tourists plus the pilot. They didn't do anything to bring their lives to a close.

Last Saturday (August 15) in the Wall Street Journal, Father Jonathon Morris-parochial vicar of St. Patrick's Old Cathedral in New York City-wrote an illuminating article. He witnessed the tragedy while hitting a few golf balls off the 18th pier. After ministering to the families, he testifies, "I witnessed inexplicable goodness and love." This was the result of grief expressed by the surviving families of the deceased.

Seemingly all the families were of Christian faith. They affirmed that in the midst of great grief, God's promise was to bring "a greater good out of every instance of evil and suffering."

Father Morris deals with the thought of what made these grieving ones to become better rather than bitter from the tragedy. He states, in answer to the question, "What makes these families different?" with one powerful word HUMILITY. They accepted their finitude.

He denounces suave platitudes. Rather, he affirms their refusal to make themselves the center of the universe. God is their center. Deep within is this certainty and it brings solace to every grieving spirit. Thank you, Father Morris, for your insights. May we NOT ignore them!

I often receive inspiring thoughts from secular novels. In Sara Paretsky's book, Hard Time, she has a priest say to the heroine who wants revenge, "You need to remember that you are not Almighty God." This affirmation automatically creates HUMILITY.

I am indebted to Charles Roberts and Dr. Lowell Linden for making me aware of these two stories.

Amen. Selah so be it.

JOY

There are many traits that characterize the beliefs of world religions. Many of these traits are held in common. For example, the so-called Golden Rule. "Do unto others as you would have them do to you." Sometimes it is quoted negatively; don't do.

A few of the more common traits are; love, patience, altruism, forgiveness, hope and JOY. The latter trait is one of the most visible and apparent. It certainly is expressive at weddings; at births; at graduations; at athletic victories.

There is a major fallacy in the espousal of joy. It is supposedly a major characteristic of Christianity. It is testified to; it is sung about; it is read about; it is preached. Yet, and it's a big yet; there is often a sad demeanor; a somber expression; and depressive gestures. I've witnessed it. I've been to churches where "joy" is talked about and sung about, BUT THERE WAS NOT A JOY LOOK. Vibrancy; if you will. Words and actions should coincide. Talk isn't enough.

The purpose of this article is to analyze, dissect and examine the concept of joy. Why...Because joy "has a lasting positive impact on our character and on who we are." It is a noun and an emotion. The emotion of joy is evoked by well-being, success, by the prospect of possessing what one desires (like a relationship.) Synonyms would be: rapture, bliss, pleasure, glad. Antonyms would be: sad, sorrow, woe, grief, misery and unhappiness.

Since joy is often equated with our faith, we need to be

reminded what the Bible says. Psalm 16:11, "In God's presence is fullness of joy." Galatians 5:22, "The fruit of the spirit is love, JOY, peace." I Peter 1:8, "Joy unspeakable." I John 1:4, "That your joy might be full." These are but four of scores of references. In continuing this autopsy of joy, I suggest five salient facts about it.

1) Joy lasts. There are several events that brought me joy; a new car, a great meal, a beautiful sunset, a trip through the Panama Canal, a particular movie. But these joys were temporary. Not lasting.

2) Joy comes from creative activities. Joy never comes from tearing down or destroying. Maybe pleasure but never joy. Building things like relationships, friendships, projects (like writing a book.)

3) There are no negative side effects of joy. Drugs and alcohol bring pleasure. The effects are crime, accidents and disease. Joy's create good effects.

4) Joy has spiritual dimensions. It is common knowledge that pleasure effects the physical senses. Illicit sex provides a measure of pleasure, but acts of compassion and altruistic behavior brings a joy that touches the heart and spirit.

5) Perhaps most important, joy requires effort. It doesn't take much energy to be hedonistic. Pleasure is passive. Buy a joint or a fifth of alcohol-no discipline is required.

The important thought is that the reward of joy always outweighs the effort. The more effort and discipline, the more joy is experienced.

Amen. Selah. So be it.

JUDAISM

Habiru was the original name of the people called Hebrews. It meant "the wanderers." The accepted "father" of the nomads was named Abraham.

Three religions: Judaism, Islam and Christianity, all look to him as the originator of their faiths. Most scholars date his beginning as 2000 to 1800 B.C.E. (Before the Common Era). The chronology for Judaism is: Abraham, Isaac, Jacob, Joseph, Moses. An interesting tie between Joseph and Moses (which is an Egyptian name) is found in Genesis 45:8.

There are four basic views about the origin of Judaism. One is the traditional view that Genesis is historically accurate. Two, is more current, that the history begins among Canaan natives. All were native nomads. Abraham's tribe defeated all other tribes. Three, using Apostle Paul's statement in Galatians 4:22-24, the Abrahamic story must be viewed as allegory. Four, an increasing scholarly view is that all of Genesis was plagiarized from Egyptian religions.

The first five books of Genesis are referred to as the Torah or Pentateuch. It is read in part each week in the Temples or synagogues. Most Bible scholars today no longer accept Moses' authorship. Generally the date set is around 900 BCE with various authors. The letters used to define authorship are J, E, D and P. Their differing styles are obvious. J stands for Jehovah, E for Elohim; D for Deuteronomy and P for Priestly.

Then, between 300 and 200 BCE the Septuagint (LXX)

translation was written with the use of Greek as the language. This was the translation used by Jesus, the Disciples and Paul. In addition to the Torah and the rest of the Old Testament, there is the Apocropha, which is included in the Catholic Bible.

Since the first century there has been the Talmud, which is a description of some 650 laws that interpret the Law. The Mishnah is the beginning of the Talmud that gives illustrations that helps define the Talmud.

As Christianity is divided into branches of Catholic, Protestant and Eastern Orthodox, Judaism is divided into: Hasidic, Orthodox, Conservative and Reformed. The local Temple is reformed.

The basic beliefs of Judaism are found in the Ten Commandments. (Decalogue) They are found in Exodus 20:2-17 and Deuteronomy (Second Law) 5:7-21. In the time of Jesus there were four distinct belief groups: Pharisees, Sadducees, Essences and Zealots. Only the Pharisees lasted.

The word "covenant" is repeated often. It was between God and Abraham and his descendants. If they obeyed and followed God, He would make them a great nation (20 million today) and bring them into the Promised Land (Canaan-Israel.) The latter is the basis for conflict today between Jews and Palestinians.

A major source of discussion about Jews is whether they are ethnic or religious in origin. The ethnicity is divided into Ashkenazi and Sephardic; Very similar to Nordic and Hispanic. The Ashkenazi is primarily white from central Europe and Russia. The Sephardic are dark skinned primarily from Spain, Italy and Africa.

The largest concentrations of Jews today-outside of Israel-are New York City and Los Angeles. The Jewish religion revolves around laws. Not only acts of worship but behavior, dress, sexuality, medicine, hygiene and diet. The book of Leviticus gives extensive prohibitions.

The word "kosher" is common to our vocabulary. It refers to the preparation of foods that make them acceptable to Jews. Also no pork and certain foods cannot be eaten together.

The rites and rituals of Judaism are vitally important. The most important is Passover. It is observed every year in the spring. It concerns the Jews deliverance from slavery from Egypt. Special foods are eaten and songs sung.

Rosh Hashanah is the Jewish New Year. It takes place roughly in the middle of September. Yom Kippur follows Rosh Hashanah. It is the Day of Atonement No food, no work and Jews repent of their sins from the year past. Sukkoth is the harvest celebration and lasts for eight days. It is in October.

Hanukah is often called the "Jewish Christmas." Most often referred to as the "Feast of Lights." The menorah is used during the holiday of eight days.

Purim is celebrated in remembrance of Queen Ester. It is usually in February and includes gift giving. Other important celebrations in Jewish tradition are: circumcision (Genesis 17:10,) bar mitzvah (boys) and bat mitzvah (girls.) These are the essential elements in the Jewish faith.

Amen. Selah so be it.

KNOWLEDGE

Knowledge should be a shared commodity. At least that's my opinion. A few years ago I served as Protestant Chaplain on the S. S. Hope in Columbia, S. A. It meant Health Opportunities for People Everywhere. A major problem encountered was with the local oligarchy. It was comprised of the wealthy and educated people. Its base philosophy was: "whatever we have or know is ours and we won't share it." They were appalled that we Americans would teach them what we knew.

We accumulate knowledge and information from various sources: from parents, teachers, friends, television, radio, newspapers, books, etc. We are indebted. Among the contributors to my fund of knowledge is the philosophy of Satchel Paige. He is the memorable baseball pitcher. One time, before integration, he struck out Babe Ruth, Lou Gehrig and Joe DiMaggio in one inning. His philosophy was simple. He said:

1. Avoid fried food which angry up the blood.
2. If your stomach disputes   you, lie down and pacify it with cool thoughts.
3. Keep the juices flowing by jangling around gently as you move.
4. Go very light on the vices, such as, carrying on in society-the social ramble isn't restful.
5. Avoid running at all times.

6. And don't look back-something might be gaining on you.

I particularly like his statement: "How old would you be if you didn't know how old you were." My second bit of wisdom comes from Robert Fulghum in his book: "All I Really Need to Know, I Learned in Kindergarten."

1. Share everything.
2. Play fair.
3. Don't hit people.
4. Put things back where you found them.
5. Clean up your own mess.
6. Don't take things that aren't yours.
7. Say you're sorry when you hurt somebody.
8. Wash your hands before you eat.
9. Flush.
10. Warm cookies and cold milk are good for you.
11. Live a balanced life-learn, something and think some and draw and paint and sing and dance and play and work every day some.
12. Take a nap every afternoon.
13. When you go out in the world, watch out for traffic, hold hands and stick together.
14. Be aware of wonders.
15. My suggestion. Read all of Fulghum's books. They are good.

Mike Trent recently sent me an article written by Regina Brett, 90 years old, who writes for The Plain Dealer of

Cleveland, Ohio. Here are a few of her suggestions to celebrate growing older.

1. Life isn't fair, but it's still good.
2. Life is too short to waste time hating anyone.
3. Your job won't take care of you when you are sick. Your friends and parents will. Stay in touch.
4. Pay off your credit cards every month.
5. Its OK to get angry with God. He can take it.
6. Make peace with you past so it won't screw up the present.
7. Everything can change in the blink of an eye. But don't worry; God never blinks.
8. Take a deep breath. It calms the mind.
9. Get rid of anything that isn't useful, beautiful or joyful.
10. Be eccentric now. Don't wait for old age to wear purple.
11. No one is in charge of your happiness but you.
12. Forgive everyone everything.
13. What other people think of you is none of your business.
14. However good or bad a situation is it will change.
15. Don't take yourself so seriously. No one else does.
16. God loves you because of who God is, not because of anything you did or didn't do.
17. Growing old beats the alternative — dying young.
18. All that truly matters in the end is that you loved.
19. The best is yet to come.
20. Life isn't tied with a bow, but it's still a gift.

Amen. Selah. So be it.

LA BREA

Approximately 75 miles west of Highland is one of the top visitor sights in Southern California. La Brea Tar Pits. That is sort of redundant since the "brea" in Spanish means tar. The best way to get there is to take Route 10 to LA, then continue on ten toward Santa Monica. Go north on off ramp La Brea to Wilshire Blvd. Turn left and the destination is a short distance on the right.

Rancho La Brea has an illustrious history. Obviously the original occupants of the area were Indians. The earliest fossils go back to about 40,000 years. Most of the over one million relics are believed to have lived between then and 9,000 years ago. Earliest recorded history comes from the Spanish/Mexican period. Gaspar de Portola made the first written report in 1769.

The original owner of the area was Antonio Jose Pocha. It was a Mexican land grant of 4,400 acres and was named Rancho La Brea. It was given to him in 1828.

Father Juan Crespa described the area as geysers spouting tar from the ground. The land was spouting molten tar from springs, surrounded by swamps. The area was christened Los Bolianes de Brea (the tar geysers).

In 1850, following the USA-Mexican war, the Rancho claim was challenged. However, in 1870 the US Supreme Court granted their claim. Because of the financial drain on the family, a major part of La Brea was sold to John and Henry Hancock.

In the early 1870's Major Henry Hancock assumed control of the area consisting of 4,000 plus acres. Today the area is still called Hancock Park. The original purpose was mining the tar and asphalt. Hundreds of tons were mined and sent to San Francisco for roads.

Today the tar pits consist of approximately 23 acres. This park was donated to the County of Los Angeles by the Hancock family. The understanding was that a museum would be built on-site "to house and exhibit the fossils." It is important to understand how the myriad of animals were trapped to become fossils. Obviously the tar and springs were always there.

The black tar (asphalt) was covered with water. Animals would come to the various springs seeking to quench their thirst. Upon stepping into the water, they would sink into the tar and be trapped forever or until their fossils were excavated.

An interesting feature that can be seen today is a large tank of tar with poles sticking out of it. Visitors can try to pull the poles out of the tar. It can be done only with great effort. The closest image I can think of to the tar pits is quicksand. Both can best be described as "death traps."

The grounds can be divided into two parts. First, there are beautiful park-like areas. Tar pits, small lakes, large trees, beautiful walkways and scenic animals made of concrete. Guides (doscents) are available to describe what can be seen at various times.

Second, there is the world famous George C. Page Museum of La Brea Discoveries. It was Page's vision and philanthropy that made the beautiful edifice possible. The display of fossils and reconstructed animals is awesome. There is also a gift shop with hundreds of items for sale. The first Tuesday of each month the facility is free. Other days there is a small fee to enter.

Over the years only one human remains has been found. The death of "La Brea Woman" took place about 9,000 years ago. Only the skull and several skeletal items were found. She has been estimated as being about 4 feet 8 inches tall and approximately 18 years old when she died. The cause of death is not known, outside of her remains in one of the pits. Close to the skull were the remains of a dog and a hand grinding stone.

Where did these animals come from? It is believed they arrived in the Western Hemisphere about 20-40,000 years ago, across the Aleutian land bridge, from Siberia. However, humans followed them and all scattered throughout Alaska, Canada, the US and Central and South America. In addition to the animals already mentioned, there is evidence of lions, horses, tigers, dogs, wolves and zebras.

The work goes on. Volunteers are working most everyday and the evidence of fossils is ever increasing. A trip to La Brea Discoveries is worth every effort you make. Enjoy.

Amen. Selah so be it.

LATERAL

There is more than one way to skin a cat. You need to think outside the box. Brain storming; we know what those words mean. In the early 60's Dr. Edward de Bono had a copyright for the two words that mean the same – LATERAL THINKING.

Born in Malta in 1933, his academic credentials are impressive. He has traveled the world advancing his theory. He's spoken to thousands of schools, corporations and the military in scores of countries. A major emphasis is that every school teacher should spend at least one hour per week teaching students to Think Laterally. His awards are too numerous to mention.

Many people say his approach is just common sense-which, in a way, it is. The difference is de Bono has structured the process and broadened his theories to include every aspect of life. Wherever there is a problem, Lateral Thinking is applicable.

Many years ago when elevators were just coming into vogue, a major hotel in San Diego-El Cortez-wanted one installed. Soon they found the building was not structurally sound for one. For the first time ever, the decision was made to build one on the outside of the building...Lateral Thinking.

Dr. de Bono's favorite geometric design is one I've used many times. Nine dots, three lines with three dots each, make a square figure. Draw four lines without lifting the pen; connect each dot. The answer is simple. Start at any corner with a straight line, BUT GO OUTSIDE THE BOX. Then to the right, going outside the box; finally across the bottom and up through the center…Lateral Thinking.

What does the Bible say about LATERAL THINKING? First, there is a problem. Then the God-given ability for creative thinking is exercised. Often God is asked for help. The old adage seems to apply. God helps those who help themselves. The examples are numerous: Noah, Abraham, Moses, David against Goliath and the Apostle Paul, to name a few.

Consider the story of Gideon. In the Book of Judges, chapters 6 and 7 are the story. The Midianites and the Amalekites defeated the Israelites; took their crops and animals. Gideon is finally chosen to lead the Israelites against their enemies.

Now begins the Lateral Thinking. He cuts his forces to 300 men. Those that lapped water like a dog were excused. He wanted ready and willing men. They were outnumbered to be sure. First, they surrounded the enemy in the middle of the night. Each man had a sword, a pitcher with a candle in it and a trumpet. At the given signal the pitcher was broken with the lighted candle flashing; the trumpet was blown and all the men yelled, "The sword of the Lord and of Gideon."

Talk about pandemonium. The enemy was scared out of their wits. They ran. Forgot their weapons and were slaughter. They were defeated by Lateral Thinking; thinking outside the box.

Accepting the status quo is the brain of lateral thinking. It accepts fatalism and pessimism as basic. These are contrary to Christian/Judeo presumptions. Both religions believe that mankind is created in the image of God. Not omnipotent, omnipresent or omniscient; but having limited capacity for self-realization, creativity, rational thinking and decision making. They are our potentials. It is these faculties that provide the tools for Lateral Thinking.

Dr. de Bono suggests provocative techniques of: wishful thinking, exaggeration, insight, intuition, creativity and openness.

Problem solving is the fertile area for using of such tools; "A person would use lateral thinking when they want to move from one known idea to creating new ideas."

Finally, de Bono gives a succinct explanation of lateral thinking. "It is a method that can be applied during the problem and creative problem solving processes to help come up with possible workable solutions."

Amen. Selah so be it.

LAUGHTER

Seniors have a distinct sense of humor. Hang out with a group of them and their laughter will be raucous. An example: A couple, both seniors went into town and stopped in Wal-Mart for a few minutes. Coming out they saw a policeman writing a parking ticket. They approached him and quietly asked him for consideration for a senior couple. He ignored them. The wife called him a Nazi cop and he wrote another ticket.

The husband called him a Fascist-pig. The cop wrote a third ticket. They went on for 20 minutes harassing the cop. He kept writing tickets. The couple walked off laughing their heads off. They didn't care because they had come to town on the bus. The car wasn't theirs.

Laughter at any age is important; especially for seniors. Nora is a 102 year old senior, going on 20. She has a perpetual smile, fastidious dresser, hair always neat, and sharp as a tack. How does she do it? "I eat sparingly, exercise every day, good genes and laugh several times a day."

John told me this story and cracked up laughing as he told it. A 92 year old man married a 90 year old woman. His kids asked him why he married such an elderly woman. Was she beautiful? "No," he said. "She's uglier than a mud fence." Was she rich? "No, she's poorer than a church mouse." Was she a good cook? "No, we eat at McDonald's every day." Why? His answer was classic; "Because she can drive at night."

The importance of laughter and humor reached front page and TV news in the 60's and 70's. Norman Cousins was the leader. He had been stricken with a collagen illness that affected the connective tissue of the body. He was diagnosed as terminal. Through laughter he became well.

As a professor in the medical department at UCLA, he was the person to discover ENDORPHINS. This secretion of the brain is stimulated by laughter. It affects the immune system and wellness.

Laughter seems to be indigenous to seniors. They laugh, smile, giggle and tell jokes. I know many elderly or aging people. They all laugh and make fun of each other.

No one remembers Jack Benny, George Burns, Red Skelton, Lucille Ball, Bob Hope, and Jimmy Durante as young people. In their heydays, they were seniors. So, seniors, show the way to the younger generations, Laugh a little and live a lot."

Betty Miller lived 100 plus years. She retired as chief of nurses at Patton State Hospital at age 50. She and her husband Charley raced horses until he died. Willy Shoemaker was one of their riders. She was an inveterate joke teller; Many of them a little risqué. Two I remember very well. John and Mary made a pact that whoever died first would try to contact the remaining spouse. John died and Mary waited anxiously for his contact.

Finally it happened. Mary heard a weird voice calling her. "What is it like over there?" John's answer was enigmatic. "I wake up and have sex; take a nap and have sex; eat a bit and then more sex; another nap and more sex; sex, sex, sex...all day long." "My word, John, is that what heaven's like?" "Who said anything about heaven, Mary? I'm a jack-rabbit in New Mexico."

Another one that Betty loved to tell is about an elderly Pasadena matron who drove a 1950 Packard with only 5,000 select miles. She drove into a strip mall and looked for a parking slot. Just as she was about to turn into one, a bright red corvette zipped in ahead of her.

A beautiful, sassy blonde jumped out, wiggled and yelled. "That goes to show what a young, beautiful blonde can do."

Those Packard's were big. The elderly matron backed up and with top speed smashed the back of the corvette; Three successive times. The corvette looked like an accordion. She popped out; adjusted her hat and said, "That shows you what your can do when you're a senior and rich." Every senior I know loves a joke.

Amen. Selah so be it.

LEGENDS

Midrash: parable, allegory, myth, illustration, urban legend; they all refer to the same literary style. They are stories that clarify truths and ideas. They vary with the discipline and era in which they are told. They are also timeless. For example: the parables of the Prodigal Son and the Good Samaritan as reportedly told by Jesus.

The most recent type is the "urban legend." "It entered the popular lexicon in the early 1980's." Jan Harold Brunvand, the folklorist, coined the phrase. It is important to note that none of the categories are to be considered as being historical. They are conveyors of truth.

Thalidomide is a sedative that was in use fifty to sixty years ago for pregnant women. It often caused severe abnormalities in the limbs or features of the fetus. It has since been discontinued.

Those Packard's were big. The elderly matron backed up and with top speed smashed the back of the corvette; Three successive times. The corvette looked like an accordion. She unhappy and depressed. However, he became an excellent student. Then, in his early teens a life changing event happened. Someone donated two ears for a transplant. Overnight his life was changed.

He graduated from high school with honors and attended Harvard, graduating with honors. He received a PhD and became a professor at Harvard. Happily married with two children, word came one day that his mother had died. He returned to his home to attend the funeral.

At the wake, he stood by the casket mourning his beloved mother. Tenderly he brushed back his mother's lovely hair and to his utter amazement, she did not have ears. She had been the donor of his ears many years before-without him knowing about it. The message is pretty clear. It's one of unlimited love without regard for personal convenience; A mother's love. It's the closest emotion to the love God has for each of us.

Jim Sims, local Highland resident, shared with me an urban legend that has appeal to anyone who has a seeing problem-like Jim and I both have. There was a blind girl who hated herself because she was blind. She hated everyone, except her loving boyfriend. He was always there for her. She told her boyfriend, "If I could only see the world, I will marry you." One day, someone donated a pair of eyes to her. When the bandages came off, she was able to see everything, including her boyfriend. He asked her, "Now that you can see the world, will you marry me?" The girl looked at her boyfriend and saw that he was blind. The sight of his closed eyelids shocked her. She hadn't expected that. The thought of looking at them the rest of her life led her to refuse to marry him. Her boyfriend left in tears and days later wrote a note to her saying: "Take good care of your eyes, my dear; for before they were yours, they were mine."

This is how the human brain often works when our status changes. Only a very few remember what life was like before, and who was always by their side in the most painful situations. The originator of this legend contributed several truths applicable to the story before whining about the distance you drive-, think of someone who walks the same distance with their feet. And when you are tired and complain about your job, think of the unemployed, the disabled, and those who wish they had your job. But before you think of pointing the finger or condemning another- Remember that not one of us is without sin. And when depressing thoughts seem to get you down-Put a smile on your face and think: you're alive and still around.

Today before you say an unkind word, think of someone who can't speak. Before you complain about the taste of your food, think of someone who has nothing to eat. Before you complain about your husband or wife, think of someone who's crying out to GOD for a companion.

Today before you complain about life, think of someone who died too early on this earth. Before you complain about your children, think of someone who desires children but they're barren. Before you argue about your dirty house someone didn't clean or sweep, think of the people who are living in the streets.

Amen. Selah so be it.

LETTERS

Letters and words have always fascinated me. While there are only twenty-six letters in our alphabet, there are scads of words. Those who study such things declare that the letter "e" is the most used letter, the letter "t" is second and the letter "a" is the third. The person who studies such things is called a "philologist."

The letter "a" can also become a word, as well as the letter "I". However, normally it takes two or more letters to make a word; how about, "Oh, yes."

Single words are plentiful. Who? What? When? How? Where? Yes. No. Believe it or not, they compose a thought.

As a columnist for the several newspapers, I'm called a "stringer." Webster's Dictionary gives a definition: "A part-time writer for a newspaper." That's me. What I do is "string' words together. Normally when two or more words are strung together you get a sentence. Hopefully the sentence will project an idea or thought.

Since I usually write religious articles, the above thoughts are applied to the King James Version of the Bible. For this article I want to do something different. This century has been called the "information age." So it is with Bible information. The number one word in the Bible is "and." The most common nouns are: LORD, 7970 times; GOD, 4094 times; MAN, 3323 times; KING, 2504 times and SIN, 1016 times.

Other common words are: FAITH, 247 times; JOY, 165 times; JESUS, 983 times; LOVE, 310 times; WISDOM, 234 times; MUSIC, 11 times; PRAY, 313 times and HEART, 830 times. Let's string some of these important words together. "Man sins and through faith in Jesus, the Lord God implants His love and joy in our hearts. We should remember to pray at all times."

Most Bible studies focus on authorship and interpretations of various verses and books. They are either devotional in nature or theological.

There are a total of 1189 chapters in the King James Version. The longest chapter is Psalm 119. The shortest is Psalm 117. For most believers Psalm 23 is the most comforting chapter. The central chapter is Psalm 118. There are 594 chapters before it and 594 chapters after it. The central verse is Psalm 118:8. "It is better to trust in the Lord than to put confidence in man."

The longest verse is Esther 8:9 and the shortest verse is John 11:35-"Jesus wept." The longest word is found in Isaiah, chapter 8, verse 1. There are three words in the Bible that are found only once: "Reverend," Psalm 111:9; "Eternity," Isaiah 57:15; and Grandmother, II Timothy 1:5.

The word "prayer" is mentioned 500 times and about, 450 times, the word "faith." But the word "money" is mentioned over 2000 times. There are 8,674 different Hebrew words in the Bible; 5,624 different Greek words and 12,143 different English words in the King James Version.

For you culinary experts, there are 49 different foods mentioned. Almonds and pistachios are the only nuts recorded. The only domestic animal NOT mentioned in the Bible is the cat. And, sad but true, there are seven suicides recorded. *Amen. Selah. So be it.*

LIBERALISM

The word "liberal" is often taken as a dirty word; particularly for listeners and followers of Rush Limbaugh. He has kidnapped the word and tarnished it with untruths contrary to its meaning. While Limbaugh and his ilk have blamed so-called liberals as the source for everything that's wrong in the world, they are wrong.

Webster defines liberal as: favorable to progress; views advocating individual freedom; free from prejudice or bigotry-tolerant; not bound to tradition; characterized by generosity; liberal arts. The historical defense for liberal actions and liberal people speaks for itself.

One good way to understand liberal is to look at its opposite; conservative or conservatism. Again, Webster clarifies the issue. It means: to preserve existing conditions; maintaining the status quo; limiting change; tendency to conserve; a preservative; the disposition to preserve what is established. The best way to understand ideology or philosophy is to image it through personality. Let's begin with Jesus. Based on the previous analysis, Jesus was obviously a liberal.

The Pharisees and Sadducees were the conservatives. They were maintaining the status quo of hypocrisy. The teachings of Jesus were revolutionary. Particularly the great thought that "the kingdom of God is within you." The world has never been the same.

A similar liberal attitudes and actions were reflected in

the life of Martin Luther, who started the Protestant Reformation. He challenged the authority and practices of the Roman Catholic Church.

John Wesley changed the religious scene of England and later the American colonies. His liberal views motivated schools for children, the Salvation Army and child labor laws. In fact, every religious awakening and new denominations were precipitated by liberal expressions.

Consider the advancements in science in spite of religious prejudice and scientific obfuscation. From Galileo and Copernicus to Newton to Edison to Einstein to Jonas Salk; they have been interspersed by thousands of liberal scientific thinkers.

What would our lives be without creative men and women like Gutenberg, Eli Whitney and Neal Armstrong? All progress, again, has been made and will be made in spite of the Limbaugh mentality.

I dream of the great explorers who dared to "push the envelope" against the rigid views of their times: Marco Polo, Leif Ericson, Columbus, Magellan, Lewis and Clark, Daniel Boone, Cortez, to name a few. They all faced opposition from rigid thinking contemporaries.

Education, strange as it may, is another prime example where liberal thinking is essential. Valuable college learning is even called "liberal arts" study. It refers to a wide range of study including art, science, literature, history and philosophy.

When rigid conservative thought prevails, ignorance is magnified. Think of the problems that students are having today. High percentage not graduating from high school;

minimizing science and many districts pushing creationism; cutting back on the arts while pushing sports; as sex education is eliminated, pregnancy among teens is increasing.

The founders of our nation were by and large liberal thinkers; led by Washington, Jefferson, Franklin and Adams. They challenged the stereotypes of Europe and definitely opposed a theocracy.

The Constitution advocates not so much a freedom of religion as a freedom from religion. There is a mood in our country today of conservative churches attempting to dominate the political scene. Again, unfortunately, many of the traditionally liberal mainline church are dying out. The Methodist, Episcopal, Presbyterian and Congregational are showing significant declines in membership.

They've lost their liberal edge. In times past they were on the cutting edge: supporter of civil rights and social services. While not liberal in theology, they are conservative in practice. They are the Pharisees and Sadducees of today.

The press is currently being accused of being liberal; which it should be. Whenever it begins to parrot the views of the reigning establishment, it becomes ineffective. It must always be in a position to critique the behavior and decisions of authority.

The same must be said for the pulpit. The Gospel is more than comfortable platitudes. When it ceases to be prophetic it becomes pathetic. The hearers must be challenged to THINK, as Jesus did. The hearers must be challenged to FEEL, as Jesus did. The hearers must be challenged to DO as Jesus do...The press and the pulpit can only be what they should be in a liberal context.   *Amen. Selah so be it.*

LIBERTARIAN

I seem to spend a lot of time these days trying to figure out if I'm a liberal or a conservative. Since about everyone seems to be using these words, I went to the dictionary to see what Mr. Webster has to say about them. To define Liberalism, he uses words like "free, not narrow, broad minded, progressive, independent in opinion, and tending toward democracy."

Webster then says the conservative "preserves what is established, is opposed to change and conserves the existing institutions or views." The conservative wants to maintain the old, the established and the way things were. He wants to protect his way of thinking as it has been, and change is out of the question. If change has occurred, he wants to take it back to what it was.

Hitler, Stalin, Hussein, David Duke, Joe McCarthy and other extremists, fit into this mold. If we had followed their ways we would still have slavery, one room school houses, horse-and-buggy transportation-we would still be living in the nations of our parents' origin and worshiping the gods of the shamans. Liberals have led the way for progress.

Here are a few liberals who broke away from the conservative status quo and radically changed our world: Socrates and the Greeks gave us the word democracy; Moses and the Jews started the process of freedom by declaring freedom for all; Jesus challenged the religious molds and stereotypes of his day;

Columbus pushed the frontiers of geography; Washington and Jefferson led a revolt against the status of monarchy; Lincoln demanded the end of slavery; Einstein forever changed science and the way we think.

Former House Speaker Newt Gingrich recently accused the news media of being "inherently biased toward liberalism. This is true because, whether through newspapers, radio or television, the search is for truth. The media seek to enlighten and clarify what is happening or has happened. Of course, errors are made, but that doesn't invalidate their basic objective. They seldom try to maintain the status quo.

Because I have an affinity for coal mines and the steel mills of eastern Ohio, I have a basic appreciation for John L. Lewis and the labor unions. Let me remind you that it is partly because of these unions that we have our standard of health care and safety on the job and better wages. Pensions, health insurance hospitalization and vacations were unheard of in my father's day. Child labor was an accepted fact of life. I worked in a foundry and mill at the age of twelve. It was not the conservative owners who brought change, but the liberal labor unions.

Many are unhappy with the civil rights changes, but just think about the tremendous benefits brought about by liberals:

1. Women's right to vote.
2. Social Security that provides the only retirement millions of Americans have today.
3. Equality for all races.
4. Educational opportunities unheard of before.

5. A United Nations that provides a forum for nations to resolve conflict without war. While some do not use it, it is still there.
6. Programs to help those in poverty situations.
7. Denominational co-operation is erasing bigotries.
8. Dialogue among all religions.
9. Medical research that prolongs life.

These are but a few of the benefits created by liberal minds. The real problem and danger today is when the liberal gets what he wants and becomes conservative so that he can keep it for himself. Unfortunately, age often makes conservatives out of risk taking younger liberals.

Our world is perilous and our lives are in a constant state of turmoil. Racial diversity, world-wide economic responsibility and the use of computers to distribute information demand flexibility and change. Only the liberal perspective is able to respond to these problems. The conservative is too anxious to stay the same or retreat. The conservative is a taker and keeper while the liberal is a giver.

Remember, the liberal is never satisfied, but is always seeking to improve the changes. He has an unease with status quo and an insatiable curiosity about improving the quality of life.

I guess I'm a liberal. I happily join the ranks of John L. Lewis, F. d. Roosevelt, Harry Truman, Robert Kennedy, Martin Luther King; and countless number of women who have given us their visions-and sometimes their lives-for change.

Amen. Selah so be it.

LIFE

A friend of mine, a native of Pakistan, and now a loyal American, tells a fascinating Pakistani story of the stages of human life; .Four of them. First is YOUTH as reflected in the life of a BIRD; full of life, playful, flying here and there. That is youth; vibrant and energetic...From birth through the teens.

Second is YOUNG ADULTHOOD. This is reflected in the life of a DOG: A German Shepherd; A Doberman. They are establishing values, directions and stability. Careers and families are important. The third stage is the MATURE ADULT. This animal is the respected and idolized BULL; powerful and a leader; successful as a family man and a business man. The fourth stage is obviously the RETIRED level. The animal is the OWL: the wise old owl; to be sure. He is affectionately described as sleeping all day and staying awake all night.

It has often been said that knowledge comes with youth but wisdom comes with old age. William Glasser, M.D., gave the stages of life as three-fold: BIRTH, LIFE and DEATH; certainly a sad commentary.

Erik Erikson (1902-1994) was a Danish-German who immigrated to the U.S. in 1933. He became would famous as a Developmental Psychologist. He became a psychoanalyst under the guidance of Anna Freud, the daughter of Sigmund Freud. For many years he studied the stages of human development, spanning the entire lifespan. What is seldom known about Erikson is his skill as a hypnosis therapist. His approach was different from any other hypnotist I've known of. I studied and used his method extensively. Instead of using the traditional induction techniques, he would tell a relaxing scenario.

As with most "stage" theories there are several cautions to be considered. The various stages are never applicable to everyone in the same way. Also, at times individuals may regress to a previous stage. Also, the rate of development is dependent on mental astuteness, environmental compatibility; and physical maturity.

In cataloging his stages, Erikson begins each one with a descriptive noun, followed by a psychological principle. They are followed with a detailed analysis of the stage.

Stage 1 – HOPE: Trust vs. Mistrust. This is the infant stage when the child is aware of self and developing reliance upon caregivers. Are they reliable?

Stage 2 – WILL: Autonomy vs. Shame and Doubt. This is the toddler learning and exploring his world. Is the parent neglectful or smothering?

Stage 3 – PURPOSE: Initiative vs. Guilt. Kindergarten comes into play. The child learns to make choices. Guilt is compensated by a sense of accomplishment.

Stage 4 – COMPETENCE: Industry vs. Inferiority; around age 6 to puberty. Child begins to compare self to others. Disparities are recognized. Re-enforcement is necessary from significant others.

Stage 5 – FIDELITY: Identity vs. Role Confusion. Teenager is emotional. Questioning of self and independence are dominant. Pushing by parents to conform creates confusion.

Stage 6 – LOVE: Intimacy vs. Isolation. As a young adult, major decisions are made; Marriage and vocation choices. This stage is lasting longer and longer.

Stage 7 – CARING: Generosity vs. Stagnation. This is the time for mid-life crisis. It is also the time for personal evaluation of accomplishments. Assisting the younger generation is a necessity.

Stage 8 – WISDOM: Ego Integrity vs. Despair; Senior citizens…The golden age. It is a time for reflection for life's end. Family consolidation is meaningful. Spiritual values become exceedingly important.

Amen. Selah. So be it.

LONGEVITY

Juan Ponce de Leon landed in Florida on April 2, 1513. The legend about him is that he was looking for the Fountain of Youth. He was searching for the fabled body of water that would give the drinker (basically him) everlasting longevity. The idea of discovering a magic potion that will add significant years to our lives is the dream and hope of every retiree.

Authors, theories and advice abound when it comes to the process of living longer. As mentioned in a previous article, the Psalmist said that our time on earth is 3 score plus 10, which equals 70.

Today, insurance companies set the expected mortality at almost eighty for both men and women. The consensus of most authorities in the field of longevity believe that people who have good health at age 70 have a good chance to live until they are 100.

Kinesiologists and physical therapists often use the word "core" in their assessment of body strength. It refers to the abdominal muscles as the center of human balance. Abs are pivotal for upper body, lower body and back health and strength-our CORE. When it comes to our dream of living longer, it is imperative to possess certain CORE emphases.

First, is the core value of focused PURPOSE: Having a reason to live now is absolutely essential! One writer has said, "People who cultivate reasons to get up in the morning are likely to keep waking up;" Setting goals of things to do and places to go provide incentive to live. Zorba the Greek said it beautifully, "Death is any day not devoted to living." In this vein, Michelangelo also brought life into focus by saying, "It is only well with me when I have a chisel in my hand."

Second, is the core value of FLEXIBILITY: Rigidity of thought and behavior is the bane of getting older?

In Greek antiquity the early philosophers argued over the most basic item in life: Water, fire, air, etc. Their final decision was CHANGE. Change is going to happen whether we like it or not. Friends die, bodies weaken, kids leave the area, goals are realized, and more.

Inflexibility, lack of adjustment creates boredom and subsequently the immune system is weakened. The answer is simple. When dreams/goals are realized or fizzle, new ones should be set. Never be without something to look forward to; Today, tomorrow, next week, month or more.

When old friends die or simply move away, a new social order should be created. Which leads me to the third core value, SOCIALIZE. Dan Buettner, noted authority on longevity, in his book Blue Zones, gives four of the healthiest place on earth: Sardinia, Italy, Okinawa, Costa Rica and Loma Linda. He found that the healthiest centenarians in all four places began with family contact and spread out their social contacts.

The friends you have, the more social activities you participate in, the better off you are. Go to church, be involved in a senior center, cultivate family gatherings, and join the "Y". Any place there is a group, be a part of it. Socialize.

The fourth core value involves FOOD and DRINK. The Sardinians have a glass of wine every day. The Okinawans stop eating before they are full. Most of the centenarians were slim. They all avoided meats and fried food. The "plant slant" appealed to all of them; particularly the Adventists in Loma Linda. They are usually vegetarians or vegans. For all the Blue Zoners their diet was heavy on beans, whole grains and green vegetables. Along with tofu; nuts were also common in their diets.

The fifth core value is to DEVELOP WAYS TO COPE WITH STRESS. Stress is a killer. One 107 year old stated, "Life is short. Don't run so fast you miss it." One author suggests that each person should take time to relieve stress. Buettner also said, "Every centenarian we interviewed seemed to exude sublime serenity."

The sixth core value is SPIRITUAL. It is fundamental to all centenarians studied by an objective research group. Their report said, "Healthy centenarians everywhere have faith." They further suggested that the act of worship was a habit that seemed to improve and add years to life. They also have lower rates of cardiovascular disease, depression, stress, suicide and a stronger immune system. Perhaps Genesis 6:3 can be a reality.

Amen. Selah. So be it.

MARKETABLE

Recently a friend gave me a provocative adage. DEVELOP MARKETABLE SKILLS. This is particularly meaningful in this time of economic woes and job instability. Its meaning is clear. Working people should develop optional skills. Have more than one way to make a living.

When my friend was fifty years old he lost his job after twenty-eight years. He had been in a highly specialized vocation. With a wife and three children he needed to find a job. In assessing his situation, he knew he needed a short term plan and a long term one. A natural salesman, he went into insurance and then into selling stocks and bonds. For the long term he went to graduate school for more education. He became a high school teacher and administrator.

He wrote two bestselling books and started a business He says, "When I was fired years ago I vowed that never again would I be caught with limited skills. DEVELOP MARKETABLE SKILLS.

Wisdom is vital for our economic future. No one knows how permanent our jobs are. Every current vocation is fragile at best. The key word is MARKETABLE. Basically it means a job that will bring income. I've met several college graduates recently who can't find a job. Their education has been in non-marketable skills.

I heard on television the other day of a woman who was making $50,000 a year. She lost her job, with no other source of income. Years ago I heard Dr. Robert Schuler, pastor of the Crystal Cathedral say, "Find a need and fill it." He applied this principle to church growth. However, it is also applicable to any job search.

The person above applied this to her situation. She came up with a unique solution. She learned how to shine shoes. Then she solicited executives in office buildings. Today she is an executive with several employees, making $100,000 per year.

Bonnie was a pre-school teacher and a travel agent. She lost both jobs. Her husband's job was limited and they had three children. She became a Notary, developed scores of regular customers and today makes more money per year than previously.

Karen became a massage therapist and takes her chair to business offices. She makes an excellent living.

Wayne is a retired veteran (78). After retirement he went to work for San Bernardino city; became a lawyer and a judge...Marketable skills. Homer is also an ex-military retiree. He became a fireman, an electrician and a manager of theaters. He possesses marketable skills.

Jeff is 52 years old. He's been a cook, manager of a fast food and manager of a picture framing business. He's been in charge of maintenance in a large mall. He can do plumbing, electricity and carpentry...Marketable skills.

If I was a young man today I would survey the job market for those that are doable and durable. Like barbering, bartending, auto mechanic. These are "service" vocations and are certainly marketable.

Amen. Selah. So be it.

MIND

I never cease to be amazed at the power and wonder of human insight. It is baffling, to be sure.

Robert Browning speaks of insight, its importance, and then utters an example. "Ah, but a man's reach should exceed his grasp." Webster's dictionary brings clarity to its meaning: "a natural inclination or awareness that becomes an animating principle." In my opinion, the best comment I ever heard was, "Insight is the beginning of change."

A great example of this truth is the Parable of the Prodigal Son. He thinks of his circumstances, and then Scripture says, "He came to himself." He followed this with his decision to return home.

The sources of insight are many. Basically, Wikipedia suggests it evaluates the state or condition of others or situations and these results in thought-provoking observations and opinions.

Following this "insight" we can get clarity about the words and actions of Jesus. Moffatt (Bible scholar) translates John 10:10 as Jesus offering life and having it "to the full."

William James once described the difference between man (us) and a dog in a museum. A dog has no awareness of the world of powers, ideas and values of human life. So there is a world of experiences and values that Jesus has for us humans...Life to the full.

The problem we have is that we normally live only a fraction of our possibilities. Our energy and power are marginalized. A further example of life to the full is expressed in Jesus' words, "I have spoken to you . . . that your JOY may become perfect"

It seems obvious in these days of opulence and despair, the supply of joy is tragically depleted. As one writer puts it, "We have machinery to manufacture everything except inner peace and happiness. Our spiritual inheritance seems tied up with faith in God.

Another insight given by Doctor Moffatt comes from the Book of Acts 3:15. "You killed the pioneer of life." The phrase was uttered on the Day of Pentecost by Peter. A pioneer is one who expands the possible areas of life; one who pushes back horizons and blazes pathways for others. This is what Jesus did. He expanded the lives of His followers. He stretched their minds and sympathies.

Think of other pioneers like Lincoln, Mother Teresa, Lewis and Clarke, Benjamin Franklin and Thomas Jefferson.

The basic problem that Jesus faced in His earthly life was that He would not fit into a pigeon hole. He was a square peg. The Scribes and Pharisees had a cut-and-dried world. They had a category for everyone. They judged people by where they lived, their ethnically and their religious practices. John 9:30 states, "We do not know where this fellow comes from. "Jesus just did not fit in. I like what Halford Luccock says. "When Jesus becomes to us merely one of any group He becomes nothing."

One final insight: Bethlehem was a small, rural village; a poor city, to be sure. But Matthew 2:6 says "From you shall come a Prince;" referring to Jesus.

It never ceases to amaze me how often people are

judged by their geographical heritage; from a ghetto, a coal mining community, a rural area, a steel mill town, Appalachia - otherwise known as a "'hill-billy".

The people in Jesus' day judged Him by where He came from. "Can any good thing come from Nazareth?"

A few years ago thousands of student from thirty countries were asked to vote for the ten greatest characters in history based on their contributions to humanity. The final tally included: Abraham Lincoln, Martin Luther, Benjamin Franklin, George Washington, Socrates, Joan of Arc, Johann Gutenberg, Louis Pasteur, Christopher Columbus and Alexander the Great.

Guess where they were born? Hodgenville, Kentucky; Eisleben, Germany; Boston; Bridges Creek, Virginia; Athens, Greece; Domremy, France; Mainz, Germany; Dole, France; Geneva, Italy and Macedonia, Greece.

The real measure of a "hometown" is the quality of citizens it produces...A MEMORABLE INSIGHT.

Amen. Selah so be it.

MINE

Remember! This is my history. NOT YOURS. It began on September 27, 1927. Three months later my parents divorced and my mother left me to be raised by my Dad and grandmother.

The 30's were the Great Depression years. Dad worked on the WPA and did odd jobs. We ate navy beans every day. At age nine I started a paper route and sold Liberty, Collier and other magazines. We never owned a car and always rented. I wore patched clothes and shoes. All my toys were used; a bike and a sled.

At age 12 I worked in a foundry, glass factory and an enamel factory. We walked every place. At 5:00 AM I walked to school and cleaned a restaurant for my lunch. At the close of school I would walk to the foundry, etc. and work until 6:00 PM and then walk home. My grades were lousy and I graduated from high school at the bottom of the class, and I stuttered. The Principal gave me the diploma in his office.

Today, at age 83, I consider myself a Christian humanist, a Democrat, a political and social liberal. I'm a retired minister and psychologist. I have 4 degrees: BA, MA, Rel.D, and Ph.D. I can chronicle my academic achievements rather easily; also my vocational activities. I have also visited 84 countries and have been on 102 cruises-lecturing on most of them. It is, however, much more difficult to explain the how's and why's of my philosophical, psychological and theological evolutions. How did I get to where I am today?

Why do I behave the way I do? I believe my defense mechanisms are acquired and not innate. I am outspoken, argumentative and defensive.

My hometown was a coal mine, steel mill, farming community. It was a mixture of Italians, Polish, Jews, Blacks, Slovaks, Irish and other Europeans. On Saturday nights you could stand on a corner and never hear English for an hour. For several years we lived between an Italian family and a black family. My close friends were named, Renzi, Tedeschi, Frizzi-all Italians.

In the factories where I worked, my associates were blacks and Slovaks. We were considered poor whites. We attended churches like the Salvation Army and Nazarene. Both appealed to the poor. We were the under-belly of society.

Poverty, limited education, religious minority, family outcaste all contributed to my rebellion. I stuttered and argued at the drop of a penny. I resented authority of any kind and still do. My life took a drastic change due to my conversion experience with Jesus.

My salvation was reading and music; and eventually going to college and Bishop Fulton J Sheen, who inspired me to be a minister.

I stopped stuttering but not arguing. My college year book described me as having "strong opinions;" The subjects: Minorities, labor unions, religion, business, patriotism, politics and whatever.

After college and seminary, I went to pastor in Florida. It was the 50's and a time of turbulence. I was there between 1951 and 1958. Turmoil best describes those years. Civil rights started with Rosa Parks and Emmett Till's murder. Martin

Luther King, Jr. began his marches. The U.S. declared segregation as unconstitutional.

My church was rabid; about everything. They were born again and also sanctified. They believed in perfection. However, promiscuity and factions were rampant in the church. Most of the members were from Georgia and outright racists. They opposed integration with a passion. No blacks in the churches. They believed blacks had the mark of Cain on them. Blacks and Puerto Ricans were not permitted to attend even funerals in the church.

A parochial school was started, primarily to provide a segregated education for K-12. There were farm labor camps in South Florida for Puerto Ricans and poor white trash. Black communities were separate. Their schools were shacks. Facilities were poor and education was worse. Incidentally, money was raised for missionary projects in Africa, but nothing was done for local blacks or Puerto Ricans.

My natural proclivity toward arguing had been dormant for several years. The racial injustices and the perfection hypocrisies and bigotry stimulated my latent passivity. I resigned and we moved to California in 1958.

I continued pastoring for 37 years. Today I consider myself a vocal Christian humanist, an anti-fundamentalist, supporter of minority rights and an opponent of right wing-politics.

I believe in tolerance of all contrary views and coalitions: Christian/Humanists, Democrat/Libertarian, Compassionate/Capitalist, and Tolerant/Fanatic.

A synopsis in conclusion: My answer to my original question is apparent to me. I am opinionated, argumentative, defensive of minorities (including homosexuals), and resentful of authority because of my exposure to poverty, hypocrisy, injustice, racism, greed and intolerance. I am a liberal for the same reasons.

Amen. Selah. So be it.

MONEY

There are millions of seniors that are having money problems. Obviously many are having problems because of their own faults. They never planned for the supposed "golden years." Others, through no fault of their own, have lost all or part of their pensions. One man I know lost his because of Enron. They had insisted that every employee buy Enron stock.

Another man worked for a company for thirty years and shortly before his retirement, the company went bankrupt-taking his pension with it. I know two seniors who used their savings to help bail out their children. It didn't work out. Many seniors (couples, widows and widowers) are living on a fixed income. The fragile economy has made Social Security inadequate.

Unemployment, rising cost of staples, (food, gas, etc.) personal indebtedness (mortgage, car, credit cards,) medical services and medicine costs have created major problems.

I'm not an economist or the son of one. I'm a practical and concerned senior (83) with a few suggestions that I try to live buy. (Spelling intentional)

I. There is an old adage that seniors should avoid at all costs. Avoid HAVING A CHAMPAGNE APPETITE ON A BEER BUDGET. If you have the means, live within it.

II. Selective buying is a must. By that I mean, not buying what you cannot afford. Or, only buy what you can afford. Many solvent seniors I know buy only what they can pay for in cash. No buying on credit. Why buy a new car when the moment it leaves the lot, the car depreciates 30 percent. Selective buying is a good mantra for seniors.

III. Frugal spending is thriftiness at work. Where do you shop for groceries? Why not try the 99 Cent Stores or Cardenas Grocery for great buys. Want a very good lunch at low cost? Try the Highland Senior Center Monday through Friday. The donation is a dollar seventy-five. Reservation suggested (909) 862-8104. An elegant lady I know wears stylish clothes. She knows where all the best thrift stores are, in the Inland Empire. Need a good mechanic? I know one who charges half of what a dealer charges. Check others out. I know several couples that split a dinner when eating out.

IV. Friends sharing are an open door for buyer's delight. Dave told me about two casinos in Laughlin that have great rooms for sixteen dollars plus tax. I am constantly looking for books to read. I spent a bundle at Barnes and Noble until Mike told me about Alibris. Often I pay $.99 or $1.99 plus shipping for wanted books. I've been on 103 cruises, 75 as a lecturer. By chance a dance instructor gave me the name of his agent and the rest is history; room plus all that food — free. My neighbor, Martin, gave me the names of two restaurants that are senior friendly. Friends' sharing is what it's called.

V. A follow up to the last suggestion is: My sharing. When I do it, it always stimulates a feed back. For example when I tell someone about Taco Bell's free drinks, they often respond with McDonald's discounted senior coffee and Kohl's Wednesday 15 % discount. I tell about Ross' 10% off on Tuesday, they tell me of Supercuts $2.00 off a haircut and of

Wendy's, Burger King and Chili's 10% discount...On and on. More and more businesses are becoming Senior Friendly.

VI. One last suggestion. Credit cards focus on the young and seniors, tantalizing both with offers of a credit card. Beware. Credit cards are a trap. If you use them, pay them off each month. The interest can sink your financial boat. If you can, plant a garden and raise chickens. *Amen. Selah. So be it.*

Amen. Selah so be it.

MUSLIMS

The consensus of opinions among world historians is that 570 A.D. marked the beginning of one of the greatest events in human history. It was the year Prophet Muhammad was born. He started one of the three great monotheistic religions; Judaism and Christianity the other two. Muslims belong to Islam. And they are intimately related to Judaism and Christianity.

Muhammad was born in Mecca. His parents died shortly after his birth and he was raised by his uncle. Tradition says he never learned to read or write. At age 24 he married a wealthy widow and he became a very rich merchant. She bore him five children; two died young. Fatima was the most important. At age 40 he received a series of mystical experiences. He envisioned a single God (Allah) and a unified church. He was greatly influenced by Judaism and Christianity.

Abraham was the source of his faith, but it branched off to Hagar and her son Ishmael. He was severely persecuted and in 622 A.D. he fled to Medina. That date is marked as the first year of the Muslim era. The Prophet died in 632 A. D. Incidentally, Islam accepts Abraham, Moses and Jesus as prophets and honors them. However, Jesus is not accepted as Divine or the Son of God.

The Koran is written in Arabic and is considered authoritative only in that language. It contains 112 sutras of chapters, and is the words and visions of Muhammad.

There are three kinds of teachings: direct doctrinal messages; historical accounts and mystical expressions. Several of the stories parallel events from Judaism and Christian traditions.

The Koran emphasizes Allah's unity (no Trinity.) It encourages dependence on Allah, and ultimate unity with Allah. This life is viewed as a test. Followers will be rewarded or punished. There will be a Day of Judgment and a resurrection.

The Koran (Qur'an) outlines five Pillars of Faith.

1. Confession of one's faith in Allah and His messenger Muhammad.
2. Ritual worship by observing prayer five times every day. At dawn, noon, mid afternoon, sunset and in the evening.
3. Alms giving for the benefit of the poor.
4. Fasting. It is to be observed during the month of Ramadan.
5. Every Muslim is expected to make one pilgrimage Every Muslim is expected to make one pilgrimage (Hajj) to Mecca on his in her lifetime.

In addition they are to forswear gambling, usury, and the consumption of alcohol and pork. Observers say that once away from their basic environment, many Muslims engage in all four.

There are several divisions in Islam but the basic one is between Shiite and Sunni. Most of us would agree with Winston Churchill who said, "I always get mixed up between these two." Ninety percent of all Muslims are Sunni; the largest natural population of Sunnis in Indonesia. The major country that is Shiite is Iran. While Sunni means Orthodox, it has become more tolerant and democratic through the centuries.

The Shiite is very strong in belief of individual leaders, like Khomeini. They accept successors who go back to Ali who married Fatimah, the daughter of Muhammad. Their leaders are called Imams. The "ministers" are referred to as "mullahs."

Islam has been described as the fastest growing religion in the world. There are an estimated 1,902,095,000 Muslims in the world today with Indonesia having the most 228,582,000; with Pakistan second with 172,800,000.

The United States has 2,454,000; Canada, 657,000; Mexico, 110,000. Christians number 2,500,000,000 in the world. Obviously the Muslims are catching up.

The month Ramadan is very important in the Muslim faith. The ninth month of their year, it is reserved for prayer and fasting. From sunrise to sunset no one eats or drinks, except pregnant women and nurses. At sunset, anything goes. The crowds in the streets are amazing. No travel, business or even surgery during the day.

Of interest to me is the influence of the Moors (another name for Muslims) upon Spain. They dominated Spain for 800 years. Toledo and Alhambra are evidence of that influence. All Spanish words ending in "a" are Arabic-drama, alfombra, mathamatica.

The spread of the Islamic empire is significant. But of equal importance is the rise of many centers of culture and science. They produced notable scientists, astronomers, mathematicians (initiated the zero concept), doctors, nurses, philosophers. Technology flourished: irrigation systems, canals and a high level of literacy.

A final word: We should avoid judging Islam on the basis of what happened on 9-11 or identifying them as terrorists. History records that professing Christians have slaughtered millions more Muslims than they have killed Christians. Both extremists bring discredit to their founders.

Amen. Selah. So be it.

MYSTERIES

I have a real appreciation for murder mysteries. They fascinate me. The chase, the drama, the courtroom give and take; all add up to excitement. In the conviction of any prep there are three essential elements that must be dealt with; MOTIVE, METHOD and OPPORTUNITY. Those are the three "cornerstones of prosecuting a successful murder case."

It seems to me these three elements are important in any quest for spiritual reality. The Bible seems to highlight these three in the lives of several biblical characters: Nicodemus, the Prodigal Son and Paul. Let's examine them. They were certainly MOTIVATED. Nicodemus was suffering from spiritual poverty-hunger. It was obviously a pressing need. He came to Jesus by night.

The Buddha tells a meaningful story. A lady came to him seeking enlightenment and nirvana. She asked him how she might attain it. He took her to a river and held her under water until she was almost drowned. Upon raising her out of the water he asked her how desperate she was to survive. Acknowledging her desperation he informed her until she was that desperate for salvation, she would not find it.

Motivation is the beginning step to God. The story of the Prodigal Son gives a clear picture of a METHODOLOGY. There is not one way for a conversion experience. For some it is instantaneous; for others it is a gradual process; a Billy Graham revival versus growing up in the church.

The path of the Prodigal began with a decision. He

would get up from where he was floundering and go back home. The power of choice is a unique part of each human. It separates us from all other elements in creation. Regardless of the circumstances of one's birth or subsequent environment, no one is beyond the capability of choosing the direction we seek to go or be. The method always begins with a choice.

The third element in a conviction or a conversion is OPPORTUNITY. We do not know if Jesus made the first move to Nicodemus. He probably did. We do know that in the parable of the Prodigal Son, the Father-obviously a reference to God-made opportunity for him by running to meet him. In the example of Paul or Saul at the time, opportunity for his conversion came by a revelation on his way to Damascus.

It should be noted that all three of these elements: motive, method and opportunity were present in the lives of all three men. They become viable in the process for spiritual conversion in the same way they are viable in the solving of murder.

Probably the best description of conversion is by William James, the father of American psychology, in his book, Varieties of Religious Experience. "To be converted, to be regenerated, to receive grace, to experience religion, to gain an assurance, are so many phrases which denote the process, gradual or sudden, by which a self hitherto divided, and consciously wrong inferior and unhappy becomes unified and consciously right, superior and happy."

Amen. Selah so be it.

MYTHS

For many years I've had an insatiable curiosity about the Middle-East: The culture, the history and the religion; in particular the latter. My academic credentials are meager but thorough; a BA and MA in mid-eastern history. I have also visited extensively: Israel, Egypt, Turkey, Lebanon, Syria, Jordan and several close-by countries. Unfortunately, I have not been able to visit Iraq and Iran. I have also studied in depth the Sumerians, Babylonians, Assyrians and the Muslim, Zoroastrian, Mithraism, Hebrew and Egyptian religions.

As a Christian minister for 57 of my 82 years, I have been particularly interested in the connection between the Egyptian religion and my own Judeo-Christian faith. A survey of the Bible indicates several references to Egypt. In Genesis 45:8, Joseph is speaking and says, "God has made me father of Pharaoh" Many scholars believe that Moses (which is an Egyptian name) and Akentonen were the same. In Acts 7:22 it states, "So Moses was instructed in all the wisdom of the Egyptians."

Bible readers are well aware of the many connections between the Jews and the Egyptians: Joseph, their slavery, Moses and the escape into Egypt by Mary, Joseph and Jesus. I suggest a different perspective. In Galatians 4:24, the Apostle Paul says the Abraham story should be interpreted as an allegory-or a myth or parable.

Rabbi Abraham Heschel and Rabbi Harold Kushner also make the same observation. Stories like the creation, the flood, Jonah and Job can easily fit the description of allegorical. What evidence is there to believe that the entire Old and New Testaments are to be viewed as allegorical?

Do the names Massey, Kuhn, Harpur, Pagel, Budge, Robertson, Schweitzer, Spong, Kingsford, Freke, Fry and Crossan sound familiar? They are all world renowned Bible scholars. All of them also support the views in this article.

Kingsford doesn't mince words. "The Hebrew sacred books were all Egyptian in origin." Another erudite scholar states, "The Bible is total plagiarism of the Sumerian and Egyptian mythologies." Parallels in the Old and New Testaments with accounts in Egyptian writings are striking. The difference is basically between mythologies and history. What the Egyptians viewed as mythological, the Hebrews and Christians made into history.

It is important to understand the basic meaning of myth. It is fictional, but reflects a significant truth, a timeless truth. The Greek myths of Oedipus and Narcissus are good examples. Tom Harpur clarifies this issue in a succinct way. "Ancient people did not believe their myths. They believed IN them, in the sense that they believed in the truth beneath the stories." The conclusion is that Biblical accounts are not to be taken as literal. They are only vehicles for sublime, divine truths. The most basic and important truth that was out-sourced from Egypt is the concept of the INCARNATION-God with us and in us.

The Gospels of Matthew and Luke emphasize this truth. Emmanuel in Matthew and in Luke 17:21, "The kingdom (spirit) of God is within you." The Apostle Paul also stressed the Spirit within. Have you ever wondered why Paul ignored the historical Jesus? In the Gospel of John, Jesus is referred to as "logos" or truth; a spiritual reference. Both Paul and the author of John were plagiarizing Egyptian religious ideas.

St Augustine, along with St. Thomas Aquinas was the architects of most of Roman Catholic theology. In his book Retractions, Augustine says, "The very thing which is now called the Christian religion also exist among the ancients, nor was it wanting from the inception of the human race until the coming of Christ in the flesh, at which point the true religion which was already in existence began to be called Christian."

For those of us who are believers it is important that "the fact that most of the material in the Jesus story was previously present in other sacred literature of the ancient world in no way detracts from its power and relevance for our lives today."

Gerald Massey, noted authority of Egyptian religion, discovered nearly 200 parallels between Egyptian material and Christian writings about Jesus.

The Horus myth was the equivalent of Jesus-the Christ. Almost all the miracles in the Gospels, the events in Jesus' life-including death on the cross and subsequent resurrection- and the sayings of Jesus are found in Egyptian writings.

As noted above, the major parallel is the incarnation; the presence of Christ within mankind. Note Paul's view in I Corinthians 3:16, *"the spirit of God dwelleth within you;"* Very Egyptian. He also speaks of "putting on Christ" and each of us having the 'mind of Christ." Up to 8000 years before the accepted birth of Jesus, Horus was referred to as "the light of the world that is in every person," as was Jesus. (John 1:9)

Again Paul speaks of "putting on Christ," and of each of us having the "the mind of Christ." Tom Harpur puts it, "The Egyptians believed that each of us is intended ultimately to be a Christ, anointed for an eternal destiny with God." What could be more Christian than that?

Amen. Selah so be it.

NAVIGATING

I recently heard an apt description of living life as a senior person, navigating through the years; an appropriate analogy.

When Jesus was crucified at age 33, He was considered an old man. At the beginning of the 20th century, mortality was approximately 45. When Social Security was established in 1937, the age it was to begin was 65. Our government didn't expect people to live much longer than that. How foolish. Today there are 150,000 citizens living in the U.S. over 100 years of age. The mortality age for men is close to 88 and for women it's 90. No wonder Social Security is going bankrupt.

We are an anomaly. To change the analogy, we are blazing new trails. As a simple illustration will suffice- Alzheimer. It is a relatively recent invasion into senior culture.

As the Captain of our boat, what should we expect as we NAVIGATE down or up this waterway called the senior life?

Whatever comes our way we should adopt the philosophy of Epictetus who lived 100 years before Jesus. He said, "While we have no control over the things that happen to us, we have ABSOLUTE control over how we react to those things."

Getting back to my analogy; whether it be the great Mississippi, the Ohio, the Amazon, the Nile, the Yukon or the Missouri rivers, they all constantly change. The Captains or Pilots MUST expect and adapt to the changes.

It is reported that Adam said to Eve as they left the Garden of Eden, "We're living in a time of transition." So are seniors. Rocks, sandbars, debris of all kinds affect the journey. They are represented of our health, our income, our family, our relationships, our social activities, our marriages, our religious beliefs, our relatives, our political beliefs; society values our appetites, our sex drive, our goals. They all are in a constant state of flux. Navigation through these variables demands flexibility and acceptance of shifting changes for seniors. There is no room for rigidity of thought, bigotry, and racism or prejudice because the changing times and rushing waters demands navigational flexibility.

As with the Captain of a riverboat, seniors must be alert to impediments. No dullness of mind or a couch potato attitude. James Baldwin, the famous black novelist said it best, "The challenge of living is to be present in everything we do; "from getting up in the morning to going to bed at night."

The navigational log for seniors includes the following lines for optimal living.

1. <u>WE NEED SOMEONE TO LOVE</u>. This is what keeps seniors resilient in an uncertain future. Rod McKuen, the noted poet, has written, "There is no harm in not being loved, only in not loving." Growing older demands it; whether a person, a cause, an animal or God or grandchildren. An emotional attachment stimulates longevity.

2. <u>WE NEED SOMETHING TO DO</u>. Succumbing to laziness, do-nothing, lethargy are the eternal enemies of aging. Vigilance must be the watchword for seniors to our dying moment-and even then. Michelangelo said it was only well with him when he had a chisel in his hand.

To maintain a healthy attitude, agile mind and physical well being: read a book, go for a walk, plant a garden, do a crossword, knit, bake a cake, have lunch with a friend, volunteer, be active, PERIOD. William James, the greatest of American psychologists said, "Act the way you want to feel and pretty soon you'll be feeling the way you're acting.

3. WE NEED SOMETHING TO LOOK FORARD TO. How long do you want to live? Read Genesis 6:3. It says man's allotted years are 120. The Psalmist said 3 score and 10 after a bad night with Bathsheba-I'll take Genesis.

Plan something for tomorrow, next week, next month, and next year; and beyond. If you don't make it; so what! It's better to plan ahead than not to have planned at all.

4. WE NEED SOMETHING TO BELIEVE IN. Everyone, especially seniors, need a belief system: Religion, country, family or oneself.

Remember Rose Kennedy? She lived to be 105. I heard her interviewed a few years ago. He reminded her of her life's troubles. A mentally ill daughter, one son died in a plane crash and two sons were shot, an unfaithful husband. "How have you survived," he asked. She stood and with fire in her eyes, said, "I refuse to be vanquished." By the way, she attended Mass every day.

A belief provides a focus for living and a direction. It adds years to our living.

Amen. Selah so be it.

NEGATIVISM

I am often amazed at the spirit or attitude of negativism that often prevails; in society, in government, in politics and even in families.

"These are the worst times ever," so say many. Crime is on the increase. Poverty and sickness afflict the world; as well as economic dilemmas. Moaning and groaning is reflected in the media-newspapers, TV, and radio. It makes little difference the sources; whether they be conservative or liberal, rich or poor, uneducated or educated, racially diverse.

From whence does negativism come? Is it hereditary? Is it an ethnic thing? Does environment play into it? I'd like to say "no" to all of these, but I'm really not sure. St Augustine and his sympathetic religionists blamed it and more on "original sin." People are born bad, evil a negative. Not just a few but all of us. A newborn baby has it too.

Everyone is born with the tendency to do wrong or to behave well. Much of conservative religion endorses this view. Incidentally, this theological concept reflects the thinking of St. Paul and the Greek philosopher, Plato.

Another prevalent source is to blame our environment. The child is conditioned by the parents and family. Horace Bushnell created the battle between "nature and nurture." He was on the side of nurture as the most important.

The question often arises, why does a person raised in a negative environment sometimes become very positive and also the reverse. Humanistic psychologists talk and write a great deal about choice and free will; either an emotional or intellectual experience occurs that stimulates change.

Charles Manson chose to become a murderer. His personal traumas contributed to his decisions. Billy Graham credits his evangelical fervor to being a born-again Christian. They made choices.

"There is nothing as powerful as an idea whose time has come," said Victor Hugo. That's descriptive of the human intellect that is influenced by a book, a poem, a movie or a conversation. Even a sermon or lecture can trigger a response.

I believe the decisions we make are dependent on the benefits received. Consequences are always the motivations. For example; negative attitudes bring a feeling of superiority. They can also engender excuses-of all kinds.

If you don't know the name George Carlin, you will not appreciate his article as much as I do. Enjoy anyway. It's a fitting answer for negativism. His article follows.

The paradox of our time in history is that we have taller buildings but shorter tempers, wider Freeways, but narrower viewpoints. We spend more, but have less, we buy more, but enjoy less. We have bigger houses and smaller families, more conveniences, but less time. We have more degrees but less sense, more knowledge, but less judgment, more experts, yet more problems, more medicine, but less wellness.

We drink too much, smoke too much, spend too recklessly, laugh too little, drive too fast, get too angry, stay up too late, get up too tired, read too little, watch TV too much, and pray too seldom.

We have multiplied our possessions, but reduced our values. We talk too much, love too seldom, and hate too often.

We've learned how to make a living, but not a life. We've added years to life not life to years. . We've been all the way to the moon and back, but have trouble crossing the street to meet a new neighbor. We conquered outer space but not inner space. We've done large things, but not better things.

These are the times of fast foods and slow digestion; big men and small character, steep profits and shallow relationships. These are the days of two incomes but more divorce, fancier houses, but broken homes. These are the days of quick trips, disposable diapers, throwaway morality, one night stands, overweight; bodies, and pills that do everything from cheer, to quiet, to kill. It is a time when there is much in the showroom window and nothing in the stockroom. A time when technology can bring this letter to you, and a time when you can choose either to share this insight, or to just hit delete.

. . Remember; spend some time with your loved ones, because they are not going to be around forever. Remember, say a kind word to someone who looks up to you in awe, because that little person soon will grow up and leave your side. Remember, to give a warm hug to the one next to you, because that is the only treasure you can give with your heart and it doesn't cost a cent. Remember, to say, "I love you" to your partner and your loved ones, but most of all mean it. A kiss and an embrace will mend hurt when it comes from deep inside of you. Remember to hold hands and cherish the moment for someday that person will not be there again. Give time to love, give time to speak! And give time to share the precious thoughts in your mind. AND ALWAYS REMEMBER: Life is not measured by the number of breaths we take, but by the moments that take our breath away. *Amen. Selah so be it.*

NICKNAMES

My name is George William Abersold. My father's name was George Henry Abersold. His brother, my uncle was William Gale Abersold. I presume my name was taken from their first names. I've never been called George. I guess my parents didn't want my Dad and me to be confused. In my earliest years I was referred to as Billy; that I always hated.

There are certainly several famous men named Billy: Billy Graham, Billy Sunday, Billy Martin, Billy the Kid, Billy Eckstein, Billy Crystal and Billy Wilder to name a few. In spite of this pantheon of greatness, I still dislike being called Billy. I also dislike being called by my last name. Most controlled groups like the military, prison inmates, school classes and sport teams call members of their opponents by last names. Why? Psychologists see it as a form of depersonalizing. I don't answer to "Hey, Abersold."

My ancestors came from Switzerland; around Berne; specifically, Zingenfelgen. In fact, there is a mountain close by named Aebersold. The Swiss, and there are many Abersolds there, spell it with an additional "e." The earliest clan goes back to the thirteenth century. They were mostly farmers. In the mid-1800's, several brothers immigrated to the U.S. Many settled in Pennsylvania. My Dad's family settled in Monroe County (called little Switzerland) Ohio.

There are several families of Abersolds, Aebersolds and Ebersoles in America. I've met doctors (M.D), teachers, Judges, accountants, a mayor, criminals, prostitutes, farmers, plasterers, detectives, minister (me), professors, missionaries, foundry and steel workers, etc.

Through the years I've been called by several names and titles. As a minister I've been called Brother Abersold, Pastor Abersold, and Reverend Abersold. Since getting a doctorate, Dr. Abersold or Dr. A has been added. The young people started the Dr. a moniker.

As a kid, my friends and I all had nicknames. Two of my best friends were Baa and Tunner. I was called Ram. Why? Because I came from a place called Ramcat Alley. It was one of the "hollers" or "cricks" or "runs" in the area.   My current nickname is "Doc." Stella (my wife) started calling me that about fifteen years ago. Through the years most everyone calls me Doc. I sort of like it. However, the name I like above all other is DAD.

Surnames and their origin have always interested me. European surnames first appeared between the 11th and 15th centuries. Population growth made surnames a necessity. Class, economics and mobility demanded a better way of recognition. Thus surnames.

During Biblical times people were often referred to by their given names plus residence as "Jesus of Nazareth."

Patronymics are forming surnames from the father's given name. Example: Johnson, Peterson, Samson, Williamson, Davidson, Robertson, Jefferson, Jackson and Stevenson.

Then there are surnames that are derived from vocations. Such as: Carpenter, Miller, Smith, Washer, and Washington. Abersold originated in Berne, which means "bear." A ber (bear) sold (seller), Taylor, Cook, Mason.

A person's character was often identified with an animal: gentle/Lamb, sly/Fox, predator/Hawk, talker/Parrot, dangerous/Wolf. Status was also used: Bachelor, Knight, Squire, King, Prince, Farmer, Ryder, and Carver.

Genealogists identify many surnames as being changed from their origin in native countries to phonetic sounds in English. Bauch became Baugh, Micsza became McShea, Siminowicz became Simmons and Schwerz became Black.

Perhaps the most prevalent origin of surnames comes from the use of famous personages: Paul, Lincoln, Franklin, Samuel, Noah, Adam, Abel, Wesley, and Stewart. Time has been the test of their choice.

I've often wondered what surname I would have chosen. Fortunately I like Abersold. However, when I face my last living moment I would like to hear God say, "Well done thou good and faithful SERVANT, enter thou into the joys of thy Lord." (Matthew 25:21)

Amen. Selah. So be it.

NO

As a minister and therapist I have often been confronted by members and clients who posed questions about God, doctrines, faith and life. I, too, have had questions about the same subjects. Sometimes, well meaning clergy, but ignorant, have chastised believers for having doubts or questions.

Obviously such chastisers have not studied the Bible. It is filled with the records of those who questioned God. Atheists and agnostics are not among them. We would expect those two groups to throw out questions; but believers? Yes, believers, even Jesus.

Since the Bible is the best seller every year, and the least read, let me remind everyone what a few so-called heroes said. Consider Abraham the father of all Jews and all Arabs, and the beginning of Judaism, Islam and Christianity. He really argued and confronted, in Genesis 18, God over the future of Sodom and Gomorrah. Abraham questions God. "Shall not the Ruler (Judge) of all the earth do right?" He goes round and round with God and God seemingly doesn't get angry with him. WOW!

Moses even questions the intelligence of God. He feels inadequate and feels God has chosen the wrong person to lead the Jews out of slavery.

David is a real case. In Psalm 13 he asks, "How long, Lord? Will you forget me forever? How long will you hide your face from me?"

Consider Job. His miseries have been well recorded. It is filled with questions about "why?" "Why do the righteous suffer?" is the basic theme of the book.

Mary, the mother of Jesus, responds to the information that she has been chosen answers with astonishment, "How can these things be, seeing I've never been with a man?" Of course it was addressed to an angel, but he was God's representative.

Jesus, on the cross, uttered the question of all question, "My God, my God, why have your forsaken me?"

You and I, we are not the first ones to question God. Why do the righteous suffer? Why are there earthquakes and tsunamis? Why are there Alzheimer's, cancer, pre-mature deaths, and even arthritis? …Questions, questions and even more questions.

I must confess, though, I've received very few answers. I can identify with the Apostle Paul when he questioned God about his thorn in the flesh. God told him, "My grace is sufficient for you." Perhaps the following anonymous bit of verse will bring some insight.

AND GOD SAID "NO"

I asked God to take away my pride, and God said, "No."
He said it was not for Him to take away, but for me to give up.

I asked God to make a handicapped child whole,
and God said, "No."
He said her spirit is whole, her body is only temporary.

I asked God to give me patience, and God said, "No."
He said patience is a by-product of tribulation:
it's not granted it's earned.

I asked God to give me happiness, and God said, "No."
He said He gives blessings, happiness is up to me.

I asked God to spare me pain, and God said, "No."
He said, "Suffering draws you apart from worldly cares
and brings you closer to Me."

I asked God to make my spirit grow, and God said "No."
He said I must grow on my own,
but He will prune me to make me fruitful.
I asked God to help me love others,
as much as He loves me,
And God said,
"Ah, finally, you have an idea."

Amen. Selah. So be it.

OROZCO

Carlos Slim Helu; have you heard of him? He's considered the richest man in the world; more money than Bill Gates and Warren Buffet. He's a Lebanese/Mexican. He and his wife and their children were all born and raised in Mexico. He owns all the communication systems in Mexico, plus hotels and a myriad of other businesses. He's not alone. Mexico has more millionaires in proportion to their population, than any other country; including the U.S.A.

Mexico has and has had an illustrious and violent history: Revolutions, genocide, social upheavals and political unrest. The recent drug crimes and murders are devastating the entire Mexican economy. Tourism is particularly in jeopardy. There are a number of Mexican features that are worthy of notice. The tourist centers like Acapulco, Cancun, Cabo and Puerto Vallarta are known worldwide. They still attract millions of visitors each year.

The ruins in Mexico are still a major attraction for natives and tourists alike. The pyramids outside of Mexico City; the ruins in the Yucatan, Palenque, Monte Alban and countless others offer exciting viewing. However, one of the least known and most important venues was the advent of the Mexican muralists. Their emergence followed the Mexican Revolution. Their emphases were often political and social. They depicted violence and conflict.

Four men in particular received international acclaim: Jose Clemente Orozco, Diego Rivera, David Alfaro Siqueiros and Rufino Tomayo. They were all left-wing liberals and anti-establishment. In fact, Siqueiros was an out and out communist. To see their murals, many of Tomayo's are in a museum in Oaxaca; Rivera's in Cuernavaca, Siqueiros' in the government buildings in Mexico City, and Orozco's in Guadalajara. My personal favorite is Jose Orozco. He was a liberal Christian. One of his most dramatic murals is in Baker Library at Dartmouth College. It's called, "The Revolutionary Christ." I have a copy of it; a gift from the college.

Some years ago I read an impression of it by Bishop Garfield Oxnam of the Methodist Church. He described it this way. "My first reaction was one of revulsion! The painter's brush had become party to blasphemy. Orozco had gone too far. Had he not made caricature of the Christ and brought contempt upon the Cross? Strangely enough, the painting possessed sufficient magnetic attraction to hold me fast; suddenly its meaning gripped me, and my mood became one of repentance.

It was Orozco's last panel, done in rich colors — the deep browns of the soil, the deeper reds of blood. A towering figure of Christ dominates all. He stands with feet apart, flesh torn, triumphant. At his side is an ax, the handle grasped tightly by his right hand. In the background are temples and tabernacles overturned in ruins amid the spoils of war, as though some terrible earthquake had made scorn of the religions of man.

Rising above shattered stone and splintered timber is the Christ. Then one sees that the ax has been laid to the root of the tree. The cross itself has been cut down. It lies beside the stump from which it has been severed, and the Christ stands astride it.   And then I knew that a dead figure hanging from a cross is not the sign of my faith. Our Lord is not a poor broken figure hanging from the tree — hands imprisoned by cruel nails and feet held fast by spikes, eyes that do not see and ears that do not hear, a tongue that is stilled, a body with spirit gone — whose message is Miserere.   No, He is Christ triumphant, living now and forever more, freed from the flesh, victory over men who vainly believe they can destroy the spirit by crucifying the body.

He lives; His eyes do see, beholding in every man a brother and envisioning what man may become as a Son of God; His ears do hear the cries of the oppressed, the low moan of the sorrowful, the glad shouts of children at play, and, like the sound of the sea, the swelling notes of joy chanted by the millions of men in that morrow when justice shall roll down as a mighty stream and righteousness shall cover the earth. His hands and feet are free, the hands of healing, the feet of the second mile; he speaks, and men learn of the way and the truth and hear that judgment will be rendered upon the simple rule, 'Inasmuch as ye have done it unto one of the least of these my brethren, ye have done it unto me — Enter thou into the joy of thy Lord.'

Christ, alive and free from an imprisoning cross before which many bow to worship but from which too few hear the summons, 'Follow me' — how can he march, if he be nailed to a cross? — a living Christ, who, having been lifted up, does draw all men because of his gift of self but who leads all men because of his mastery of death — this is the revolutionary Christ, whose message will be Jubilate."

OROZCO SPEAKS AS CLEARLY AND AS LOUDLY

TODAY AS HE DID A HUNDRED YEARS AGO. NO MESSAGE IS MORE RELEVANT AND DEMANDING FOR CHRISTIANS TODAY.

Amen. Selah. So be it.

PARABLES

Anyone who has ever attended Sunday school or studied the Bible has heard of the "parables" of Jesus. A parable is a figure of speech, a short allegorical story; an extended metaphor. In Jesus' day it was in common usage to illustrate or teach a truth. They usually teach a single truth.

The Kingdom parables of Jesus all begin with "the kingdom of heaven is like." That's a metaphor. In the four Gospels, Luke contains 24 parables and 10 unique to it. Matthew has 23 parables and 6 unique ones. Mark has 8 and only 1 unique. John contains no parables but several metaphors.

The two most popular parables are only found in the Gospel of Luke: the Good Samaritan (chapter-10:33) and the Prodigal Son (chapter 15).

Some years ago I was traveling by bus around the country of Austria. I became good friends with a couple from England. He was a retired colonel who had served in India. We often traded books to read and one day I saw him reading a heavy volume entitled, The World's Best Short Stories.

Upon examining it I saw the very first story was what Christians call the Parable of the Prodigal Son.

Bible scholars believe the parables reveal what Jesus was thinking about, what was on His mind. They encompass the sum of His beliefs…His theology.

While most parables have only one main emphasis, the

prodigal's story has several Christian views. It seems those views should have prominence over the Apostles Creed, the Korean Creed, the Westminster Confession and any other creed. The parable begins when the youngest son takes his inheritance and goes far from home. He chooses to waste all he has on "riotous living" and loses everything. The far country is wherever we go without God: wasting one's talents as well as substances. He ends up feeding slop to pigs; a horrible thing for Jews to do.

While there "he comes to himself" and decides to go home and seek forgiveness. These two experiences, leaving and making a mess of his life and the arising and returning home, are the most important things in what makes us what we are-the power of choice.

Anthropologists say that 98% of human DNA is found in other mammals. It's that 2% that makes us different and human. I like what Victor Frankl called it, "The indomitable power of the human spirit."

The second important belief revealed in the parable is about the father. In reality the father is a portrayal of God. It reveals the most amazing truth in Christian belief. God (father) is on the lookout for the wayward son.

THE PARABLE STATES THAT HE SAW THE SON WHEN HE WAS FAR OFF. AND THEN HE DOES SOMETHING VERY AMAZING. HE RUNS TO MEET HIM AND EMBRACE HIM. This is the only instance in the Bible of God running to meet us.

In our living room we have a 3 foot by 4 foot copy of Rembrandt's famous painting of the prodigal's return and being embraced by the Father. The original is in the

Hermitage Museum in St. Petersburg, Russia. Rembrandt has captured the real meaning of the parable. God greeted and welcomed the wayward (you and me) with unconditional acceptance and love. There is no reservation.

Rembrandt has the son kneeling and the Father has His hands on his shoulders. It is a moving scene. I like what Augustine said. "God has made us for Himself, and we can find no rest until we find our rest in Him."

Many years ago Bishop C. A. Morrison of the Methodist Church told a beautiful story. While riding on a train he noticed that a young man across from him was very distraught. His story was moving. Five years earlier he had left home in anger at his parents. He went to Chicago, got into trouble and was sent to prison. Now he was out and had wired his parents begging for forgiveness. A few miles ahead were their farm. If they forgave him they were to hang a yellow ribbon on the oak tree at the corner of their property. He was scared. Would they accept him back? ...When the train pulled close to the farm, THE TREE WAS COVERED WITH YELLOW RIBBONS. Any parent can understand that story. By the way, it was made into a popular country song.

A third truth in the parable is often neglected. There is a celebration. The Father calls for a fatted calf; puts a robe and a ring on His son; and there is music and dancing. Talk about a celebration.

This is a forgotten theme in most churches. Somber music, sad demeanors, pessimistic sermons are the usual venues.

The Early Church was different. The worshipers met for a service, had a pot-luck dinner, spent the afternoon dancing and spent the rest of the afternoon telling jokes. So states the Internet. No wonder it is called "The World's Best Short Story."

Amen. Selah. So be it.

PARKING

Some years ago C. William Fisher wrote a book entitled, Don't Park Here! The chapters related to men and women who had debilitating illnesses and how they "moved beyond their handicaps and tragedies to a fuller life." His opening sentence is a statement by the famous comedian, Jimmy Durante. "All of us have schnozzles." He meant such as blindness, deafness, dyslexia, amputation, depression, disfigurement, etc.

Harold Russell lost both hands during World War II. In the movie made about him, there is a statement he made that epitomizes his philosophy. "It is not what you have lost that counts, but what you have left."

CONSIDER THESE EXAMPLES OF PEOPLE WHO REFUSED TO BE VICTIMIZED BY THEIR ADVERSITIES. Franklin Delano Roosevelt had polio and was on crutches most of his life. Yet, he led our nation through the Great Depression and World War II.

Many intellectuals today refer to Stephen Hawking as the most brilliant man on earth. He cannot walk or talk and lives attached to a breathing machine. He is renowned as a physicist. His views have changed our views of the universe. At age 51, he has had Lou Gehrig's disease for 30 years.

Epilepsy is a dreaded illness. Vincent van Gogh, Sir Isaac Newton, Napoleon Bonaparte, Agatha Christie, Charles Dickens, Alexander the Great, Michelangelo, Leonardo Da Vinci, Julius Caesar, Aristotle, Theodore Roosevelt are just a few of the thousands who have suffered from it. Think how our world would be deprived without their contributions.

Consider Helen Keller. No one has ever been more physically abused-borne blind, deaf and dumb-and accomplished more than she did. Her achievements stagger the imagination. Considering all the physical ailments that can afflict us humans, they seem minimal in the light of the staggering amount of emotional and mental ailments that confront people today.

Depression is number one. Consider mood disorders. Bi-polar and schizophrenia take a horrible toll on millions every day. Abraham Lincoln, Buzz Aldrin, Harrison Ford, Mike Wallace, Dick Cavett, Jim Carrey and Brooks Shields to name a few.

Since Christianity is my major focus and Christian music is my avocation, I'll emphasize three composers: George Frederick Handel, Martin Rinkart and Annie Flint. Handel's great oratorio "Messiah" is world famous. However, he suffered from epilepsy, chronic illnesses and extreme poverty. It speaks for itself. Martin Rinkart was a minister in Germany. In 1637 the plague killed 8000 people in his village. It was followed by a severe famine. His wife and children died in a horrible fire.

Shortly before his death in 1649, he penned these words. It is a favorite Thanksgiving hymn. What a testimony to his faith.

Now thank we all our God
O may this bounteous God
With heart and hands and voices

Through all our life be near us,
Who wondrous things hath done,
With ever joyful hearts
In whom his world rejoices;
And blessed peace to cheer us;
Who from out mothers' arms,
And keep us in His grace,
Hath blessed us on our way
And guide us when perplexed,
With countless gifts of love,
And free us from all ills
And still is ours today.
In this world and the next.

Annie Johnson Flint wrote two of my favorite Gospel songs. Her parents died when she was a child. She became a devout Christian at an early age. At the age of 23 she became afflicted with severe arthritis.

She became a cripple and bed-ridden. She earned money by writing poems and publishing them. My two favorites are "God Hath Not Promised" and "He Giveth More Grace." One verse and chorus from each:

God hath not promised skies always blue,
He giveth more grace when the burdens grow greater.
Flowers strewn pathways all our lives
He sendeth more strength when the labors thro' increase.
God hath not promised sun without rain,
To added affliction He addeth His mercy;
Joy without sorrow, peace without pain.

To multiplied trials.
His multiplied peace.
But God hath promised strength for the day,
His love has no limit,
Rest for the labor, light for the way,
His grace has no measure,
Grace for the trials help from above,
His pow'r has no boundary known unto men;
Unfailing kindness, undying love.
For out of His infinite riches in Jesus,
He giveth, and giveth, and giveth again!

Amen. Selah. So be it.

PERSECUTION

I heard a Christian minister declare the other day that persecution is no longer a part of the Christian life. He further stated that he no longer expected to be persecuted for his faith. That affirmation bothers me. So, this article will contradict the minister's view.

Martyrdom and early Christian prosecution go hand in hand. The first Christian martyr, as recorded in the Book of Acts, was Stephen. He was stoned to death. Of the disciples of Jesus, all were martyred except John the Beloved, and possibly Thomas.

Tradition says that Peter was crucified upside down. The apostle Paul was beheaded. In his book, The Blood of the Martyrs, Fox documents hundreds of Christians that died for their faith. Through the centuries the number has grown exponentially. The issue should be viewed currently rather than from a historical perspective.

One major source for persecution is political. Without successful contradiction we can assume that our country is basically Christian. That means that any political discussion will affect most Americans.

Poverty and its elimination is a political matter; unemployment or an inadequate minimum wage. Politics is involved in both of them. Free enterprise is certainly commendable, but when poverty prevails in so much of our citizenry, it is persecution.

Outsourcing of jobs is also a form of persecution. The

loss of jobs to third world countries deprives Christians of meaningful employment. It is persecution perpetuated by political forces.

Christians today are also being tormented by mental persecutions. We're naïve if we think racial prejudice is a thing of the past. While the racial killings and the obvious types of discrimination are no more, the subtle expressions are still in evidence. Not just blacks and Hispanics, but also women and homosexuals.

Abuse and bullying teenage homosexuals is on the increase. The result is often suicide: hangings, guns and even jumping off bridges. This is certainly evidence of mental persecution. Unfortunately it is on the increase. Persecution also has an emotional component to it. Countries like Cuba, Jamaica and several countries in West Africa practice witch-craft otherwise known as babilao.

I've attended a séance when the so-called "doctor" was practicing his craft. An example would be hanging a dead chicken in front of a house. No one was permitted to speak to the designated victim. The emotional strain often caused his/her death.

Perpetuating fear is a strong emotional persecution technique. Seniors in particular are victims of emotional persecution. They face the future with a fixed income and the possible reduction of Social Security. Fear is their constant companion.

As with the early disciples who were persecuted with the threats of death, the current persecutions, as mentioned, can only be dealt with by trusting God.

The recent trauma and drama of the Chilean miners

provide a good example. One of them is reported as saying, "There were not 33 miners in the tomb for 69 days, but 34." How could that be? His response was simple. "God was the 34th one. Each man carried a Bible and all of us prayed. That's what helped us through." So it is with persecution.

Amen. Selah. So be it.

PHOTOGRAPH

There's an old, old humorous story about a nine year old boy. He's drawing a picture and his mother asks what he is doing. Jackie informs her that he is drawing a picture of God. Mother informs him that no one knows what God looks like. He informs her, "They will know when I get finished." The story is old but apropos.

E. Stanley Jones was a great Methodist missionary to India. In one of his books he says, "Jesus was the greatest photograph God ever had taken." The implication is clear. If you want to know what God looks like, look at Jesus. Likewise, if you are curious about God's view points, examine the words of Jesus. In John 10:30 it says, "I and my Father are one." John 1:1 is very specific, "In the beginning was the Logos (Word) and the Word (Jesus) was with God and the Word was God."

The Gospel writers are clear in their portrayal of Jesus as a reflection of God. The Apostle Paul picks up on the same theme. "At the name of Jesus every knee shall bow." Then, "Every tongue shall confess that Jesus Christ is Lord." However, for the purpose of this article I will limit my conclusions to the four Gospels. My method is called "profiling." It is more commonly used by the FBI in identifying criminals; in particular serial killers.

The method is also used by other disciplines in their search for clarity of personality types. Since history does not give a picture of the historical Jesus. I will use the aforementioned method. Since Jesus was a Semitic Jew of the first century, He was short of stature (about 5'4"), dark complexion, with a hooked nose, dark hair and eyes. He was muscular with a wiry physique, since He was a carpenter and builder. Jesus was also a farmer. He knew about crops and weeds. He was acquainted with animals: camels, cows, donkeys and pigs. His family was into the fishing business and it is safe to say He was also. A weakling could NOT have walked around as Jesus did. I've been to Israel. It is hilly and rocky. I've walked where He walked. It was rough going; even more so in that day.

Jesus' emotional reactions also define His profile. His emotional reactions are chronicled several times. When Lazarus died and the news was received by Jesus, the word is that "Jesus wept."

The conflict between Jesus and the Pharisees is well known. In His frustration with them Jesus reportedly called them "white sepulchers." Perhaps the most visible emotional expression is when Jesus cast out the money changers from the Temple. He used a whip to do it. He was angry.

Another insight into the personality of Jesus is to remember His interaction with people: women, children and the physically ill. He always treated women as special. Whether Mary Magdalene, the woman taken in adultery, Mary and Martha or His mother. Jewish men of that day thanked God every day that they were not a woman. Jesus respected them.

Many scholars believe Mary Magdalene was the key leader in the early church. Even on the cross, Jesus told Apostle John to care for His mother.

Think of those who were healed: the lame, the blind, and the lepers. Jesus' compassion is indicated again and again. Then there is His intelligence. At the age of twelve He confounded the elders with it. His wisdom was exceptional. It was revealed in His confrontation with the Scribes and Pharisees. He can be described as sharp as a tack, politically astute and a scholar.

But one attribute stands out above all else. He was focused. He was passionate about life and what He wanted to do. He was willing to die for what He believed. And He did.

No one has ever lived as He did; impacted the world as He has; and challenged millions of people to follow in His footsteps through the centuries as He does.

Amen. Selah. So be it.

POPE FRANCIS

Pope Francis was born Jorge Mario Bergoglio on December 17, 1936. Following in the succession of the Apostle Peter, he is the 266th Pope, elected on March 13of this year. He is 76 years old. He was ordained to the priesthood on December 13, 1969, and became a Cardinal in 2001 by Pope John Paul II.

Born in Buenos Aires, Argentina, he has four siblings and his parents had immigrated from Italy. As a teenager Bergoglio had a lung removed. However, it did not keep him from becoming a world class tango dancer, although he preferred the faster paced milonga. The future Pope also says he had a girlfriend at that time. Before pursuing an ecclesiastical career he received a master's degree in chemistry at the University of Buenos Aires.

An unusually smart man he speaks fluently in Spanish, English, Italian, Portuguese, German, and French. He also can read ancient Greek and biblical Hebrew.

After Cardinal Bergoglio was elected on the fifth ballot, there is speculation as to why the Pope chose the name of Francis I. Two historical giants were under consideration: Giovanni Francesco Bernardone, better known as Saint Francis of Assisi; and Saint Francis Xavier.

The first Francis was born in 1182 and died on October 3, 1226 at age 44. He started the Order of Franciscans that was granted permission by Pope Inncent III in 1209, with eleven followers. They became known as "the lesser brothers." Their membership is made up mostly of "Friars" that are not ordained as "priests." Notable of Franciscans was Friar Junipero Serra, founder of the California missions.

For several hours after the election of Pope Francis there was intense discussion over which Francis' name he was assuming; either Francis of Assisi or Francis Xavier, one of the founders of the Society of Jesus-the Jesuits. Xavier (1506-1552) died at age 46.

Pope Francis has settled the dilemma. He says that after the election he was greeted by his good friend, Brazilian Cardinal Claudio Hommes, when he hugged and kissed the Pope and whispered in his ear, "Don't forget the poor." At that moment Saint Francis of Assisi came to his mind, "who devoted his life to the poor, missionary outreach and caring for God's creation."

His reputation in Argentina is paradoxical-contradictory. He is the essence of humility. He lives in a small apartment, rather than the Cardinal's mansion; he cooks his own meals; he rides the local bus rather than being chauffeured. He visits AID patients, kisses and washes their feet. In every respect he is considered a humble servant of Jesus. His hope is to be the Pope of the people and the poor. His focus is on humility and poverty.

These characteristics are not denied. However, he is vilified by charging him with supporting the military regime and not supporting his priests who challenge it. The strongest voice against the military is support for "Liberation Theology," which the Pope is accused of being lukewarm about it.

His opposition is primarily from the Argentine media

and focuses on charges of the Pope's collaboration with the government. However, no charges have ever been proven against him. His open opposition to the feared dictator Jorge Videla/Cristina Kirchner and support by the victims of oppression was affirmed by many witnesses.

An additional profile of the Pope is relatively easy. As an Italian, I'm confident he loves pasta and pizza. As an Argentinean I'm also sure he loves steaks-of all kinds. Since there are many athletes from there, he undoubtedly supports them, especially Manu Ginobili of the NBA San Antonio Spurs.

The prayer of Saint Francis of Assisi is very applicable to the new Pope. Lord, make me a channel of the peace, that where there is hatred, I may bring love; that where there is wrong, I may bring the spirit of forgiveness; that where there is discord, I may bring truth; that where there is doubt, I may bring faith; that where there is despair, I may bring light; that where there is sadness, I may bring joy.

Lord, grant that I may seek rather to comfort than to be comforted; to understand, than to be understood; to love, than to be loved. For it is by self-forgetting that one finds. It is by forgiving that one is forgiven. It is by dying that one awakens to eternal life.

Amen. Selah. So be it.

PRAYER

Prayer is a fundamental expression in almost all recognized religions. In one way or another, adherents will approach their God with their petitions. They will vary. For example, Muslims will use their prayer rugs and face Mecca. Buddhists will engage in chants. Catholics will use a rosary and Anglicans will read from the Book of Prayer. We pray as a corporate group, in a small group, as a family and individually. The Bible urges us to "pray without ceasing" and "in all things to give thanks."

The so called Lord's Prayer is a misnomer. It should be called the Disciples Prayer because Jesus gave it as an example of prayer. His disciples had asked Him to teach them how to pray. Jesus' prayer is more aptly found in John's Gospel, chapter 17. It begins with the words, "These words spoke Jesus, and lifted up His eyes to heaven, and said." The following 26 verses give His prayer.

The following kinds of prayers include: Bidding prayers, Intercessory prayers. Dedicatory prayers; Special day prayers; Confessional prayers; Praise prayers; Ordination prayers; Installation prayers; Baptismal prayers and Wedding prayers.

An analysis of the so-called Lord's Prayer is rather simple. It begins with an affirmation of Adoration, followed by seven Petitions and closing with a Benediction. The prayer begins beautifully- Our Father. It is inclusive. Jesus and His disciples; which includes you and me. Father is the source of our lineage. Family is implied. Jesus ardently identified God with Joseph, His earthly father. There is an intimacy.

Forever and ever He then elevates fatherhood to a high level. His name is hallowed; sacred, holy. Along with honored, as recorded in Exodus 20:12. "Honor your father and mother." Again, memories of His earthly father were in His mind. This is followed by the petition of "Thy kingdom come." Where is it...The location? Luke 17:21 brings a measure of insight. "The kingdom of God is within you."

Then we are to pray for the will of God to be done. Here on earth as it is in heaven. God's will, His wishes, are to be actualized right here; certainly not in or on mountains and valleys or other materials.

More likely, God's will is best viewed through the words of Jesus, "You shall love the Lord your God with all your heart, soul, mind and strength; and your neighbor as yourself." This is quite a challenge and expectation and reality to be prayed for.

Asking for "daily bread" has an interesting connotation. In John 6:35, Jesus is recorded as saying, "I am the bread of life." Of course bread is symbolic of physical nourishment, but it also signifies spiritual nourishment. Through faith we receive a daily supply of hope and encouragement for living. Years ago I heard a preacher say that the letters in the word faith stand for Forsaking All I Take Him.

The next two verses are chucking full of powerful words: forgive, trespasses (debts), lead, temptation, tests, deliver, wrongdoing, evil...Powerful words.

The first phrase resounds with mercy. Forgiving and

being forgiven. They seem to be reciprocal. We need it and we need to give. All have fallen short, we've missed the mark. The concept is basic to Christianity. The cross and God's love demands it. Whether we say debts or trespasses it makes no difference. They are the same. It is unlimited mercy.

The next phrase is one of pleading. The Aramaic word for test and temptation is the same. The Muslim's Koran speaks of this life as a time of testing.

I like what one writer says, "We naturally have enough testing's in our life without God leading us to anymore." "Please, God, be chintzy with the testing." Whatever tests we have, be with us.

The climax, the pinnacle of thought, the crown jewel of the prayer is verse seven. It is God's kingdom, His power and His glory forever. Not you or me. All belongs to God.

Ecclesiastes 4:12 gives a provocative insight. "A threefold cord is not easily broken." One thread is quickly roken, but four? No way. The benediction is declarative. It is something to hang our faith on.

Amen. Selah so be it.

PREJUDICE

Frank Melton of St. George, Utah recently sent me a humorous and insightful story. A young couple moves into a new neighborhood. The next morning while they are eating breakfast, the young woman sees her neighbor hanging the wash outside. "That laundry is not very clean," she said. "She doesn't know how to wash correctly. Perhaps she needs better soap."

Her husband looked on, but remained silent. Every time her neighbor would hang her wash to dry, the young woman would make the same comments. About one month later, the woman was surprised to see a nice clean wash on the line and said to her husband: "Look, she has learned how to wash correctly. I wonder who taught her this?" The husband said, "I got up early this morning and cleaned our windows."

AND SO IT IS WITH LIFE. WHAT WE SEE WHEN WATCHING OTHERS DEPENDS ON THE PURITY OF THE WINDOW THROUGH WHICH WE LOOK.

The prism through which we view situations and other people can easily be misinterpreted and wrong. PREJUDICE IS OFTEN THE RESULT. It is an evil that is as old as recorded history. The problem is that often social prejudice becomes normative for the vast number of people.

The most visceral and deadly of all prejudice is RACIAL; white against black; black against brown; brown against yellow; yellow against red. Bigotry is a difficult attitude to defend; particularly in the light of scientific discoveries. Skin color in no way determines the quality and value of any race.

Skin color is determined by the pigment. Blood is the same in all people. We are all of one blood. So this thought is recorded in Acts 17:26. God: "has made of one blood all nations of men."

How then can religion of all kinds support racial prejudice? This brings me to the second evidence of prejudice...RELIGION. I can remember the day when animosity prevailed between Catholics and Protestants. Thank God and the wisdom of believers, congeniality is now the norm. But bitterness is strong today between fundamentalists and the more liberal brands of Christianity. The sides are prevalent in both Catholic and Protestant churches. A number of Biblical scholars are declaring that Jesus would not recognize His followers today. According to the Gospels He advocated the opposite spirit to that which is evident today.

My third prejudice under discussion is probably more relevant to me and my generation, than to others...AGE. Perhaps I should include the young (teenagers), because they too, are often victims of prejudice. The youth are often judged harshly. "They are lazy, disrespectful and have bad morals." What an indictment. I see them differently. Most of the ones I know are working and/or going to school.

What about us seniors? Consider this questionnaire. What age group supports the travel industry? What age group supports the churches and other helpful agencies? What age group has investment programs and supports all areas of the economy? If you name any other age group than seniors, you're not paying attention.

This article doesn't include the discrimination toward the handicapped; prejudice against those who are overweight; the mentally ill; and the minimally educated.

I hope that President Obama is never denigrated because he is a black man. I hope the Muslims are never excluded because they are different believers. I hope that being a certain age category is never the criterion for efficiency. As a nation and as individuals we cannot afford prejudice. Perhaps a different perspective is needed. That's just the way it is.

Amen. Selah so be it.

PROBLEMS

The Christian faith creates a lot of problems for most people. Why is there suffering and the problem of evil that has caused many to become atheists? The myriad of different denominations with contrary viewpoints has perpetuated controversies galore.

Theological concepts have done little to maintain the easily understood teachings of Jesus. Men like the Apostle Paul, Saint Augustine, Martin Luther, John Wesley, Paul Tillich and Karl Barth have tended to obfuscate His truths. What were Jesus' priorities? Of course there are those contained in His parables. The two greatest commandments are also to be considered as basic.

But there are two others that I feel are so vital they should be considered in the priorities of Jesus' most important utterances. Matthew 19:14 "Let the little children come to me and forbid them not, for of such is the Kingdom of heaven." He then placed His hands on their heads and blessed them. What an amazing revelation! Matthew 25:40. "Inasmuch as you have done it unto one of the least of these my brothers, you have done it unto Me." This followed Jesus' admonishment that His followers care for the hungry, the thirsty, the stranger, the sick, those in prison and those in need of clothing. These were the criteria for discipleship; concern and compassion for the needy.

Roxie Smith shared the following story with me. "On a cold day in December, some years ago, a little boy was standing before a shoe store barefooted, peering through the window, and shivering with cold. A lady approached the young boy and said, "My, but you're in such deep thought staring in that window!" "I was asking God to give me a pair of shoes," was the boy's reply. The lady took him by the hand, and asked the clerk to get half a dozen pairs of socks for the boy. She then asked if he could give her a basin of water and a towel. She took the little boy to the back part of the store and, knelt down, washed his little feet, and dried them with the towel.

By this time, the clerk had returned with the socks. Placing a pair upon the boy's feet, she purchased him a pair of shoes. She tied up the remaining pairs of socks and gave them to him. She patted him on the head and said. "No doubt, you will be more comfortable now." As she turned to go, the astonished kid caught her by the hand and looking up into her face with tears in his eyes, asked her. "Are you God's wife?"

Did you know that the USA is numero uno (number one) in response to world disasters: Haiti, Pakistan, Indonesia, China, etc? We send billions to Africa to help AIDS victims. Our generosity is legendary.

Did you know that we are numero uno in supplying military arms (guns, tanks, bombs, airplanes) to other countries: Egypt, Israel, Saudi Arabia, South Africa, etc?

Did you know that one out of seven families in the USA is living below the poverty level?

Did you know that Mexico has the highest percentage of children living in poverty? (26.2%) The USA is second. (22.4%) Sweden is lowest with 2.6%.

Did you know that one child under five dies every 5

seconds because of the lack of food? That is 6 million per year.

Did you know that 5 million seniors are dying each year in the USA because of hunger? Remember what Jesus said.

Amen. Selah. So be it.

PROVERBS

Proverbs (English) and dichos (Spanish) have been a part of history since it was recorded. All nationalities have them as a part of their culture.

They are not so much history as philosophy; bits of wisdom. Parents have particularly been prone to voice them as reprimands of for guidance. When a parent says, "Do you think money grows on trees?," you know you are being chastised for over spending or asking for money or "When in Rome do as the Romans do." ...Words of guidance. When visiting other countries or a neighbor, abide by the customs they have. Don't eat with your elbows on the table. Wipe your shoes off before entering their home.

The Bible is filled with proverbs. Jesus used them all the time. "Do unto others as you would have them do unto you." "Judge not that you be not judged." My favorite proverb is found in the Book of Ezekiel 18:2, 3. "The fathers have eaten sour grapes, but the children's teeth are set on edge." Israel has been taken captive. They are slaves. They were defiant. But their children are paying the price for what their parents did; a current and prevalent indictment. However, the Scripture goes on to say "As the Lord thy God liveth, NEVER SAY THAT AGAIN." (Moffat) Why? Because as with all proverbs, it is only partially true.

Children, especially teen agers are prone to blame others (parents, siblings, teachers, anyone in authority) for their failures and miscues. Of course, we parents are always quick to point out their willfulness and their tendency to follow the influences of others. That's when proverbs come into play.

There are some proverbs that seem to me to be more relevant than others. By relevant I mean applicable to everyday living. For example, <u>LIFE BEGINS AT FORTY</u>. Does it mean the young will find "life" when they get to forty; or to we seniors approach through memory? Life <u>began</u> back in time.

I reject both views. I affirm that it begins wherever we are NOW.   The Quakers had a proverb that enlightens. "This is the first day of the rest of your life."

The Life Begins at Forty also implies the challenge to be aware (alive) to all experiences. An urban legend about Thomas Edison is applicable. Remember, not the least of his hundreds of inventions was the light bulb. As the legend goes, one night his lab went up in flames, destroying all his notes and inventions.   Upon seeing it, he told his son to go get his wife and his son's mother. "Tell her she'll never see such a sight in her life. It is beautiful."

Another of my favorite proverbs is, <u>SEEING IS BELIEVING</u>. As with most proverbs, this one is only partially true. If you're scientifically oriented, then it is totally true. Scientists believe that if a hypothesis cannot be verified in a test tube, it is unbelievable. It is based on the pragmatic philosophy.

In contradiction to the scientific approach there is the RELIGIOUS approach-the reverse of the given proverb. BELIEVING IS SEEING.

LOVE, COMPASSION, INSIGHTS, FAITH, HOPE are

all intangibles. They cannot be measured or seen; only their results. But they are non-the-less real. They are all the basic affirmations of religion.

Consider this illustration. It's about Joan of Arc. She was born in 1412 and burned at the stake on May 30, 1431. She was canonized on May 16, 1920. She was militant in heading the military of France against the British in the last phase of the Hundred Years War (1339-1453). At the age of thirteen she began to hear voices, as from God. She continued to hear them until her last breath.

King Charles VII was her mortal enemy and caused her martyrdom. In a classic confrontation, he accused her of heresy and hearing the voices. He said, "Why doesn't the voice of God speak to me?" Joan responded, "He does. But you don't listen." Believing is seeing…as true today as back then.

Amen. Selah. So be it.

PSYCHOSOMATIC

Rene Decartes (1596-1650) a French philosopher, mathematician and scientist. He was the one who said, "I think therefore I am." His writings affected many intellectuals in the 17th century. However, his views drastically influenced Western medicine for 300 years. Called Cartesian; he stressed the disconnection between the mind and the body. In his view, neither affected the other. Medical schools advocated this theory for generations. Hans Selye M.D., disrupted this view. Oriental medicine always saw the connection. Younger doctors today no longer are Cartesian.

Norman Cousins PhD wrote "Anatomy of An Illness" in which he shared his views about attitudes affecting and laughter affecting body wellness. He and others like Carl Simonton M.D. debunked Cartesianism. Simonton focused on the cancer prone personality. One trait was the internalizing of negative emotions. Among several other traits, another one was ignoring the affects of stress.

In my doctoral dissertation I gave a test to several practicing doctors asking them what percentage of their patients had no real illness-outside of genetic problems (heart, kidneys etc.) and broken bones? And, they would prefer telling them to go home and rest, and forego medication? Why don't they? ...Obviously because we patients don't want to hear their suggestion. We want pills. THEY SURPRISED ME WITH THE AVERAGE: 95%. PLEASE RE-READ MY QUESTION.

Since stress is endemic to we humans, what are some viable ways to manage stress? Since maladaptive measures are unacceptable, we should engage in acceptable activities. Dr. Simonton recommended (insisted) that his clients "play" one hour per day. Everyone had to list 10 ways that didn't cost $5.00 and then 10 ways that cost $10.00 or more. Go for a walk, fix your favorite meal, read a book, a glass of wine while in the tub, make love, call a friend, write a letter, go swimming, go shopping (looking), watch a TV sit-com.

Psalm 126:2 states, "Then was my mouth filled with laughter, and our tongues with singing." Norman Cousins advocated laughter as a stress reducer. One of the benefits is that it strengthens the immune system. Laugh a little and live a lot.

Another way to relieve stress is by exercising. As with laughter, it releases endorphins in the brain. Strength exercises, flexibility exercise and cardio-vascular should all be included. A recent study of longevity indicates that those over 100 years of age, all engaged in some sort of exercise. Try taking a nap...even a powernap of three minutes. Hippocrates (father of medicine) said for maximum health to eat right, get a massage everyday and take a nap after every meal. By the way, massage dissipates lactic acid (a by-product of exercise.)

Take care of a pet-a dog, a cat preferably. A fish or a bird seems too impersonal. Stories abound about dogs that become caretakers. They love without prejudice. If you're angry, stressed out or even ignore them. Just smile and pet them, and they are yours. Being friendly with a dog is a great stress reducer.

There is another form of stress reduction that is vital. I am particularly fond of this one. It's called "deep breathing" or "diaphragmatic breathing…This in contrast to "thoracic breathing."

All musicians, especially singers breathe diaphragmatically and in doing so they maximize their lung capacity. Thoracic breathing draws the diaphragm muscle up into the lung area, diminishing air capacity a third. Diaphragmatic breathing is pushing the stomach out as you breathe in, which in turn expands the lungs to their full capacity.

Air is changed to oxygen, which in turn feeds the blood and strengthens and relaxes the muscles. Practice diaphragmatic breathing while driving, walking or watching TV.

It is absolutely important that in managing stress we develop a belief system. Attitudes that will affect our tranquility will initiate in our belief system. The Bible says, "As a person thinks, so is he." (Proverbs 23:7) A follow up thought is another Scriptural suggestion. "They that wait on the Lord shall renew their strength." (Isaiah 40:31) Other words to think about are:

1. You can alter your life by altering your attitudes (William James)
2. Believe in the capacity of your immune system (Simonton)
3. Negative emotions (anger, jealousy, unforgiveness, Etc.); contribute to illness (Cousins)
4. Life is worth living (Abersold)

5. Believe in the reversibility of negative diagnoses (Siegel)
6. Believe in the potential of lateral thinking (Di Bono)
7. Believe in the potential of your inner spiritual self. Go to church (Abersold)

Amen. Selah. So be it.

PUPPY SIZE

Writers are always looking for and expecting inspiration. It comes unexpectedly; Sometime with elapsed times of "writer's block." But when it is perceived, it's like finding a gold mine. Of course, like finding a gold mine, it must be mined. Writing takes work. Ask any writer. The work includes style and structure. When a book, article or column is finished it has often been described as giving birth.

What are the sources of inspiration? There really isn't a sure-fire answer. Every author has his or her own criteria, but my main source is other people. Many family members and friends provide me with inspirational ideas. An example of what I mean comes from my daughter, Pamela. It is one of the neatest stories I've ever heard. You will know precisely what this little girl is talking about at the end.

"Danielle keeps repeating it over and over again. We've been back to this animal shelter at least five times. It has been weeks now since we started all this," the mother told the volunteer. "What is it she keeps asking for?" the volunteer asked. "Puppy size!" replied the mother. "I know...we have seen most of them," the mom said in frustration. Just then Danielle came walking into the office "Well, did you find one?" asked her mom. "No, not this time," Danielle said with sadness in her voice. "Can we come back on the weekend?"

The two women looked at each other, shook their heads and laughed. "You never know when we will get more dogs.

The two women looked at each other, shook their heads and laughed. "You never know when we will get more dogs. Unfortunately, there's always a supply," the volunteer said. Danielle took her mother by the hand and headed to the door. "Don't worry, I'll find one this weekend," she said. Over the next few days both mom and dad had long conversations with her. They both felt she was being too particular. "It's this weekend or we're not looking anymore," Dad finally said in frustration. "We don't want to hear anything more about puppy size either," Mom added.

Sure enough, they were the first ones in the shelter on Saturday morning. By now Danielle knew her way around, so she ran right for the section that housed the smaller dogs. Tired of the routine, mom sat in the small waiting room at the end of the first row of cages. There was an observation window so you could see the animals during times when visitors weren't permitted. Danielle walked slowly from cage to cage, kneeling periodically to take a closer look. One by one the dogs were brought out and she held each one. One by one she said, "Sorry, you're not the one."

It was the last cage on this last day in search of the perfect pup. The volunteer opened the cage door and the child carefully picked up the dog and held it closely. This time she took a little longer. "Mom, that's it! I found the right puppy! He's the one! I know it!" she screamed with joy. "It's the puppy size!"   "But it's the same size as all the other puppies you held over the last few weeks," Mom said. "No not size--- the sighs. When I held him in my arms, he sighed," she said. "Don't you remember? When I asked you one day what love is, you told me love depends on the sigh of your heart. The more you love, the bigger the sigh!"

The two women looked at each other for a moment. Mom didn't know whether to laugh or cry. As she stooped down to hug the child, she did a little of both. "Mom, every time you hold me, I sigh. When you and Daddy come home from work and hug each other, you both sigh. I knew I would find the right puppy if it sighed when I held it in my arms," she said. Then holding the puppy up close to her face she said, "Mom, he loves me. I heard the sigh of his heart!"

Close your eyes for a moment and think about the love that makes you sigh. Not only find it in the arms of loved ones, but in the caress of a sunset, the kiss of the moonlight and the gentle brush of cool air on a hot day. They are the sigh of God. Take the time to stop and listen; you will be surprised at what you hear. "Life is not measured by the breaths we take, but the moments that take our breath away."

Amen. Selah. So be it.

PURPOSE

The other day I watched a remarkable display of artistic expressions. An artist carves or molds very small figures. They cannot be seen-only through microscopes. Many of them are so small they can fit on the end of a pin… believe it or not. It's amazing the affect that small things have upon our lives. A mustard seed is one of the smallest seeds on earth. Yet, Jesus said it we had faith the size of a mustard seed amazing things could be accomplished.

George Washington Carver changed the economy of the South with his work with the lowly peanut.

One of the most valuable of jewels is the pearl; totally different from gold, silver or diamonds. It is created by the oyster. A small, very small, grain of sand lands in the oyster shell. It is an irritant, abrasive. But the oyster secretes a miraculous substance that covers the grain. Eventually a pearl is formed.

It is common knowledge that human cells make up the substance of our bodies. The small egg produced by a woman is fertilized by a small sperm from a man. They multiply until they become an embryo. In the early stages of development, the embryos of a chicken, whale, rabbit (or other mammals) are similar to the embryo of a human. After several months a fetus is formed and after nine months a human baby is born. From two cells to a 6-9 pound baby.

The parallel between the above and the "germ" of an idea is similar. One becomes a baby and the other an article.

Think of a few world changing documents: The Declaration of Independence, the Gettysburg Address, the Mayflower Compact, Monroe Doctrine, the Bill of Rights. Through the centuries there have been many significant documents: the Code of Hammurabi, the works of Plato and Aristotle, the King James version of the Bible, to name a few.

I'm sure you have had ideas cross your mind that have inspired and motivated you. The ideas were small but large in significance. To enforce this concept I suggest the words of Victor Hugo who said, "There is nothing as powerful as an idea whose time has come." The significance if it should be obvious.

Aside from verses of Scripture, I've respected short, pithy statements that inspire. Victor Frankl, PhD and MD, the father of humanistic psychology, spoke often of the Indomitable Power of the Human Spirit. He saw the ravages of Hitler's death camps and witnessed survivals. There is that which we all possess that wills us to persevere.

Karl Barth, the great theologian from Basel, Switzerland said, "There is a saving element in every situation." Sometimes it is hard to find and hard to recognize. But it is there. A friend of mine told me in a time of great personal depression: "Jesus was only on His cross for three hours."

I was told recently that. "The purpose of life is to FIND A PURPOSE." It took me a minute or two to get it. George Burns challenged his audiences to: DO WHAT YOU LIKE AND LIKE WHAT YOU DO.

One idea that I've tried to practice daily comes from James Baldwin. He said, "The challenge of living is to be PRESENT in everything you do from getting up in the morning, to going to bed at night. *Amen. Selah. So be it.*

REGULATION

I am not an economist and struggle trying to understand the problems in our country. I do know we are in a mess. However, I recently learned a great deal about the major cause from the Rachel Maddow Show on MSNBC. She interviewed Senator Byron Dorgan who explained de-regulation as that cause.

An important factor in coming out of the Great Depression (GD) was President FDR and Congress passing a REGULATION law which governed the activities of big business. Monopolies and free enterprise were running amuck. Business was doing whatever it pleased. In 1999 President Bill Clinton and Congress eliminated Regulatory laws with only eight Senators voting against. One of them was Senator Byron Dorgan.

He was prophetic and said and wrote that within ten years our nation would rue that day that large companies could do just what they wanted. Hello, AIG and all the other companies that benefited from de-regulation.

A good friend shared with me this insight. "Every great discovery or program benefit has a potential for the opposite." Take fire for example. It can cook or heat, but also burn and destroy.

In regard to REGULATION; President Obama warned that as important as it was, we should NOT disparage company expansion or a justifiable bonus for effective executives.

Ever since the Apostle Paul started Christianity regulations have been a part of it. Women shouldn't cut their hair or wear jewelry; be silent in the churches; wives should be submissive; slaves should obey their masters, are a few examples. Later on, doctrines were established and to doubt them caused excommunication. In every generation there has been regulation.

I grew up in a fundamentalist denomination: no dancing, no movies, no make-up, no wedding rings, no TV, no mixed swimming, no booze-even wine, no card playing or smoking, etc. Other churches today have similar regulations.

The Bible is replete with thousands of rules, guides, advice otherwise known as regulations. Sifting them out, what three would you designate as the top three? I would give number one as what Jesus said the greatest commandment. *"You shall love the Lord your God with all your heart and with all your soul and with all you mind and your neighbor as yourself."* Even though Jesus was quoting Deuteronomy 6:5, it does not diminish the importance that Jesus placed on it.

The word regulation has a sense of obligation in its meaning. It is a demand without equivocation. It is a principle of Christian living. The second regulatory law that is a guideline comes from the Old Testament. Micah 6:8 states unequivocally, "What does the Lord require of you, but to do justly, and to love mercy, and to walk humbly with God." Another translation puts it very succinctly. Here's what we are to do: "To be fair, just, and merciful and to walk humbly with God."

While the Ten Commandments are often described as the center of Jewish thought, most Jewish scholars say these words from Micah are the core of Judaism. It has nothing to do with circumcision or kosher food. The standard for following and worshiping God is spiritual: fairness, mercy, love and humility.

The third element of religious regulation is what Jesus said in Matthew 6:33 "Seek you first the kingdom of God and His righteousness."

Ralph Sockman, a great Methodist preacher in the1930's and 40's, called this, The Higher Happiness. He affirmed that Jesus cured base desires by creating higher hungers. This premise was a regulation for sure.

Continuing the aforementioned analogy, there is a bonus for those involved in the business of being Christian. The bonus is the acquisition of the kingdom. And where is it? The Gospel of Luke is clear. (17:21) "The Kingdom of God is within you." That is more valuable than any monetary bonus.

Amen. Selah. So be it.

REMINDER

The word "reminder" has a provocative connotation. It can be meaningful or it can be unfortunate. Psychologists tell us that our memories are the depository of everything we have ever thought, heard, read or done. They reside in our sub-conscious. Reminders are the triggers that bring them to our conscious minds. Such reminders can contribute to our unhappiness and depression.

All of us have been the victims of unpleasant reminders. Some time ago I heard of a young boy who was adopted into an unhealthy home.

The father was constantly REMINDING the boy how appreciative he should be for his adoption. This was followed with constant criticism of everything he did or didn't do...worst of all, the father had taken his baby shoes and had them bronzed. They were placed on the mantel where everyone could see them. They were obviously old and poor. The father used them as a reminder to the boy of what he had done for him. One can well imagine the affect on the young boy.

Using the modality of prayer, I'd like to address God and request of Him a few reminders. O God, remind us of our humanity...our mistakes. Things we should do, but don't. Things we should not do, but do. Remind us O God, to be generous with our applause for those who excel and to be stingy with our criticism for those who do poorly.

O God, remind us of Your mercy that is from

everlasting to everlasting. That our sins are removed from us as far as the east is from the west and they are placed in the sea of Your forgetfulness.

Remind us O God, of your providence. As we count our many blessings. Your watch and care over us is revealed as the count increases.

O God, remind us to forgive others as You have forgiven us. As You forgive us of everything, remind us to forgive everyone everything.

Remind us O God, to have faith even if only as small as a mustard seed and to couch our faith in thought, because faith without thought is superstition.

O God, remind us of the importance of our families and friends. Relationships are not automatically enhanced. It is not necessarily true that families must accept us but friends we choose. Even Jesus had problems with his family. Cultivation for both is essential. We must not take either for granted.

Remind us O God, of your promises; particularly those that we make personal. The Psalmist was right on when he said, "Yea, thou we walk through the valley of the shadow of death, Thou art with us."

O God, remind us that if we draw near to You, You will draw near to us. Also, "Your ear is not heavy that it cannot hear; neither is Your arm shortened that it cannot save."

Remind us O God, even though it's beyond our comprehension of Your great love that sent Jesus to earth. Through His life and death we have salvation and hope of eternal life.

Finally, REMIND us O God, of the words of Your servant St. Frances of Assisi.

O God, make us instruments of your peace,
Where there is hatred, let us sow love;
Where there is injury, pardon;
Where there is discord, union;
Where there is doubt, faith;
Where there is despair, hope;
Where there is darkness, light;
Where there is sadness, joy;
For Your mercy and for Your truths sake.

Amen. Selah. So be it.

RESURRECTION

The most important doctrine of the Christian faith is the resurrection of Jesus. The issue of disagreement is whether Jesus' resurrection was physical or spiritual. I was confronted with this dilemma a few weeks ago. The following is a summation of some of my thoughts.

Chronological authenticity begins with historical knowledge about Jesus. Using our current calendar, He was born in zero A.D. At the age of 33 He died.

Peter and Paul were killed by Nero in 64-65 A.D. History records Nero's death in 65 A.D. This means that everything Paul wrote had to precede 65 A.D.; 32 years after Jesus' death.

Not one Gospel- Mark, Matthew, Luke, John-was written before Paul's death. Biblical scholars agree that Mark was written first, about 70-75 A.D.; Matthew and Luke around 85-90 A.D., and John's Gospel about 100 A.D.

A basic approach used by historians to establish veracity is to RECONSTRUCT verifiable data. Therefore I will rely on what Paul wrote in the Corinthian letters. Many scholars believe the two are really a compilation of four or five letters.

By omission Paul never mentions Jesus' birth, baptism, family, transfiguration, miracles, prayers, words of wisdom, temptation, appearances before Herod and Pilate, and so on. Paul does describe the Lord's Supper and affirms his belief that Jesus died and was raised. The ascension is not mentioned. Paul also mentions that Jesus appeared to Cephas (Peter) the twelve disciples, His brother James, over 500 others and himself.

The empty tomb, those who visited it, the eating of fish and other incidents recorded in the Gospels, are NEVER mentioned. In chapter 15 Paul mentions twice the words, "in accordance with scriptures." To what scriptures does he refer? It's too much of a stretch to equate such words as "He died for our sins" as fulfillment of Old Testament prophecies.

Since Paul's letters were the first books in the New Testament, it must be assumed that the words "according to the scriptures" were a later redaction. Few details of the resurrection are included.

The most important assertion by Paul is that God raised Jesus. The power of the resurrection resided with God. Jesus was the recipient. Paul uses this phrase thirty-seven times.

Jesus went from the grave directly to God's right hand. Bishop John Spong states: "There is no sense at all in Paul of a physical resurrection of Jesus back into the life of this world." It was a spiritual resurrection.

The much later Gospels distorted the resurrection of Jesus. That, for Paul, was Easter. Paul introduces Jesus as having "died for our sins." He becomes the ransom, the atonement for mankind. These concepts changed the direction of Christian theology. The Christ of faith subverted the Jesus of history.

The sacrificial lamb goes back in Hebrew history to Noah and the patriarchs. The belief in the sacrificial death of Jesus is also a paradigm that has its origin in Mithraism and the ancient Egyptian religions that were plagiarized into the

Old Testament stories.

The word "appearance" is similar to the one Paul had on the road to Damascus. The same revelation came to others Paul mentions; including the 500. None of them in Paul's writings had a physical encounter with the resurrected Jesus. It is called a revelatory manifestation.

The word used for revelation or insight is OPHTHE. To have one's eyes opened. For Paul this was the raising of Jesus by God.

Amen. Selah. So be it.

REVERSAL

Seniors are very vulnerable to certain illnesses: Pneumonia, cancer, heart attacks, arthritis, Alzheimer's, among others. Medical research places the cause of many of their illnesses, at their weakening immune system.

The human immune system is weakest when we are children; when we are elderly; and when we are under stress. That is why children need to have their shots. The elderly need shots, good food and plenty of rest. Everyone needs to manage stress in creative ways.

The standard Holmes/Rehe stress test indicates the number one stressor is the loss of a loved one. Second is divorce and third is the aging process.

In recent years there has been a growing awareness of two subtle, insidious and debilitating causes of Senior's stress: ROLE-REVERSAL and ABUSE OF SENIORS.

I became aware of the problem of role-reversal a few years ago while visiting a museum in Bozeman, Montana. While waiting for a movie on dinosaurs to start, an elderly couple and obviously their daughter sat on a bench beside me. The daughter got up and with a dominate tone advised her parents to stay where they were. She was going shopping but would be back. "Stay right here. Don't leave," she said as if they were children. As soon as she left, they took off Role-Reversal.

I witnessed the same situation and dynamics a few weeks ago in the Inland Center Mall with two senior parents

and a 40 year old son. He demanded obedience to "stay put."
When he left them, they disappeared in the opposite direction.

Role-reversal is children assuming the role of parents
while parents become the obeying children or child. Parents
are told what to wear, eat and where and when they go.

A senior friend told me recently, children also tend to
control what their parents think –on a variety of subjects from
religion to politics.

Control and independence are the dominant issues. The
children feel obligated to watch over their parents by
controlling what they do. Parents are reluctant to yield their
independence; in spite of diminishing physical skills. Of
course, there will come a time when the parent or parents
need the care and "watching over" that only children can give.
Until then, role-reversal is too often a bossy trend.

The same principle can also occur between a husband
and wife. Because of illness or other negative circumstance, a
wife may take control of their lives; driving, paying bills,
shopping and planning activities. Monetary control is often a
source of both parental/children and wife/husband role-
reversal.

SENIOR ABUSE: They can include physical,
psychological, neglect or financial exploitation. Physical
abuse can be readily detectable: broken bones, bed sores,
internal bleeding, medication overdose, pressure ulcers, head
injury, falls, malnutrition, bruises and even death.
Psychological abuse is often evident by: depression, agitation,
withdrawal, fear, frequent crying, anxiety and complaints of
improper treatment.

Sources for abuse are often family members, spouses,

neighbors and even a medical caretaker.

Both role-reversal and senior abuse can be referred to as "silent killers." They are subtle and destroyers of happiness. Mainly because most seniors are reluctant to voice unhappiness or report conditions to others and often they are too ashamed that their children (relatives or guardians) are mistreating them.

It is important to remember there are times when role-reversals are important and beneficial. A friend's mother developed Alzheimer's. For several years she cared for her and then had to put her in a home-care. She bathed her; changed her stained clothes; gave her medication; handled her money. Role-reversal took place. That kind of situation happens too often. However, there is no excuse for senior abuse-at any time. The most subtle expression of abuse is neglect.

Through the years I've had many opportunities to visit convalescent hospitals and retirement communities. The greatest tragedy is to meet seniors who never have a visitor or a family member. That is abuse....Shame.

Amen. Selah so be it.

SENSES

I heard the other day that in the early 1900's the longevity of U.S.A. citizens was 45 years. Today it is approaching 85 for men and 90 for women. The Bible in the Book of Genesis 6:3 indicates that the allotted years for men and women are 120. I like that.

Hardly a week goes by but what some study is printed defining the traits of seniors. Smelly, crippled, cantankerous, are just a sample. From my stance based on observation and personal experience I suggest the following criteria. However, only from the neck up, eyes, ears, nose, mouth and brain. These five physical attributes are drastically affected by the aging process. For example, take senior EARS. As a person gets older they very naturally lose distinct hearing ability. Of course, this is often remedied by hearing aids. Unfortunately they often are costly and seldom work.

The vast majority of seniors have a gradual loss of hearing. Conversations are lost; in a noisy environment, hearing words is difficult. Going to movies and listening to the TV is an ordeal. "What did she/he say?" The scene is changed before an answer is given.

Fast food places are a real pain. Foreign languages (especially Spanish,) are often common. Seniors find them hard to hear and understand. Seniors often have a hearing problem with those who speak rapidly. English and Spanish both are spoken fast and softly.

What about seniors and their EYES. Cataracts,

glaucoma and macular degeneration are common ailments with the aging population. Of course glasses and laser surgery is helpful, but the process of eye degeneration is rapid. With a fixed income many seniors cannot afford correction.

The landscape is one of recognition. The elderly often see people-even friends and things-through a fog. Please don't assume they are ignoring you.

The next appendage that diminishes with the passing years is the NOSE. It is often the object of ridicule because they are too big, too crooked, too flat, too hooked, etc.

German noses are usually big; Jewish noses are normally hooked; Indian noses look thin and sharp. Orientals have small noses. Blacks often have large nostrils. Aside from these characteristics, noses have two other basic ones. They are prone to bleeding because of the many capillaries. In fact, they bleed easily.

Then, their primary purpose is for smelling. They detect odors. Good smells like pies and bad smells like skunks. But most seniors lose their sense of smell. Elderly women often wear an inordinate amount of perfume and men too much cologne. Fortunately seniors have taste; sometimes.

This brings me to the fourth example, TASTE. It is a wonderful asset. The tragedy is that like the previous examples, it begins to diminish as a person grows older.

This became apparent to me a few years ago when a friend of mine-a senior lady-was in convalescence. A genteel lady, she had always preferred to eat at elegant restaurants. However, in her state, she always wanted to eat at "fast food" places. She wanted ketchup, French fries with salt, mustard, onions, and pickles. It dawned on me that those condiments were pungent, strong and satisfied her need for taste.

The fifth characteristic is the BRAIN; which is the location of memory. It also diminishes with age. I had some things to say about it but I can't remember what I was going to write.

If you're young or middle age, you have the five signs of aging to look forward to. They really are not as bad as I've depicted.

Amen. Selah. So be it.

SHACK

THE SHACK by Wm. Paul Young is a book of fiction that reads like Pilgrim's Progress. It speaks of sorrow, guilt, repentance and redemption.

Mackenzie Allen Phillip's (Mack) daughter, Missy, is brutally killed. For four years he is under a great sadness-depression. He receives a message to go to the Shack and while there he encounters God (Papa,) Jesus and the Holy Spirit.

The saga unfolds with a series of questions from Mack and answers from the Three. The most penetrating question comes when Mack asks Poppa, "Where were You when Missy was killed?" The answer is astounding and revelatory and inspirational. For me, it is the most meaningful book I have read in five years. The following are a few of the insights that have triggered a personal response.

Mack is overwhelmed in his first confrontation with Papa (God the Father.) She is in the form of a large black woman who is wearing a long billowing dress. She listens to contemporary jazz and loves cooking.

In The Shack, Papa challenges Mack's acceptance of certain stereotypes. His religious conditioning inhibits his acceptance of God being neither male nor female. Papa reminds Mack that the abuse he suffered at the hands of his father would have closed his mind to a male God/Father. She also challenges him to move beyond the stereotype of God being an old man with a long beard. Neither is God a celestial

Santa; very white and very male.

This propensity to associate the Divine with our own stereotypes is counter-productive. Our view of Jesus is more like Salman's head of Christ. Delicate features, somewhat effeminate, classical Aryan, WASP features.

Some years a new church building was built. The building committee instructed the architect to put a picture of Jesus in the narthex. At the dedication, when it was unveiled, to their chagrin it was a modern figure of Jesus in a grey flannel suit; so contrary to their stereotype.

The historical Jesus was a man's man. He walked everywhere He went. He was a carpenter. He used a whip to chase the buyers and sellers from the Temple. He was to be admired, not to be pitied.

The literary structure of The Shack is very interesting. It definitely is dramatic. Each page is filled with drama. Sentence structure is picturesque and filled with metaphors and analogies. The basic grammatical structure is made up of questions by Mack and answers by Papa, Jesus and the Spirit.

Many of the basic Christian subjects are discussed. In a moving scene, Missy is seen by Mack on the other side. Question: "Is that you, Missy?" "Yes." And then she mouths the words, "its okay. I love you."

Question by Mack. "She's really okay, isn't she?" Answer. "This life is only the anteroom for a greater reality to come." Mack asks about being a Christian. Jesus says, "Who said anything about being a Christian. I'm not a Christian."

Question: "Do you enjoy punishing those who disappoint you?" Answer. "Sin is its own punishment. It's not my purpose to punish; it's my joy to cure it."

Here's a very important question. "Was Missy alone in her death?" Answer. "Mack, she was never alone. I never left her, not for one second." Question: "Did she know you were there?" Answer. "Yes Mack, she did."

There are at least 70 questions and often multiple answers; creation, redemption, the cross, salvation, punishment, the Bible, the Trinity, etc. I recommend the book whole heartedly.

Amen. Selah. So be it.

SILENCE

I have a good friend who has a scientific background. He is a brilliant thinker with extensive knowledge. He is also a prolific writer. In a recent monograph-he wrote an article entitled, "The Silence of God." His contention is, "There is in fact not a shred of evidence that God ever spoke a single word directly to anyone."

The words 'and God said,' "had to be recorded by someone into myth and story long after the fact." An example of my friend's argument is Genesis 1:26. God says, "Let us make man in our own image." WHO WAS THEIR WITNESS TO HEAR THESE WORDS? ...And subsequently to record them. So much of the Bible reports God speaking to one person without reliable witnesses: Adam, Noah, Abraham, Moses, Jacob, the Prophets and even David.

My friend declares, "So much for inerrancy." His conclusion is the "silence of God." I concur with him when it comes to the infallible, inerrant words in the Bible. With copying problems, there are at least 200,000 errors in the Bible. With all of that I still believe the Bible contains the truth of and about God.

To my way of thinking, God is NOT silent. The writer of the Book of Hebrews gives a clarifying insight. THE WAY translation says in chapter 1 verse 1 and 2, "Long ago God spoke in many different ways to our fathers through the prophets (in visions, dreams, and even face to face,) telling them little by little about His plans. But now in these days He has spoken through His Son." How? Through the story of His life, His parables and advice, His actions and what His followers came to believe about Him.

Prophets were revealers of truth as they perceived it. Modern day prophets would be Mahatma Gandhi, Sister Teresa and Maya Angelou. Listen to Maya, conveyor of truth.

"Thank you, Lord. For life and all that's in it. Thank you for the day and for the hour and for the minute. I know many are gone, I'm still living on, and they've gone away. You've let me stay. I want to thank you." WOW!!

It seems to me that God speaks to humans in a myriad of ways. Plagiarizing Elizabeth Barrett Browning, How do we hear from God, let me count the ways.

A beginning affirmation comes from the Psalmist. "The heavens declare the glory of God, and the firmament (earth) reveals His handiwork." This appeal to the human capacity is to see and appreciate God's revelation.

Richard G. Colling, PhD is an outstanding Professor of Biology. In his book, Random Designer, he states, "To deny evolution is to insult God's intelligence and creativeness. Evolution is His tool to establish and nurture all life." The human intellect is the apex of Divine initiative in creating the process of evolution.

Our capacity to think, to feel emotion, to rationalize, to be logical, to be appreciative and to be creative become brain waves over which God speaks. The human conscience should not be ignored. God's will is often clear and strong in convicting our senses of right and wrong. Specifically, what practical method will translate God's messages to us? There's the wisdom of parents and significant others or the wise words of a spouse or good friends.

Certainly God speaks through the language of books, DVD's, ministers and school teachers. The thought processes of our minds will stimulate ideas that convey God's truth.

Even the Bible, that contains truth without being inerrant, will resonate with the voice of God.

Joan of Arc was the great hero of France and saint of the Catholic Church. Born in 1412, she was burned at the stake on May 30, 1431. She was called to lead the French forces against the British.
George Bernard Shaw's classic story, Saint Joan, graphically tells her story.

One particular event applies to the basic purpose of this article. Upon hearing that she has visions and hears the voice of God, King Charles VII asks, "Why doesn't He speak to me?" Saint Joan of Arc replies just before her death, "He does. You just don't LISTEN."

Amen. Selah. So be it.

STORIES

A basic approach in conveying truth began with shamans, the first religious leaders among Homo sapiens. It was the telling of stories; the regaling a clan or family with common events. Pictures on cave walls were a favorite way. Later on the parables were basic when Jesus was conveying truths.

Consider the methodology of Mark Twain, probably the greatest of all American story tellers.

I love to tell stories in lecturing or preaching. In my opinion, nothing reveals truth better than a well-turned story.

Mike Trent, local resident, recently sent me a most provocative story with a great moral. The only survivor of a shipwreck was washed up on a small, uninhabited island. He prayed feverishly for God to rescue him. Every day he scanned the horizon for help but none seemed forthcoming. Exhausted, he eventually managed to build a little hut out of driftwood to protect him from the elements.

One day, after scavenging for food, he saw the hut in flames with smoke rolling up to the sky. He felt the worst had happened, and everything lost. He was stunned with disbelief, grief, and anger. He cried out, "God, how could you do this to me?" Early the next day, he was awakened by the sound of a ship approaching the island! It had come to rescue him. "How did you know I was here," asked the weary man of his rescuers. "We saw your smoke signal," they replied.

THE MORAL OF THIS STORY: It's easy to get

discouraged when things are going bad, but we shouldn't lose perspective, because God is at work in our lives, even in the midst of our pain and suffering. Remember that the next time your little hut seems to be burning to the ground. It just may be a smoke signal that summons help from God.

Another story comes out of the tragedy of Katrina. It seems the levee had broken not far from a man in his home. He was fearful and prayed earnestly but wasn't too concerned. Soon a patrol car showed up but he was feeling safe. The water was only up to his yard, so he refused to leave. Soon the water was in his first floor. He began to get worried. A neighbor stopped in a rowboat, but he still felt a measure of safety.

Then the water was up to the second floor. Now he was becoming desperate. A police boat showed up to rescue him, but he trusted God and refused to leave. As he climbed to the roof a helicopter showed up to rescue him, but he said, "God will deliver me." He eventually fell off the roof, drowned and ended up in heaven.

He was distraught and asked God why He didn't save him. God's answer has the moral. "I did," God said. "I sent the police car, then your neighbor, followed by the police boat and finally the helicopter." God works in mysterious ways but He works.

One of my favorite stories is about a farmer. As is the custom in the mid-west, he had several barns of various sizes. On top of the largest barn and steeple there was a weather vane. For the farming illiterate, the vane would move in the direction the wind was blowing; thus the name weather-vane. It was usually a long spear with an arrow at the end. This particular farmer was a devout Christian. On his vane he had painted the words. God Is Love. The answer and moral was simple. He explained, "Whichever way the wind is blowing, Always God is love."

Amen. Selah. So be it.

TED

As with most Americans I have a modicum of mixed emotions regarding the death of Ted Kennedy. On balance I come down on the side of respect for him, admiration for his accomplishments and appreciation for his legendary issues. He certainly was a "lion" among politicians. He knew what made people, friend or foe, tick. His compassion for humanity has been well chronicled. As one politician said, "He transcended most mortals."

But aside from that, he certainly was human. There were several blotches on his record. He admitted years ago of cheating on a Spanish exam at Harvard. He was kicked out. His bouts with alcoholism are also well known.

The darkest period of Kennedy's life began on July 18, 1969. Following a small party on Chappaquiddick Island, he drove his car off a bridge, killing Mary Jo Koechne. Kennedy managed to escape, but was unable to rescue her.

He denied being under the influence and tried repeatedly to free her...unsuccessfully. The physical and emotional trauma affected him. He later said, "I regard as indefensible the fact that I did not report the accident to the police immediately.

To believe or not to believe him is the question. The view of many is similar to that expressed by a gal on the Bill Handel morning show. She said, "I never liked him (Kennedy) and I hope that Mary Jo met him at the gate of heaven and sent him to hell." This from one, who is an addicted gambler, drinks excessively and lives with a boyfriend. (Unmarried) She is also an avowed antagonist to President Barak Obama.

There's no denying that Kennedy worked for over forty years to put the tragedy behind him. He was, above all else, passionate for the needy and less fortunate of our citizenry. He considered managing the Civil Rights Act in 1964 and elimination of the Poll Tax in 1965, as his greatest accomplishment as a Senator.

Here's my evaluation of Ted Kennedy? I think his life and work was one of redemption. Who am I and who are you to question that he didn't receive it. Like his mother, Rose, he always looked ahead. She is quoted as saying, "Do not grieve over the past." She didn't and neither did her son. Both mother and son were very devout in their loyalty to the Catholic Church. They attended Mass on a regular basis.

With all due respect to those who have opposed Kennedy throughout the years, I suggest two basic insights. First, the support that he received through the years from fellow Senators who were Republicans. Two leaders of that party are Senators McCain and Hatch. They worked together often.

Second, I appeal to the basic message of the Gospel. Forgiveness is a fundamental belief in Christianity. It is for everyone, including Senators. All sins and deviations are forgivable.

Along with the record of Edward Kennedy of support for equality for everyone, his fighting for the down trodden, he also possessed a strong spirit of patriotism.

I make no apologies in affirming for him what I hope to

hear for myself: "Well done thou good and faithful servant; enter thou into the joys of thy Lord."

Amen. Selah. So be it.

THERMODYNAMICS

Thermodynamics is associated with the phrase, "the Second Law of Thermodynamics." It was first mentioned by Sadi Carnot in 1824. In the field of science it is considered right up there with the "Law of Gravity," so named and discovered by Sir Isaac Newton. Scientists today describe it as the motivating force, the driver, the stimulus, for all of life on earth; from the smallest amoebae to we humans.

The word itself is a combination of two Greek words like Philadelphia-the city of brotherly (adelphos) and love (phileo). The words are "thermos and dinamos." The first means "heat" and the other means "power or energy." We get the words dynamite and dynamo from it.

So, thermodynamics is best expressed as "entropy," which means gradual or instant destruction, rot, deterioration, falling apart, or, disorganization, decay and death. As Dr. Richard Colling, in his book, "Random Designer," describes it, "In its primary role, it directs the directional flow for all physical and chemical reactions." Basically all structure tends to become unstructured.

While I make no pretense to understand Albert Einstein's theory of relativity (E=MC squared), quoting Colling again, "when matter breaks down into simpler components, it is accompanied by the release of large quantities of energy."

The universe, with all its galaxies is considered to be between 13 and fifteen billion years old. At that time all matter was concentrated in one area of space. The Big Bang explosion generated an unbelievable amount of energy and power. The universe was born. Around 4 to 5 billion years ago our earth came into existence and the laws of gravity and thermodynamics were activated.

The first Law was initiated at the time of the Big Bang. Gravity held the planets and stars in place. If the earth was too close or too far from the sun, chaos would result.

Genesis chapter one verse one indicates the start of the whole process. "In the beginning God created." The following are phrases that define and clarify this creative process: Intelligent Design, Theistic Evolution and Random Designer.

I can understand this Law when it comes to our physical world: plants, fish, animals, primates and even the 98% of our DNA that is similar to chimpanzees.

But the problems of Original Sin and Human Suffering are another matter. The traditional explanations leave me cold. I believe, "THE SECOND LAW OF THERMODYNAMICS" is the answer.

Since it is the cause of physical disorder, disintegration and ultimately death, it seems natural to assume the same process affecting the spirit of humanity. Unfortunately, tradition and orthodoxy has emphasized the doctrine of Original Sin. Countless creeds have tried to define it. Reinhold Neihbur described it essentially as "pride." A more descriptive word would be "selfishness;" Self before others and self before our Creator God.

Innate to our nature is self-preservation; climbing over anything or anyone to achieve personal objectives. It is basic to biological survival. The concept of "survival of the fittest"-

which was originated by Herbert Spencer-is based on it. Dr. Colling says, "Squarely embedded at the epicenter of this survival instinct is the behavioral element of selfishness or self-centeredness."

Another scientist puts it this way. "Selfishness drives the evolutionary process." The unselfish died off. The selfish creatures flourished and passed on their genes. After many generations, selfishness was in our genomes until it became a part of human nature.

What better way to describe the actions of Eve and Adam in the Garden of Eden. It is the taint upon the spirit of mankind from then and forever. The only substantial answer is John 3:16 and the truth of the gospel of Christ's redeeming grace. Selfishness becomes selflessness.

DNA studies reveal a remarkable truth. Every person ever born is uniquely different from every other person who ever lived or will ever live.

Why do we suffer? And why does every person have different ailments? It seems to me the answer is obvious.

IT GOES BACK TO THE SECOND LAW OF THERMODYNAMICS. THE DIRECTION AND RATE OF DISINTEGRATION AND DECAY OF THE PHYSICAL IS CONDITIONED BY THE UNIQUE DIFFERENCE IN EVERY PERSON.

The illnesses can be as diverse as heart attacks, stroke, infections, cancer, respiratory problems, Alzheimer or simply old age...All part of the Second Law of Thermodynamics.

Amen. Selah so be it.

THINGS

There are certain things that tweak my curiosity: The novel, the ancient, the controversial and the newly discovered; in particular. Recently there were three items that met one of more of these criteria. Sixty-five million years old dinosaur tracks, two million years old human skeletons and an amazing savant.

In February 2000, Dr. Sheldon Johnson, a retired optometrist living in St. George, Utah, made the discovery of his life. While using his tractor to level a mound on his small farm on the outskirts of St. George, he turned over a large rectangular slab of rock and saw dinosaur tracks that had not been visible for at least 65 million years. He saw knuckles, claws, scales and three big toes. Over the next few years thousands of tracks were discovered.

Stella and I first heard about the discovery about seven years ago and drove to St. George for a timeshare vacation. The location was just a tin roof shed over hundreds of tracks.

Since then Johnson has donated his find to the State of Utah and there is a modern edifice covering many of the tracks. It is now called the St. George Dinosaur Discovery Site Museum.

Scientists are now convinced that Sheldon Johnson had "stumbled onto one of the world's most important dinosaur tracking." The importance is based on the fact that Johnson's discovery was "tracks." Fossils are great, but "tracks are very dynamic. They show things like speed, individual behavior, social behavior and animals starting to run." Believe it or not, paleontologists are saying the tracks reveal the evolution from sea animals to birds. If you can possibly make the trip, I assure you that your visit will be memorable.

I have followed my second interest on 60 Minutes for several years. It concerns an amazing savant. I had a casual interest in savants until I saw the movie, The Rain Man, in 1988, starring Dustin Hoffman.

Leslie Stahl has been especially interested in musical savants. Derek Paravicini of England is such a one. Now thirty years old, he was born blind and his mental capacity is severely limited. "The savant syndrome is believed to be caused by injury to the left hemisphere of the brain, which results in compensation from the right side, leading to enhanced abilities on one level and disabilities on another."

In the Rain Man, Dustin Hoffman had unusual skills with numbers. With Derek he is a musical genius. He can play a song he hears immediately. He can remember all of them. He then can play them in different keys and styles. He can also improvise a new selection in the styles of jazz, classical, R & B, Dixieland, marches or symphonic. However, he cannot tie his shoes, or add 2+2, or dress himself.

Leslie has also followed Rex Lewis-Clack who is also a musical savant. Both young men have performed before thousands. They have astounded medical experts as well as musical authorities.

The third interest that stimulates my mind was published on April 9, 2010 in The Science Daily Magazine. An amazing skull fossil plus 40 percent of an entire body was found. It was located in a World Heritage Site in South Africa.

The use of X-ray synchrotron micro tomography by Prof. Lee Berger (noted paleoanthropologist) enables him and other scientists to set the date of the fossil at 1.9 million years.

The skull is that of a 9 year old boy that is named "Sediba," which means "source" The skull is so well preserved "that you can count his teeth-so very much like ours."

Berger is convinced that his discovery that was really made by his son Mathew is the "missing link." It is the bridge between ape-man and human....A primate like us.

The first piece of fossil that led to the skull was a clavicle, a collar bone. In addition to the skull of a nine year old boy, a skeleton of a thirty year old woman was also found. When Leakey examined the bones he said, "It's almost too much to digest. WOW. It is a treasure trove."

In the near future Dr. Lee Berger believes the find will show what the 1.9 million year olds were eating, what their skills were and what they were doing in the cave area. These three items certainly simulate my curiosity. As I'm sure they do yours.

Amen. Selah so be it.

TODAY

One of the most inspirational verses of Scripture is found in Psalms 118:24. "This is the day the Lord has made; let us rejoice and be glad in it." For many years as pastor of a church I would begin each service by repeating those words. Each morning upon awakening, I begin the day by singing (often badly) these words. To me it is a good way to begin the day. The meaning of the verse speaks to me in an unmistakable way. I hope to make it meaningful to the readers of this column.

How often have we heard the words, "This is the first day of the rest of our lives?" In the stage play and musical Zorba the Greek cries out, "Death is any day not devoted to living." Henry Ward Beecher, the great preacher in the 1800's, challenged his parishioners by saying; "God asks no one if they will accept life. Our only choice is what we do with it." In the classic movie, Dr. Zhivago utters these provocative words. "Man is born to live, not to prepare for life." All of these phrases compliment the statement by the Psalmist.

The inspiration for this article came to me while reading a romance novel by Julie Garwood, "One Red Rose." Her handsome hero says, "Living is an adventure."

Elsa Maxwell was a great comedienne of the 1940's and 1950's. She once said, "I have so many chins that I often lose my necklace in them." She also was a provocative homespun philosopher. She is quoted as saying, "I wake up every morning and wonder what wonder I'm going to see or what interesting person I'm going to meet." For her, truly "living was an adventure."

Some years ago I was having a delightful dinner with a dear friend. In the course of our conversation she said something that I've never forgotten. The gist of it was: "Doc, this is a special time for us. No matter how long we live, no one will ever share this time with us. Also, we will never experience this time again. This time is priceless; it is etched forever as a segment in our lives."

That is true for everyone no matter what is done or isn't done. Regardless of the number of years we live on this earth, the time is special. No one else can live it for us.

The challenge is: TO MAKE TODAY COUNT. According to Douglas Brinkley in his monumental book about Teddy Roosevelt, he describes Roosevelt as believing that death constantly loomed over him. This view challenged him to live each moment. He maximized his time on earth to the fullest. He refused to squander a second.

Micro-biologists tell us that cells are the building blocks of our bodies. We have between ten and one hundred trillion of them. They also affirm that Homo sapiens and chimpanzees have 98 percent of DNA that is the same.

That 2 percent makes us special. THEN, they also declare; that each person who is alive or lived in the past or will live, is UNIQUELY different. No two people have the same DNA. We implement this difference by how we live and rejoice in each day.

Amen. Selah so be it.

TURKEY

The country of Turkey is a Muslim nation. However, along with Indonesia, it is a Democracy. It is also called a "Secular Democracy." It is a member of NATO and very definitely a friend of the United States.

The archaeological history of Turkey goes back 100,000 years. Most of those early inhabitants lived in caves. I've been in several of them and all kinds of sand buildings were in the caves. Through the centuries many Empires dominated what was called Asia Minor or Anatolia: Mongols, Persian, Greeks, Assyrians, Romans and the Byzantines or Islam.

The name Turkey has an interesting origin. For several thousands of years the various languages of the people were called TURKIC. It was very easy to name their country after their language.

By the year 500 B.C.E. the Turks had established several symbols and practices: the star and crescent, the primacy of wolves, the color blue, iron and fire. They also were practitioners of Shamanism. The darkest page in Turkish history is obviously the Holocaust of the Armenians. Millions of the Armenians were slaughtered and it has not been forgotten to this day. Turkey is rich in archaeology and Biblical history.

A few years ago I spent a month traveling around Turkey. I carried an ancient map, a modern map and the Bible with me. It is often called "the second Holy Land." However, from my experiences in the land and reading of the Bible, especially the New Testament, it could reasonably be called the "first Holy Land."

The Apostle Paul traveled and lived in Turkey for years. The Apostle John and the Virgin Mary lived in Ephesus and were buried there. But one of the earliest mentions in the Bible is Mount Ararat; the story of Noah. The Ark landed on Ararat after the great flood.(Genesis 8:4) In recent years there have been expeditions on the mount to try and find the remains of the Ark.

The Apostle Paul was born in the city of Tarsus (Acts 9:11). In his day it had a population of a half million people. It had the second greatest University at the time-second only to Alexandria, Egypt. Tradition says that Seneca, the great Greek Stoic, lived there at the time of Paul. Tarsus was the center of many ethnic groups and various religions.

Another famous Biblical fact is the city of Antioch. Acts 11:26 states that the followers of Jesus and Paul were first called Christians in Antioch.

One of the greatest ruins today is in the city of Ephesus. Paul wrote several of his Epistles from there. Ephesus was also the home of one of the Eight Great Wonders of the World...The statue of Diana.

Santa Clause (Saint Nicholas) actually came from the city of Demre. He was the area Bishop. Tradition says that on Christmas Eve he would deliver gifts to the children.

The most famous Council of the early church was in 325 A.D at Nicaea...about 100 miles from Istanbul. Today it is a tourist resort, alongside a beautiful lake.

The Epistle to Philemon was sent to the church at Colossae, Turkey. The letter concerns Onesimus, who was a slave; one relevant point that is outside the Bible. The city of TROY, which is significant in Greece mythology, is on the West coast of Turkey. They even have a huge wooden horse.

One final Biblical reference is in the Book of Revelation, chapter two and three, there are seven churches mentioned: Laodicea, Sardis, Philadelphia, Ephesus, Smyrna, Thyatira, and Pergamos; All in Turkey. Galatea, Bithynia, Cappadocia was all areas of Turkey in Paul's day.

Amen. Selah. So be it.

TWAIN

Larry Burgess is considered by many in this area to be the history laureate. He is certainly knowledgeable of the Inland Empire's history. In a seminar he conducted, I heard him say the 19th Century was his favorite time of all time. Why?

I presume because of so many historic events in that time frame. Consider Napoleon. He changed the face of Europe. The political climate was never the same. Philosophers by the bushel, Karl Marx and Hegel; to name just two: Beethoven and Mozart again representative of many; Newton, Fleming and Pasteur in science.

The Western hemisphere, including Canada, Mexico and South America were in total revolutions. But the world-all of it-fades into the shadows compared with the United States in the 1800's. Abraham Lincoln and the Civil War; the annexation of the Southwest, the Louisiana Purchase: the buying of Alaska and the discovery of gold in California.

The great Industrial expansion and inventions: telephones, steam engines, guns and powder, railroads, ships, etc; and the development of churches; Methodist, Catholic and Baptist. Education went wild with colleges and universities plus public education being established. Cowboys and lawlessness were riding rampant. I'm sure that it was an exciting time to be a part of history being made.

What impresses me most was the intellectual influence on our American culture by three significant writers and minds: Mark Twain, Henry Thoreau and Ralph Waldo Emerson. They were all products of the 19th century. All three expressed religion insights but all were skeptical of organized religion. Politically they would be described as LIBERTARIANS, in today's parlance.

MARK TWAIN (Samuel Clemens). Without a doubt, Twain was bigger than life. He traveled throughout the world and had opinions on everything he saw. It is hard to imagine anyone covering more subjects than he did. In the book, "The Quotable Mark Twain," R. Kent Rasmussen gives hundreds of quotable quotes. Under the title are the words: His Essential Aphorisms, Witticism and Concise Opinions.

A few examples are:

BIBLE: "It's not the parts of the Bible that I don't understand that bothers me, but the parts I do understand." Again "It is full of interest. It has noble poetry and some clever fables; and some blood-drenched history; and a wealth of obscenity; and upwards of a thousand lies."

JESUS: "If Christ were here now, there is one thing he would not be-A Christian."

The CHURCH: "It means death to human liberty, and paralysis to human thought.

RELIGION: "I cannot see how a man can ever be religious-except he shut the eyes of his mind and keep them shut by force."

SATAN: "I have always felt friendly toward Satan. Of course that is ancestral; it must be in the blood."

RALPH WALDO EMERSON and HENRY THOREAU: Even though Thoreau was the younger by fourteen years, they undoubtedly knew each other. They lived just a few miles apart. They were both philosophers, poets, historians, transcendalists, abolitionists, anti-government and writers. They were also graduates from Harvard University.

How did they differ in many ways? Emerson was outgoing and a foreign traveler. Thoreau was a hermit and a recluse. Emerson was married while Thoreau was a confirmed bachelor. Emerson was a fluent speaker and distinguished in appearance. Nathaniel Hawthorne described Thoreau, "as ugly as sin, long nosed, queer-mouthed, uncouth and rustic." Emerson was a lapsed Unitarian minister and Thoreau seemed religious only toward nature. A classic statement by Emerson is, "God enters every life through a private door." Thoreau's most famous statement is, "I went to the woods that I might live deliberately and not come to the end of life and find that I had not lived at all." Needless to say, both men were fiercely independent and truly marched to their own drumbeat.

Amen. Selah so be it.

UNIVERSE

The Discovery channel has had several programs on the origin and development of the universe. Its origin has been established as 14-15 billion years ago.

Stephen Hawking is quoted frequently. His insights and projections are worthy of consideration. Such words as galaxies, asteroids, the Big Bang and the Black Hole were described and explained with more or less clarity. Considering the immensity of the universe is staggering, to say the least. Is there life on other planets? Hawking's latest contention is in support of aliens that travel through space and very possibly are heading toward earth.

With all the space searching by telescopes, the most interesting revelation comes from the Bible. The Psalmist categorically stated, "The heavens declare the glory of God." Obviously the assumption of this phrase is that God the Creator was the source of the universe coming into existence.

Consider aspects of the heavens that are easily visible to the naked eye. The sky that changes from dark to various hews of blue. Clouds that roam the sky like great puffs of cotton. Lightning and thunder that shatters the tranquility of the heavens; rain, snow, hail, sleet and wind that provide a backdrop for various cosmic scenarios.

The Gospel song writer caught the wonder of God's creativeness when he wrote,

"O Lord my God, when I in awesome wonder;
consider all the worlds Thy hands have made.
I see the stars, I hear the rolling thunder,
Thy power throughout the universe displayed.

Chorus
Then sings my soul,
my Savior God to Thee;
How great Thou art, how great Thou art.
Then sings my soul, how great Thou art.
How great Thou art."

My rationality insists that such wonder and orderliness has to be the product of a Designer. Randomness is an affront to my intelligence. Ten billion to twelve billion years after the Big Bang, a glob of meteors and asteroids came together-by design-to form the planet earth.

My preference for the process of creation is THEISTIC EVOLUTION. This equates with Genesis 1:1, "In the beginning God created the heavens and the earth."

The evolutionary process includes the universe, our earth and life on it. It was initiated by the Divine. From one isolated cell, that divided and multiplied: came mankind-you and me. With the capacity of choice, thoughts, imagination, emotions, values, and all other things that make us human created in the image of God.

Amen. Selah. So be it.

WEAKNESSES

I know my weaknesses; at least most of them. Since I'm eighty plus years of age, some of them I no longer have. Others that were detrimental to my health, I've eliminated. Several of them are included in a working to improve agenda. Like my pleasure at eating fattening food. I'm on a diet; which seems to be perpetual. I hope in my next life I'll come back as a skinny guy.

I have an ego, like everyone else. It doesn't seem to be clear-cut. It's a mixture, of inferiority and the opposite, superiority. It affects me somewhat like a bi-polar condition. Sometimes I'm down and other times I'm up. I call it my male PMS. For about a day I get depressed; feeling inferior because of age, my health and my lack of motivation. It only lasts for no more than twenty-four hours. My bounce back is tremendous. The energy level is high and my creative juices are running.

Most people have heard of the Holy Trinity. It refers to the Father, the Son and the Holy Spirit. My ego excursions give me an Unholy Trinity: me, myself and I.

I become open to any slight, a word of criticism or a denigration of any kind. A balance I do not have. My only refuge is compensation. From a young man who stuttered and got lousy grades in school, I've compensated by studying and getting several degrees.

My only hope is that my weakness seems to be a little stronger; which leads on to my second weakness. That weakness is an insatiable curiosity. I'm constantly wondering what's around the curve. Or, what's on the other side of the hill.

I'm especially curious about people. What they do for a living; where they're from; their age, their family, do they travel, etc? My curiosity about places is insistent. I want to know about places I've never visited like Galapagos, Antarctica, Iceland, Cameroon, the Congo, Bolivia; and many others.

I'm curious about animals: the blue and sperm whales, the gray back gorillas, and especially polar bears.

I have a curiosity about history. What was the world like 1000 years ago or 10,000,000 years ago? Was man created or did he evolve?

I have a great curiosity about words and ideas. If I don't know about them, I'm bugged until I learn.

So, I talk to people, I travel as often as I can and I read, read, read. My favorite book is Webster's Dictionary. These are a few of the ways I alleviate some of my curiosity. This weakness is obsessive-compulsive.

Going back to my first sentence, my greatest weakness is mediocrity. Socrates is reported to have said, "The unexamined life is not worth living." True or not I'm constantly battling my prevailing sense of mediocrity.

I possess a measured skill in many endeavors. Music is an avocation of mine. I can play several instruments: trumpet, bass fiddle, drums, valve trombone and baritone. But none of them exceptionally well. I've played in bands, orchestras and symphonies, but never the top player. I also sing and read music; however, I'm not bass, baritone nor tenor. My skill is mediocre.

I've played most sports; football, basketball, golf, racquet ball and tennis; but never well. I can dance; from ballroom to Latin to swing; but with limited finesse.

I preach, but with marginal ability. I'm a student of the Bible, anthropology, Spanish and history, but not a scholar. I do magic and write articles, but again my skill is with reservations.

There are many other areas that I can speak with some knowledge about; but never with an assertive ability. However, there is one area that I excel with enthusiasm. I thoroughly enjoy my participation in whatever I do. Each day I approach with pleasure and try to end the day with satisfaction. Weaknesses all: inferiority, curiosity and mediocrity.

Amen. Selah so be it.

WORDS

John Wooden died recently at the age of ninety-nine. He was affectionately called the "Wizard of Westwood" (UCLA). As a coach he won ten NCAA basketball championships. Kareem Abdul Jabbar and Bill Walton were two of his famous players. As good a coach as he was, he was an even better man and a devout Christian. His pyramid of success is still being taught by scores of coaches.

Coach Wooden was fastidious in his demands for his players. They were even taught how to tie their shoes. Of all the things I've read about him, one of the most unique concerned behaviors on the court.

The five <u>must</u> play as a team. Whenever a player made a basket, he must immediately <u>in some way</u> acknowledge the player who had fed him the ball or set him up. Teamwork was essential; such a little thing, but so important. Incidentally, the first team to win the NCAA championship did not have a player over 6 feet 5 inches tall. A small band of five players, relatively short, started the Wooden dynasty.

The words of Margaret Mead-great anthropologist-said, "Never doubt that a small group of thoughtful, committed citizens change the world. Indeed, it is the only thing that ever has." I never cease to be amazed at how little things, small events, incidental words can affect major decisions. They can inspire and be helpful or they can depress and be hurtful.

On the positive side, Dr. Victor Frankl said, "There is a

saving element in every situation." Or as one novelist suggests, "There's opportunity in every mishap." It's often difficult to accept this principle and make it a rule of life, but it is a good rule to live by. It's a small idea, with grand consequences.

I think of many people who have guided me with their influence and casual compliments. One friend lifted my spirit by reminding me that Jesus was only on His cross three hours. I had prolonged mine by weeks. Often a small gift, a card, a phone call, a hug or handshake can lead us through the maze of depression or indecision.

There is a Greek legend about a labyrinth on the island of Crete. A monster, Minotaur, lived there. It had the head of a bull and body of a man. Humans trapped in the mage were eaten by the monster. No way out. But the hero, Theseus, was aided by Ariadne. She had Theseus tie one end of a ball of thread to the door and he would find his way out by following it.

The destruction of Minotaur was at the hands of Theseus. As so often happens; a friend and a wise action brought the victory.

Many assume the basic issues in our world are complex. In fact, they are rather simplistic. There's the world of bad people who are self-centered with only self-interests. There is also the world of people who are compassionate and interested in making the world better. Jesus described it this way, "You can't serve God and materialism both." It's one or the other.

Robert Ludlum's books always have a bit of wisdom and advice included in the drama of his stories. In "The

Ambler Warning" he repeatedly says, "People see what they want to see." I can see the world as dirty, corrupt, antagonistic, racist, bigoted, sickness, sorrow, smog, dog eat dog; and when I do I feel depleted with a sense of guilt or I can admire myself by seeing goodness, human potential, love, compassion, sunshine, rainbows, wellness and happiness. I see what I want to see.

I began this article by emphasizing the value of little things. Among those values is our awareness of human community. Someone has said that we are a part of everyone we have ever met. We each have more to gain by accepting this than by ignoring it. Our world depends on it. We need more people like John Wooden.

Amen. Selah. So be it.

YEARS

When the Prime Minister of India visited the White House recently, he quoted Abraham Lincoln in his toast. "It's not the years in your life that count, but the life in your years." These are wise words; to be sure...A fitting description of life at its best.

The Book of Numbers in the Bible is a tragic book. Mainly because it lists the chronology of so many who just "lived and died." They didn't follow the admonishment of President Lincoln, "life in their years."

I read a book years ago entitled *"Locked In A Room With Open Doors."* It describes people who have allowed various conditions and phobias to so debilitate them that they become imprisoned. This in spite of the fact the door is open for them to get out. It is a self-imposed incarceration. Google identifies 40 different phobias. Two of the best known are agoraphobia and claustrophobia. Both conditions inhibit a person from living a carefree life.

Three women that I know are the very opposite of that. Their names are Berniece, Carmen and Nora. As far as I know, they do not know each other. Berniece lives in Highland, Carmen in San Bernardino and Nora in Redlands. Berniece is ninety years old; Carmen is eighty-seven; and Nora is one hundred and two years old. Since I did not interview any of these ladies, my comments are based entirely on my observations and listening to their comments.

All three do like to talk. Not one is timid about

expressing opinions. However, I know very little about their feelings on POLITICS. I'm sure they have them, but not to my knowledge. All three are extremely attractive. In fact, beautiful could be applied to each. Even at their ages today. I have seen all three in a variety of circumstances. Never have I seen them without make-up or hair in disarray. They are stylish in attire and appearance. I'm sure that in their youth, they would have been called a "Beauty Queen."

All three are extremely active. They belong to organizations and participate in family activities. The history of all three is filled with surgeries and grief. All three endured the Great Depression, World War II, the Korean War, the Vietnam War and the Iraq and Afghanistan conflicts.

Yet, all three are very positive and radiate optimism. Certainly their religious faith is an important factor in their lives. At one time or another I have been the minister for all three. Their faith is real.

Let's look at each of them, beginning with Berniece. She has remained strong in faith through the death of her husband, preceded by his Alzheimer. In spite of colon cancer and knee surgery, she continues line dancing to this day; and exercises every morning. For many years she has been a volunteer at St. Bernadine Hospital as a "pink lady." Incidentally her home should be showcased in a design magazine. She has scores of plants, appropriately placed in her home. She certainly fulfills President Lincoln's admonition.

Nora is an effervescent person. She simply radiates her personality. She exercises six days a week. Her specialty, believe it or not, is spending twenty minutes on the "stepper."

That is similar to climbing stairs. But what I like best about Nora is her love of humor. She remembers jokes and she tells them-all the time.

An example, I always begin my sermon with a joke. Each time I saw her she could remember my joke from the previous week and would tell me another one. She, also, fulfills the admonishment of President Lincoln.

Carmen is Hispanic; having been born in Barcelona, Spain. During World War II, she and two sisters were imprisoned in a Japanese camp in the Philippines. Through the years she has suffered great grief: the death of her two sisters, the suffering of one son with schizophrenia and eventual death and the death of a grandson. Today she is an accomplished painter. Her home is filled with them-and best of all-she has given me one which I display in our home. She has recently taken up the monumental task of writing her memoirs. She uses the unique style of relating her life's experiences in the third person. Most certainly, she is an example of President Lincoln's urging.

Nora, Berniece and Carmen are ladies to be admired. I do. Maybe I admire them most because each has purchased several copies of my recent book, "Words to Live By."

Amen. Selah so be it.

ZOROASTRIANISM

Have you ever wondered about the influences on Jesus? Who and what were they? Obviously, we can assume that He grew up in a typical Jewish home. His parents certainly influenced Him. He was conversant with the Scriptures and the cultural advantages of the day. The give and take of family life (parents, siblings, and relatives) would affect Him.

The pressing question for centuries has been where was Jesus from age twelve to age thirty? Tradition does give a few indications. The best way to solve the mystery is to examine His words and deeds that are found in the Gospels.

Does the word "Zoroastrianism" sound familiar? It sounds like a disease, but it isn't. It's the name of a religion. In fact, it is considered the oldest of all recognized religions. Most scholars date its origin back to 3800 B.C. to 6000 B. C. The earliest date would make it 2000 years older than the time of Abraham. (1800 B.C.)

Religious historians have been able to catalog its history. The founder is Zoroaster and he lived in the land of Persia. He was married and the father of four children. He and his entire family were tragically murdered.

However, he left two significant books, The Avesta and The Gathas. His basic emphases are contained in them. History records that Zoroaster was the creator or inventor of magic and astrology. Interestingly, the last letters of his name (aster) mean "star."

Consider the first – supposedly- contact between Jesus and Zoroastrianism. Matthew records the Magi, from the East, followed a star and brought gifts to the Christ-child. Is this event accidental or intentional?

One of the major traditions about Jesus' early life places Him in the area of Persia studying Zoroastrianism. This view is substantiated by the correlation between the teachings of Jesus and the views of Zoroaster.

A basic tenet was the belief in and the use of apocalypticism. It means "unveiling" or "revelation." Around the time of Jesus there were scores of such writings.

Albert Schweitzer in his classic book, "The Quest of the Historical Jesus," calls Him an "apocalyptical preacher." Schweitzer's view is based on what Jesus is recorded as saying in Matthew, chapters 24 and 25.   In addition, The Book of Revelation, and the Books of Ezekiel (chapters 37-39) and Daniel (chapters 7-12) have significant apocalyptical messages.

The Dead Sea Scrolls also reflect the Zoroastrianism influences. Most Christian scholars also believe that Jesus was influenced by the Essenes.

Basic expressions of apocalypticism are: a belief in an end-time conflict between good and evil; the use of figurative language like dragons and angels; they always reflect their times and that the end was near; so expressed in Ezekiel, Daniel, Matthew and Revelation. The figurative language was used to confuse the PERSECUTORS. For example, in the Book of Revelation, Babylon was really Rome; the whore was Nero or Domitian ((Emperors).

Another purpose of the apocalyptical writings was to

encourage the readers and to give them hope that good would conquer evil and that God would conquer Satan.

All the major writings were in tough times for people and persecutions; The Assyrian and Babylonian captivities; the Greek and Roman persecutions.

ZOROASTER'S MESSAGE BEGAN WITH A BELIEF IN MONOTHEISM. He was the first in recorded history to assert this belief.

Other beliefs of Zoroaster as recorded in his books:

1. God is not about fear, guilt or condemnation.
2. God is wisdom, love and logic.
3. God does not have favorites or discriminate.
4. God treats humans with dignity and respect.
5. God is not jealous, wrathful or vengeful.
6. Man is not sinful, fallen or depraved.
7. Man was created to progress in likeness to God and to eliminate wrong in the world.

These beliefs give an amazing similarity to original Christianity. However, in no way do they diminish our faith in Jesus as the Son of God.

Amen. Selah. So be it.

Made in the USA
San Bernardino, CA
27 March 2014